THE
BORDER
WARDENS

THE
BORDER
WARDENS

BY

JOHN MYERS MYERS

PRENTICE-HALL, INC.
Englewood Cliffs, N. J.

ISBN 0-13-080218-2
Library of Congress Catalog Card Number: 70-129819
Printed in the United States of America   T

Prentice-Hall International, Inc., London
Prentice-Hall of Australia, Pty. Ltd., Sydney
Prentice-Hall of Canada, Ltd., Toronto
Prentice-Hall of India Private Ltd., New Delhi
Prentice-Hall of Japan, Inc., Tokyo

To

MRS. MARY C. CECIL

*for her graciousness in bestowing
on a stranger the treasured
clipping collections upon which
several chapters of this book
are based.*

ACKNOWLEDGMENTS

It had been the good, or hot paving intention, to cite all the Border Patrolmen whose cooperation made this book possible; but for reasons given in the Foreword some jotted names got lost, while others weren't noted because of clouding circumstances. Certain officers are named in the text, as what they said happened to be suitable for inclusion at this point or that; the accidents of literary composition left out others who were equally helpful. But they were universally fine fellows, patient and frank with an inquisitive author, tagalong while they went about tiring and often rough enough rounds; and the same held true of such Customs Agents as were encountered. So herewith a tip of the Stetson to the courteous lot.

Meanwhile special thanks are due: Gordon R. Pettengill, Deputy Border Patrol Chief for the Southwestern Region, for arranging the tour of the Mexican boundary essential to this work; Robert J. Seitz, Public Information Officer of said Patrol region, for faithfully and promptly answering all queries flung in his direction; Gary E. Heath, a Customs Bureau opposite number in Washington, for being usefully informative; Border Patrol old-timers A. E. "Dogie" Wright, Harlan Carter, Robert Sparks, Fletcher Rawls, and John E. Eagar for reports on early policing along the line; Senior Patrol Inspector Drexel B. Atkinson of the Douglas Station, and Assistant Chief Patrol Inspector Donald F. Johnston of the Yuma Sector, for furnishing valuable literary material which else would have been overlooked.

FOREWORD

A grasp of what is afoot along America's Southwestern line asks knowledge of a zone as remarkable for breadth and scope as for the little that has been written about it. Considered as a whole, that is. Many books have dealt with separate features or aspects of it. But it has not been treated as the entity, distinct from the country's norm, which natural, political, and social forces have brought into being. An attempt to impart and explain the flavor of the border is a goal of the chapters to come, second only to citing it as the arena of important action.

The documentation is personal as much as literary. For if I have probed the lore of the region for nearly two dozen years, I have been present in one or the other of the border states for a like span of time. And the nature of my activities has forced me to view the extreme Southwest from many angles.

In two border states a newspaperman, I have covered its modern actualities as a reporter, a feature hand and an editorial writer. As a free lance, I have published its traditions in poetry and fiction as well as in the factual works listed in the bibliography. And while I was working on various phases of a strange geographical belt, it was working on me. Starting as an incredulous outsider of a burning, bright land, I have become used to being in the tiger, and use its eyes when regarding the rest of the world.

As for the International Line itself, I have surveyed it from end to end under the guidance of its manning officers. In the course of a protracted tour I was posted on its problems by experts who also told of their own as frontier guards.

I made notes when it was feasible; quite often it was not. While jackrabbiting over desert ridges in a scout car, for instance, or when prowling with a shift on night duty. Some of the notes I did take I couldn't later decipher, because they were made in dwarf airplanes that bucked as never bronco did when caught in choppy currents amongst mountains. However, things heard or seen under such circumstances get a better hold on the memory than the foundlings of comfort, and the gist of what I was told or observed stayed with me.

Aside from the legible portions of my notes, the written sources of this book are official printed matter, sector portfolios, albums of old press clippings, recent newspaper columns, and books of today, yesterday and long ago.

When any of this material is directly drawn upon, the fact is mentioned in the text. Plenty of statements are not so supported, though. I drew them out of my own spread of regional books or learned the incorporated truths by watching and listening attentively.

Among those I was lucky enough to listen to were a number of now retired Border Wardens, old enough to have been active when the present band of guardians was first organized. Through their courtesy I am able to assert else missing details of a panorama which I have tried to make comprehensively clear.

J. M. M.

CONTENTS

THE
BORDER
WARDENS

INTRODUCTION

THE
THEATER
OF GRAVE
ACTION

The Mexican Border is the scene of two threats to the safety of the United States, one of which has been given wide publicity through the avowed will of the Federal Government to quash it. This, of course, is the northward flow of narcotics.

The other menace is a migration across the line on a scale to damage the nation's economy in several serious ways. That, too, is being opposed by Federal officers, but their struggle has so far drawn neither the floodlight of national news coverage nor the marshaling of massive resources.

While the volume here offered will deal with both national perils, it will give more attention to the battle being fought, as it were, in the dark than to the generally understood combat. An odd but in focus incident should serve as well as any to introduce those striving to hold back invasion.

On the afternoon of March 24, 1969, a team of United States Immigration Service Border Patrolmen stationed at El Centro, California, joined a hunt for a child lost in rough desert fifty miles north of the boundary. In charge by right of rank was Assistant Chief Patrol Inspector Allon C. Owen.

At nightfall an assortment of other officers and volunteers had to give up the search for want of a way of sifting a wilderness in the dark. The border wardens, though, owned a skill linking today's astronautic America with its woodcraft beginnings. Trained trackers and used to plying that trade at any hour, they continued to pick out such prints as slight weight could leave on hard scrabble.

Rocky patches further slowed men whose methods of combing huge wastes will be dealt with later. The point here is that the faintest of traces led Owen to his bewildered goal soon after the turn of midnight.

The combination of craft and dogged application that achieved that feat is common to a force engaged in stemming mischiefs which are, in general, as little understood as the nature of the Border Patrol. It would be difficult to overstate the dangers to the social structure which the force is called upon to deflect. It would also be hard to overvalue what the corps has accomplished with slender resources, in spite of handicaps imposed by officials safely away from the international front.

One reason for the small notice paid a crucial matter is that not many Americans know their nation is guarded by such a unit as the Border Patrol. Even most of the people in border states are not aware of a force which operates so much in empty country or under the hat of darkness. Residents of the interior may recall that on their way back from Mexico or Canada they passed a Patrol traffic checking point. Few have any notion of what is being searched for, or what the corps does besides stopping motorists impatient to hurry home with the liquor or racy pictures they've bought.

The Border Patrol is the law enforcement arm of the Immigration and Naturalization Service, itself a branch of the United States Department of Justice. It is a force of some 1,500 men charged with keeping aliens from illegally crossing America's 8,000 miles of international boundaries.

Most of the Atlantic Coast doesn't form a border. Because of nearby islands owned by foreign nations, the toe of Florida and a couple of thousand miles of adjacent Gulf of Mexico shore were declared a boundary in 1925. The nearly 4,000 miles of the Canadian, and the 2,013 miles of the Mexican Border, have histories dating from the eighteenth and nineteenth centuries respectively.

But if the Mexican is the shortest of the three boundaries, it is the real trouble zone. By official count 5 percent of Border Patrol action takes place on the other two lines and 95 percent on that of Mexico. And as it is the seat of the cited threats to national health, it will be the sole boundary treated in this work.

A thing to be said of the Mexican Border at the outset is that it is as little known as its Patrol. Two thirds of it lie in country that is either utter wilderness or has been developed to only a primitive degree. Industry on any scale has taken root only in El Paso and San Diego—which as a seaport and naval base is not really a border-oriented town. Tourists cross the line in force here and there, but most such visitors glance only at the showcase froth of the Mexican communities and take no notice at all of the American ones.

Probably the last time Americans as a whole were aware of this zone was in 1916. On March 16 of that year Doroteo Arango, who preferred to be known as Pancho Villa, led 400 liegemen over the line and into Columbus, New Mexico, which they partly burnt in the course of killing sixteen United States citizens. Pursuit by General John Pershing, then but a year away from commanding the American Expeditionary Force of World War I, fizzled when the Mexican Government failed to give a reach for Villa's scalp the expected blessing.

Thereafter, the boundary lapsed from national note again. For even when an occasional report of some portion found its way into big town newspapers, little or no impression was made on the average reader. The place names were too unfamiliar and the geography too vaguely understood; and it was all so far away from what were deemed the main American currents.

Yet it can be said of this boundary that it has been the most consistent theater of dramatic action in the history of the United States. Other frontiers have quieted, but the border has never known a placid year since it emerged from the Mexican War of 1848. Next followed Indian and bandit raids, filibustering, cattle rustling, silver smuggling, and the counter strokes of soldiers, rangers and Custom guards. Then came the running of contraband Chinese and the Wild West show staged by Prohibition. Now there is the infinitely more sinister narcotics problem. And now from end to end the line is the scene of desperate trespass and the traps and chases by which Patrolmen combat its ever mounting force.

The adversary is officially styled "an illegal alien immigrant." He may be an Asiatic, a European, a Central American or a Cuban fugitive from Castro's Communism. Sometimes, surprisingly, he is a French Canadian, trying to sneak in over the southern door instead of jumping over his own sill. But in the overwhelming preponderance of cases, he is a Mexican, and along the border he is called a wetback.

The term stems from the theory that he illicitly entered the United States by swimming the Rio Grande. In practice he often finds ways to avoid immersion in that river when crossing into Texas, and it never has been any trick to slip into New Mexico, Arizona or California dryshod. But once adopted, catchwords have a way of holding their own, and a flip for logic. Wherefore the Mexican invader is as thorough a wetback when nabbed on a cool mountain slope as he is when fished from water in subtropical parts near the Gulf.

The wetback is referred to as "he" advisedly. Although this has not always been so, the number of Mexican women now trying to crash the border is negligible. Whether or not married, and Mexico is a land where the practice is to wed young, the trespassers enter America stag.

They seek lawless entry because they cannot meet this country's immigration requirements. Many have criminal records. Many have good reasons for not wishing to face a physical examination. Most either have no education or have barely crossed the threshold of literacy. All are seeking employment in fields where non-citizens are barred by Federal laws and often state ones as well.

If historically America has been settled and developed by men hailing from a gamut of countries, the wetback is not of a piece with these. Although willing to claim United States citizenship in pursuit of his designs, he typically has no thought of cutting his ties with his own land by becoming a true part of this one. He comes to make money, of which as little as possible, in the majority of cases, will be spent north of the border. The rest will be sent or brought back to Mexico.

His thinking is as simple and primitive as a cat versus a fish store. Knowing or having been told that what he wishes is to be found north of the line, he comes to get it by any means possible. He is no more troubled about being unwanted than yellowjackets at a picnic. The door barred, he stands ready to jimmy the window, squeeze through the coal chute or slide down the chimney.

In concrete terms, the wetbacks jump the line at all hours and seasons, via bridges, ferries, rafts and fords, by city streets, roads, trails or no path at all. They cross alone or in troupes, afoot or in vehicles, by air as well as by land or water. They find their own way or are guided by ever more numerous and progressively vicious smugglers.

Waiting for them at as many points as their numbers make possible are the men of the Border Patrol. For the wading wetbacks or the walkers with dry feet they keep line watch by day and night and in heat or frost. Or to get on the trail of successful river crossers as well as those stealing in overland, they patrol drag-roads and other traps by cars and planes. In towns they check all forms of public conveyance capable of bringing invaders across the line or funneling them away from the border. Along secondary highways and farm road networks patrolmen forever coast in prowl cars, their purpose to look for any signs of wetbacks or people who might be able to furnish leads. On throughways and other traffic mains they stop all cars and trucks which suggest smugglers to trained eyes. Or they spring aboard their own vehicles and chase non-compliers. In the air, pilots cruise in search of craftily hidden wetback camps, summoning ground aid by radio as soon as one is spotted. And meanwhile smugglers of live bodies are ceaselessly active, as well as spies serving both the law and its breakers.

These activities, together with the seizures of drugs which are also often involved, would stand journalism on its head, had they happened elsewhere. But except for the noticed anti-narcotics drive conducted by the Customs Bureau, the border has been little patrolled by scouts for national news media. There are reasons for this that can be better understood after an appraisal of the line's natural and social properties.

From a California point on the Pacific to a Texas one on the Gulf of Mexico, the border stretches unevenly south and west for 2,013 largely uninhabitable miles. For the first 700 it courses overland, less the seventeen in which the Colorado divides Baja, California from Arizona. East of the Colorado the line severs Arizona and New Mexico from Sonora and Chihuahua as far as the Rio Grande, known to Mexicans as the Rio Bravo del Norte. For the remaining 1,300 miles, the boundary runs down the middle of the river, with Texas successively facing Chihuahua, Coahuila, Nuevo Leon and Tamaulipas.

The physical aspects of the overland section (defined by white monuments and barbed wire stock fences), are mostly grim and common to the United States and Mexico. Moistened by the Pacific, the Coast Range is verdant, but to eastward, barrens frame the border for hundreds of miles. Broken but to a small degree by irrigation, the Colorado Desert is a mix of rugged heights, flats and dips below sea level. Beyond the Colorado River the even fiercer Arizona Desert is followed by a series of bleak ranges, piled up as high as two miles or better. Not counting a few valleys where streams or springs make farming possible, that's the way of it far down the Rio Grande.

Seasonally no more than a string of pools in spots, the Grande can be itself a part of the general drouth. Along that river, however, a difference in the terrain of the border's two countries at last becomes marked. The separating feature is Mexico's great Central Plateau, whose face towers unbrokenly over the south bank, while the mountains on the northern one give way first to the scattered hills of the Great Plains and then to the flatter Grand Prairie zone. Only in the sub-tropical Gulf coastal belt do the border's two halves resemble each other again.

Such is the physiology of the border, except for its overland markings. In chief these consist of white cement monuments placed on sighting points at irregular intervals. Sometimes the only boundary line is the imaginary one running between any two markers. More often a barbed wire stock fence defines it, while for miles on each side of ports of entry there are 10-foot cyclone fences.

But a description of the border isn't complete without noting other man-made additions. Two are the dams backing up the waters of Amistad Lake and Falcon Reservoir. Crucial are the Border towns, the communications which serve them and the bridges inviting international traffic.

To give only the main ones, and starting with that nearest the Gulf, they link Brownsville with Matamoros, McAllen with Reynosa, Laredo with Nuevo Laredo, Eagle Pass with Piedras Negras, Del Rio with Ciudad Acuna, Presidio with Ojinaga and El Paso with Ciudad Juarez. But if the towns are thus paired, they are not matched, any more than are the ones which face each other where the line runs west of the Rio Grande. With a single exception, the Mexican city is much more sizable than its American neighbor.

But that statement falls far short of suggesting the Border's ratio of Anglos—or native speakers of English—to those born with Spanish tongues. Laredo, Texas, for example, is 95 percent Hispanic, and many smaller communities on the American side of the border are entirely so. The language of Spain, not of England, is the dominant one all along the line, and fluency in it is a demanded qualification of all Border Patrolmen.

Much of the architecture of the American side pairs with that to be found south of the boundary. So does much of the cooking. Even the English of the border is separate from that of the rest of the country, borrowing as it does many Hispanic terms as well as the Indian ones imbedded in Mexico's version of Spanish.

To get back to the zone's urban centers, those of the United States are relatively small except for El Paso, for San Diego, as has been remarked, is little concerned with the border and differs from the other towns near it by being dominantly English speaking. But out of the seventeen largest cities in Mexico, on the other hand, seven are on or near the boundary. The situation, then, is that the border has two different ratings, depending upon the country considered. Seen from the point of view of the United States, it is largely out of the swim. Yet in Mexico it approaches the status of main line.

When it comes to rural development, however, America is far ahead. In part this is due to the Great Mexican Plateau, which limits irrigation south of the Rio Grande in stretches where it is extensively practiced north of the river, while as grazing land it is not the equal of the Great Plains and prairie belts on the American side.

West of the Rio Grande, though, nature has dealt more evenly with the two nations. The border regions of New Mexico and Arizona share with those of Chihuahua and Sonora about the same proportions of barren mountains, desert flats and watered valleys where grazing and even some farming are possible. Also the Colorado distributes irrigation water to both the American and Mexican parts of the desert named for it. And lastly, the fine cattle country of the Coast Range lies in both Californias.

But cities and agriculture notwithstanding, the border's dominant note is savagery. Rough country is near neighbor to all the towns. Tilled land is dwarfed by waste, and the range that nurtures cattle, sheep and goats, feeds antelope, deer, wild burros, javelinas and bighorn sheep as well as being the hunting ground of panthers, wild cats, coyotes and occasional bears, wolves, ocelots and jaguars. Among the smaller fauna are foxes, raccoons, badgers, skunks, armadillos and the ring-tailed bassaris or cacomixls.

The snake-slaying bird elsewhere known as the chaparral cock or the road runner is called "paisano" along the Border. The chacalaca, the only American guan, is found here, and quail, ducks, plover, doves, buzzards, hawks, owls, egrets, flickers, thrashers, mocking birds, turkeys and eerily whistling jackdaws.

The border is well fixed for rattlesnakes both as to numbers and varieties. The coral snake, kin through its venom to cobra, makes its home there and the also colorful and poisonous lizard called the Gila Monster. There are still a few alligators in the Rio Grande but oddly, in view of its abundance in other Texas streams, the water moccasin is said to be absent. This lack is in some degree offset by a wealth of centipedes and scorpions—often known locally as vinegaroons—lurking on the line's terra firma.

The flora there range from the canebrakes to be found on the lower Rio Grande to the green but leafless palo verde, spiny mesquite and spinier ironwood of the desert, while ponderosa pines thrive near the crests of some of the highest mountains and live oaks shade certain intermediate levels. There are grasses and such innocuous shrubs as sage, burro bush, greasewood and Indian broom, but the border is par excellence the home of spiked plant life. Chaparral will scratch, cat's claw is as good as its word and yucca's other name is Spanish bayonet. Ocotillo is as bloodthirsty as graceful, and cacti bristle with everything from the needle pointed hooks of the little pin cushion to the serried spines of a forty-foot tall sahuaro.

Some of the cactus grows where man has lived but does so no longer. There are the husks of towns, preserved in something like their entirety by dry air which once flourished by the mining pits and horizontal shafts which dot mountainsides and canyons. There are old American forts and older Spanish missions. There are Pueblo ruins and other places where Indian potsherds or weapons may at any day be stumbled on. There are, too, caves where Mexicans as well as Indians have dwelt.

Going back of man's earliest residence, the border boasts stretches where sea shells are common, for the Colorado Desert and its Arizona neighbor were once the floor of an ocean. Yet the named desert is the site of a new water body of considerable magnitude, formed by the overflow of the Colorado in this century. That is the Salton Sea, whose surface is 235 feet below sea level in general.

Although water is the zone's abiding dearth, it is the seat of cloudbursts which can, in jig time, turn dry washes into destructive torrents. If snow only pelts its mountains, winds whip up dust storms capable of shutting down traffic not only on open roads but in towns where visibility has been all but blotted out. Walking columns of sand known as dust devils can strike with semi-cyclone force.

But the border's norm is far visibility and the glare of a hot country sun that is seldom missing two days together. It allows cold winds and some frost in the winter, of nights, which can be chill in high deserts even in the summer. But while up, it mostly sticks to its business of keeping the country warm—delightfully so for eight months of the year. The other four are strictly for salamanders, and no Chamber of Commerce poet has been able to think of a word in their praise.

That in brief is the anatomy of the area about the line. It is America's most exotic region as well as its current danger zone. As varied as it is vast, this is where 1,200 members of the bilingual Border Patrol keep active watch the clock around.

PART

I

*THE
PATROL'S
ANTECEDENTS
AND
EARLY
YEARS*

1

STIRRINGS ON THE LINE'S AMERICAN SIDE

There was a thing that happened away from the border and as far back as 1867 which was to induce the original invasion by illegal Mexican immigrants. In that year an adventurer named Jack Swilling passed through uninhabited desert at about the site of Phoenix, Arizona, and rightly guessed that the series of shallow depressions he noticed were ancient irrigation canals. Flush with the profits of gold prospecting in the Wickenburg area, he there formed a company which undertook to clear out channels that Indians had abandoned a half a millennium before.

Thus watered, the desert proved capable of blooming with such crops as American farmers had never previously seen. And because frost was a seldom visitant, fields could be made to yield at almost any season. The region's blessing was also its drawback, though. The supplying Salt River would go on a rampage every spring and whenever there were heavy rains at other times. Then it would sweep away the beaver style diversion dams and damage other construction.

Farming about Phoenix was therefore limited, but the basic success of Swilling's enterprise inspired Charles D. Poston with a desert rehabilitation scheme in which he was determined to get the Federal Government to invest. Among the border's pioneer industrialists, Poston had been sent to China in 1868 on a diplomatic mission. That accomplished, he had continued around the world, studying irrigation methods in Asiatic and Egyptian parts where it had been practiced for thousands of years. When he returned to Washington he became a lobbyist for desert reclamation, with the result that in March of 1877, Congress passed the Desert Land Act.

But a measure that was to bring greenery to many arid sections of the border had proved its worth only in a small way a quarter of a century later. The Salt was still regularly destructive, and so were other streams which had been tapped for irrigation purposes. The remedy lay in a chain of storage and regulatory dams, not built in the farming zone but at strategic points up the Salt and its chief contributor, the Verde. But farmers didn't have the money for such a massive undertaking and neither did a frontier territory. It was, as Poston had foreseen, something that only Washington could manage. The scheme of a man who died that year became something more than a hope when a Bureau of Reclamation was added to the Department of the Interior in 1902. The following year the Salt River Project was approved by the bureau, and in 1905 work was begun on the Roosevelt Dam, its site a great natural basin where the Salt and the Tonto joined forces.

In California at this period, plans to put the Imperial Valley in bloom were being undermined by the tilt of the Colorado Dersert toward the Salton Sea. With its belly 287 feet below sea level, this suddenly great lake threatened for a time to be the outlet of the Colorado rather than the Gulf of California. It was not until 1907 that the irrigation system—of which a main feature was a canal which dipped below the Border into Baja, California—was brought back to sound working order by a system of levees. These put the skittish Colorado back where it belonged and made sure that water diverted from it would flow where it was wanted.

As consulting engineer for the Reclamation Bureau, Louis C. Hill designed not only the Roosevelt Dam but the also mighty Elephant Butte check athwart the Rio Grande. Built in New Mexico, this likewise supplied the El Paso area of Texas. Providing electric power and changing the face of grim deserts, these were great undertakings. So was the border-nudging All America Canal which Hill ran through Southeastern California. They did everything expected of them and one thing besides. The crop they reared which had not been counted on was a lawless Mexican immigration horde.

But that was of the future, and in the twentieth century's first decade, the Chinese were the problem. An Exclusion Act, outlawing Chinese immigration for ten years had been passed in 1882, and Congress had repeatedly extended it. But the men from Asia kept coming, and on the whole they were better received in the pioneer inland West than in industrialized California. Many ranches were happy to have them as cooks. They performed chores around mines that organized hard rock hands would not. In market towns as well as mining camps they performed as was remembered of early Phoenix by Charles A. Stauffer. "The principal restaurants," he declared in *The Westerners*, "were run by Chinese." And, of course, the Chinese laundry was a Western institution as well as an Eastern one.

So jobs were open, and except for an occasional United States Marshal there was nobody to question the Chinese who arrived to fill them. Sheriffs and Texas Rangers weren't concerned with Federal offences, nor was the Army marshaled for immigration service. As for the Mounted Customs Inspectors, which had been established in 1853 by the Secretary of the Treasury to guard against smugglers and illegal immigrants, they had been relieved of immigration duties in 1891 by the special inspectors of immigrants stationed at border points of entry. These could not function in the needed fashion, though. So eighteen years after the original Chinese Exclusion Act the twentieth century arrived on time without erasing the fact that the Government had passed and renewed a law it had not equipped itself to enforce.

The situation remained the same a year later, when the Arizona Territorial Rangers were organized. Like those of Texas, they were in the saddle to chase rustlers and calm excited bad men. A coolie quietly on his way to find work as a dish washer or clothes cleaner was not what they wore guns for.

Three more years, during which there was another extension of the law prohibiting Chinese, were to pass before somebody thought of doing anything about the anomaly. Then inspiration fired the brain of a Customs officer named Sam Webb. Stationed in Nogales in April of 1904, he looked at the problem from the point of view of smuggling. Most Chinese came over the Border as contraband. He was supposed to stop that and was in no position to. What the situation demanded was a rider with no other duties but to rove in search of man smugglers.

Luckily, or nothing would have been done about the notion of a minor employee in a far away post, Webb did not have to feed his suggestion to the Treasury Department. Through a chain of fine arranged circumstances, this frontier tariff collector hooked up with the White House. It could not have happened if Arizona had been a state, but it was a territory and its governor, like Webb himself, was an appointed Federal official. Specifically he was James O. Brodie, and he owed his governor's chair to the fact that he had been an officer in President Theodore Roosevelt's Rough Riders.

Always open for new ideas, Roosevelt liked the one that Phoenix got from Nogales. Webb had told Brodie that the right man for the job was Jeff Milton. The President naturally accepted the recommendation of his old wartime friend, and Sam Webb's thought became a fact, with a minor change. Because people formed the contraband to be watched for, Roosevelt assigned Milton to the Commissioner General of Immigration, then a hand of the Department of Commerce and Labor.

Destined to be the ancestor of the Border Patrol, Jefferson D. was the son of John Milton, Governor of Florida during the Confederate years of 1861–65. As he found a biographer in a well known Western historian named J. Evetts Haley, a great deal more about him is on record.

With help from Reconstructionists, the Miltons changed from prewar riches to post-bellum rags. Without prospects at home, Jeff let the carpetbaggers and alligators go snacks on Florida and beat his way to Texas. Managing to pass as older than he was, he joined the Rangers although years below the legal age limit. First, though, he had to prove he knew how to handle a gun. This he was able to do then and to the satisfaction or downfall of all who met him ever after. In a region where pistol skill was one of the important talents, he won the rating of genius.

In the course of time he peopled a private cemetery which he viewed without brooding. "I never killed a man who didn't deserve it," Jeff informed Haley. Yet if there were headstones over some that met him, many among the living rejoiced to know him. He had the gifts of friendship, humor, yarn spinning and holding his liquor.

He was not quite twenty-six when, in 1887, he became a Mounted Customs Inspector at El Paso, where the man in charge was Joseph Magoffin, son of the town's founder, James. After trying him out for a couple of weeks, Magoffin assigned him to the Tucson sub-office of his sector. In charge was William S. Oury, on his last legs then but one of the great adventurers of the West. Fifty-one years earlier, to name but one of his ploys, he had stolen through Mexican lines in a vain effort to rally aid for the Alamo. It was Milton's odd fate to meet this great old timer and never serve under him. He reported to Oury on March 31. That same day his chief collapsed in Jeff's arms, his malady a fatal stroke.

In the upshot Milton patrolled the border about Tombstone, and a rover had found a home. Appointed under Cleveland's Democratic regime, he was out of the Customs Bureau when a Republican administration took control two years later. But Jeff and his gun managed to find employment that kept him near the boundary for most of his life.

In 1900 he was a guard riding the "Burro Line" from Benson to its meeting point with Mexican trains at Nogales. His career nearly ended that year, when bandits held up the train he was on at a point near Tombstone called Boquilla. What happened then was told by Arizona historian James H. McClintock. "The hero of the affair was Express Messenger Jeff D. Milton, who fought till incapacitated by a bullet wound that terribly shattered an arm . . . The bandits numbered five. One of them was captured the next morning six miles from Tombstone, where he had fallen from his horse and had been abandoned by his companions . . . He died a few days later in the Tombstone hospital, having received in the body a buckshot load from Milton's shotgun."

The only factor that saved Milton's trigger arm was that Dr. George Goodfellow, a Tombstone medic during its liveliest days, had gone on to San Francisco and national renown as a surgeon. His Tombstone years had given him priceless clinical practice, of course, and from it he had evolved methods of treating shattered bodies that raised him to the top of his field. Although bone had to be removed from Milton's right arm, that wing was so restored under Goodfellow's care that after a couple of years Jeff regained his uncanny speed and gun sureness.

He was thus in prime form when Webb's sound thinking led to his appointment as Chinese Inspector. His position was that particular-

17

ized because no other illegal immigrants were then thought of. There was a district immigration inspector that Milton was technically under, but he saw as clearly as Jeff that nothing in his training qualified him to direct a new order of police. Neither did anybody in Washington try to guess how Chinese invaders and their border abettors could best be foiled. The one man patrol was left to make up his own rules and regulations. He went where he thought best when he chose to do so. Occasionally, and this, too, only when the spirit prompted him, he scrawled reports of developments along the line to a Commissioner General of Immigration, flabbergasted by news so remote from the department's norm.

But where smugglers were concerned, it was not against Mexicans that Milton operated. He told Haley that in the district he was assigned to, all the runners of human contraband were Americans. The trails they used were in general two. East of Nogales one ran from Cananea, Mexico, down the San Pedro to Tombstone or its Fairbank railhead. The western one coursed from Altar, Mexico, to the Border town of Sonoyta. From there it led to railway stops at Gila Bend, near Phoenix, or Wellton, toward Yuma.

Billy Stiles, an outlaw long known to Jeff because they both made Tombstone their base, was one that he found to be in the traffic. He and an ally named Charlie Hood were said to have shot and thrown into a well in Ephraim Canyon sixteen Chinese who had paid a hundred dollars apiece to give them the chance. There were those who did not betray their salt, though. It was the brag of honest Charlie Foster that he had been the Moses of several hundred Celestials who safely passed through the desert.

This meant he used the western runway. Its advantages were that nobody else ranged its vicinity but uncaring prospectors or Papago Indians. Its bad traits were that it was Gobi dry at all times and hell's hinges hot six months of the year. As some of its few water holes were seasonally parched, only the well posted could count on not leaving bones as well as tracks there. But Indians and gold seekers had schooled Milton about the area when he was a Mounted Customs Inspector in the 1880s. Confident of his desert training, he began his lone tour of duty with swings through southwestern Arizona at its worst.

He did not limit himself to the American half of the border, though. Finding it a good observation point, he for long camped at Quitovaquita, Mexico. Thus dug in near the traffic channel, he could

18

confer with smugglers before they committed the crime of bringing Chinese across the line. After such heart to heart talks some outlaws decided not to risk being a great gunman's target by walking contraband over the American boundary.

Still this was a big dike for one finger to plug. Smugglers did get troupes of Asiatics across and on to a railway, whence many made for California. They could travel by rail openly, if they were provided with a "chock gee" or forged residence certificate. Those that lacked this convenience were given secret passage by railroads paid to be sympathetic. One method was to mix Chinese with inanimate cargoes and place them in the sanctuary of sealed freight cars. Without specific grounds an officer could not demand the right of inspection.

Getting wind of this practice, Jeff went to Yuma to see what could be done about it. How to crack the seals proved baffling until he passed a store with a patented bee smoker on display. His next stops were a tobacco store, a pharmacy which stocked sulphur and a grocery well supplied with cayenne pepper. When he had combined these, he returned to the Yuma freight yard and set them alight. As warranted, the bee smoker huffed and puffed, emitting a gas to give dragons emphysema. On his way up a line of freight cars, the Chinese Inspector would hold his dire contraption where it could waft fumes into the cracks around car doors. On his way down he would listen for coughs and wheezing, thus several times bagging not a few illegal aliens and spoiling what had seemed a foolproof dodge.

Yet his best hunting ground was east along the San Pedro. From the border in this sector, trails led to underground distribution points known as Chinese farms. Otherwise they wound to Tombstone or as far north as the copper mining town of Globe, where fellow countrymen would either employ new immigrants or pass them on to jobs elsewhere. Milton found that every Chinese man's house in Tombstone had a cellar which was part of the smuggling network, and doubtless that was true of every other border camp.

Any abandoned mining shaft or natural orifice might turn out to be a smuggler's respository. Once when riding up the San Pedro, Jeff noticed a cave along the stream's farther bank. As instinct whispered it was worth probing, he fired a shot at the top of its entrance which flushed seven repentant Celestials.

As Sam Webb's idea had proved a worthwhile one where Arizona's section of the line was concerned, a few other Chinese Inspectors in time patrolled other parts of it. Who they were and just what they did are matters that got lost in a place and time of scanty record keeping.

But after Milton had been on the job six years, Chinese smuggling no longer formed the border's chief news. The consequence of the Mexican Revolution of 1910 was that dictator Porfirio Diaz was driven from power. Whatever may be urged against a hard-handed man, he had suppressed the banditry long rampant in northern Mexico. With him gone, there was no one to check what he had contained, and a new era of international bandido operations began.

At first only isolated ranches on the High Plains or in the Big Bend region were subject to Mexican assault. But within a few years, villages in the Lower Rio Grande Valley were raided, and attacks on detachments of United States troops were made.

Fortunately for history these activities found a chronicler in the person of Mrs. Maude T. Gilliland, who was living in the vicinity at the time. "By August 1915," as she observed in *Rincon*, "hardly a week passed without raids or rumors of raids . . . soon there was one raid after another."

Cameron County is the one of which Brownsville is the seat. On the sixth of August in the named year a bandido gang rode into a settlement in it called Sebastian. After robbing its chief and perhaps only store, they shot an American and his son for no greater offense than operating a cornsheller.

Upstream in Hidalgo County, four days later, Mexicans killed a member of an Army patrol near Mercedes. But when they attacked an American detachment in the vicinity of Donna the following week seventeen bandidos paid for their mistake. In September there were several more raids upon Hidalgo points, in one of which the river town of Ojo de Agua was pillaged. That month also saw clashes between bandits and soldiers. Of these the fight near Progreso lasted two hours.

Mrs. Gilliland was careful to distinguish between the general run of Mexicans, whom she found decent and likeable, and the savage bandido strain. She characterized those of this blood as being "unbelievably cruel," a point carried by an incident connected with the battle at Progreso. An American trooper captured there served as entertainment viewed by witnesses below the border. His ears were first cut off, then his head, which was stuck on a stick and borne about in triumph.

The raids went on in October, on the eighteenth of which bandits wrecked a passenger train but six miles north of Brownsville. The engineer was killed by the derailing. A civilian and four soldiers were shot to death and other passengers were wounded by random firing.

And so it went for months that stretched into the next year. If these things had taken place anywhere else in the United States, there would have been a national uproar which would have forced Washington to take action. But the border was too far from the general ken, and William Jennings Bryant contented himself with writing notes to a Mexican administration which was having all it could do to stay in control of its capital.

Meanwhile there was one border development of 1915 which was not wrought by bandidos. Although it never produced the insurrection that was hoped for, there was a scheme to recover for Mexico all the territory north of the boundary which it had once owned, plus some that Spain had ruled when in charge of Louisiana. Named for the small Texas town in which it was hatched, the plot was known as the San Diego Plan.

Its father was a school teacher called Basilio Ramos Garza. Its exposer was a deputy sheriff of Hidalgo County named Tom Mayfield. Having some grounds for suspecting Garza, Mayfield arrested him on January 19, 1915, in McAllen and found the San Diego Plan among his effects. Written in Spanish, it called for the uprising, at two o'clock in the morning of February 20, of all Latin American residents of Texas, New Mexico, Colorado, Arizona and California. As Arizona and New Mexico had become states in 1912, all five were in that category. Fused as a separate Mexican republic, they would jointly seek annexation by the already extant one. But while waiting to be welcomed into the pan-Mexican fold, the people of the new republic would not be idle. Rather they would take over six more American states, these being Utah, Wyoming, South Dakota, Nebraska, Kansas and North Dakota.

The fate of the author of this romance doesn't appear to be known. It can be affirmed, however, that a year after his arrest, one that was not a day dreamer was raising some of the international hob that Garza had hoped to.

After some hesitation, the United States had recognized the administration of Venustiano Carranza, thereby enraging Pancho Villa. Hoping to get a crack at the presidency himself, Villa resented anything which would bolster the regime of his rival and announced that the American Government had betrayed him. To get revenge for

21

said miscarriage of trust, and in order to embarrass Carranza diplomatically, Pancho advanced on the Mexican mining town of Santa Ysabel. There on January 9, 1916, he massacred eighteen resident Americans.

When that failed to cause the international trouble he had counted on, Villa led some five hundred bandidos into Columbus, New Mexico on March 9. In the course of burning most of the town they murdered sixteen of its sparse citizenry.

That outrage stirred Washington where the ones perpetrated in Texas had failed to. To protect towns in Texas the entire National Guard was at length sent to the Rio Grande in June. Three months earlier General John J. Pershing had led 12,000 regulars over the border, his mission to seize Villa.

President Woodrow Wilson had authorized the expedition with the thought that Carranza would be in favor of a move against a murderous international nuisance. What came to light, however, was that Carranza hated America even more than he did Pancho. By protesting Pershing's foray, he protected an enemy who did not again visit the United States until his pickled head turned up in El Paso in 1923.

What happened to the arch bandido's noggin is a matter of debate among authorities on southwestern Texas lore. But it is not the only unusual Villa memento with a lost location, if yet the rarist. Judge Fletcher Rawls of Del Rio had an uncle, Thomas Rawls, who had known Villa during one of the several times that the brigand had found Texas safer than his own country. In return for some favor that the elder Rawls had done him, Pancho had presented the American with six solid silver dice. As temptation proved too much for a souvenir collector to whom they were proudly exhibited, this breaker of hospitality walked off with them without troubling to mention the fact. But if they can ever be found and identified, they will stand for the only treasures that the collective banditry of Mexico ever voluntarily left on American soil.

2

THE
OPEN
DOOR
CLOSES
SOME
MORE

The records are so scant that historians have nothing but traditions to go on, but 1911 would appear to be the year in which the border was patrolled by more immigrant inspectors than Jeff Milton. They were not watching exclusively for Chinese, since most of Asia had been classed as a barred immigration zone. No longer a specialist himself, Milton began to pick up Hindus and Japanese.

But a trend away from the "Open Door" policy had begun as far as Europeans were concerned, too. Having drained western Europe of its restless and deprived, the voracious factories of the Atlantic Seaboard states had commenced the intake, late in the nineteenth century, of central and eastern European peoples. The earlier immigrants either spoke some form of English, French or German—the three modern languages then taught in American schools—or, like the Scandinavians, they looked as if they could. None of them so varied from the national norm as to startle thoughtful viewers. But when the Open Door let in hordes that neither sounded nor looked like parts of the established pattern, men with an eye to the future started to challenge the policy.

As the Atlantic Seaboard was where the portents of change were greatest, that region was where critics first came forward. The earliest note of warning by an important political leader was voiced by Senator Henry Cabot Lodge of Massachusetts in 1896. After some introductory appeals, he made a point that is well worth today's notice. "There is no one thing which does so much to bring about a reduction of wages and to injure the American wage-earner as the unlimited introduction of cheap foreign labor through unrestricted immigration. Statistics show that . . . the number of skilled mechanics and of persons trained to some occupation or pursuit has fallen off, while the number of those without occupation or training . . . has risen in our recent immigration to enormous proportions . . ."

Wishing to restrict immigration, Lodge did not propose banning the people of any nation. What he offered was a plan which would keep out doubtful bargains, while giving competence and education a chance to enter. This could be done, as he said, by requiring all immigrants to be able to read and write the languages of their respective native lands.

Lodge's recommendation got lost, for the time being, in a muddle of "melting pot" bombast. But Congress, which had already barred lunatics a couple of earlier times, did it again in 1903, closing the door likewise on professional beggars and anarchists. In 1907 there were more repetitions of acts already on the books, together with a new wrinkle that made immigration read like youthful entry into an "adult" movie. Children under sixteen would not be admitted unless accompanied by their parents.

The border was not glanced at while these laws were being passed. It was seemingly believed that only Chinese and occasional other Asians would stoop to crossing the line at points where Immigration Inspectors were not on hand to examine credentials. But somehow the Commissioner General of Immigration must have learned that not all European felons, professional beggars, anarchists and runaway juveniles were honest johns either. For this reason Jeff Milton was reinforced with a few more men, their mission to watch for whites without proper tickets as well as most from east of Suez.

While Mexican insurrectionists and roving banditti were rampant along the line, most of it was as unsafe for illegal aliens as for others. But after American troops arrived in sufficient force to daunt raiders, the border again had immigration problems. And this time, notice was taken of them in Washington, for thanks to Villa, the boundary had briefly become a point of national interest.

For nineteen-sixteen was the year in which a definite if severally named corps of patrolmen was assigned to the border. Along the Rio Grande they were first called the River Guards or River Riders. Elsewhere they were originally known as Mounted Watchmen. Eventually they all saddled up as Mounted Guards. They appear to have been without coordinating liaison, and certainly they kept few records. It is believed that they numbered about seventy-five, of whom the names of quite a few are preserved.

Two that still view the Rio Grande scene are Robert L. Sparks of Del Rio and the aforementioned Judge Fletcher Rawls of McAllen. From them it was ascertained that the Mounted Guards were assigned in pairs to points from which they rode fifty miles east and as many west. No more in uniform than Jeff Milton, they carried the weapons of their choice. They also rode their own horses, for which they drew a feed and shoeing allowance.

The force formed the Federal Government's response to two factors. One was that many aliens who crossed the border were smugglers operating at points not covered by the Mounted Customs Inspectors. The other was that the American public had at last grown alarmed at the myriads of all ilks streaming through the Open Door.

In 1917 the first general immigration act, aimed at keeping out more than freaks, halfwits, subversives, beggars, incompetents, convicts and brats, was finally passed. Twenty-one years after it had been proposed by Lodge, the ability to read and write was made a port of entry requirement.

The "Asiatic Barred Zone" was enlarged, besides, by the addition of the Pacific Islands. Also, a good conduct clause was appended. Those could be deported who followed up lawful entry by committing certain specified crimes.

The year of that measure was the one in which the United States joined the Allies opposing Kaiser Wilhelm's Germany in World War I. President Wilson's administration, therefore, paid even closer attention to what was afoot on the border. Carranza's anti-American leanings aligned him with Germany. Hopeful of clearing the way by submarines for invasion of the United States via Mexico, the

25

Kaiser's government had promised Carranza a reward that would have reversed the outcome of the Mexican War of 1848. In return for giving Germany a base for striking north of the boundary, Mexico was pledged the return of Texas, California and all points in between.

So all the Army's old Indian fighting posts were manned again in force. Yet in the end, it was not the war which wrought upheaval all along the line. For there the Women's Christian Temperance Union proved much more shattering than the Kaiser and all the dread arrows of war in his quiver.

While the nation's fighting men were abroad, or afloat or in training camps, the W. C. T. U. teamed up with enough nonfighting ones to bully Congress into voting the country dry. What was called the "War Prohibition Act" was voted ten days after the Armistice of November 11, 1918, ended hostilities. The act said that the United States could not provide food for military forces that were about to be disbanded or spare grain for distilling purposes *"except for export."* That phrase inserted with a straight face the measure remained in effect for more than a year. By then Volstead's National Prohibition Act had been passed, vetoed by President Wilson and passed again by the necessary Senate and House majorities on October 28, 1919. The Eighteenth or Prohibition Amendment, that was ratified in January of 1920, put the War Prohibition Act out of business, but did not change a picture already painted by Volstead.

Or perhaps it would be more accurate to call it an engraving in dry point. In either case a part of his accomplishment was the violence that roused even the placid Canadian boundary. As for the ever hectic Mexican Border, the cheers of delighted smugglers resounded from sea to sea.

Nothing could have been more timely as far as the bandits south of the line were concerned. For in the West, the day of the English Hereford had replaced that of the Mexican longhorn. Rustling along the border had been hard hit by this change; although still a pursuit, it was a fading one. Many former rustlers had already switched to other sorts of smuggling, while hampered by the small American demand for most Mexican dry goods. Now they began pushing products which had abruptly won hordes of admirers in the United States.

Away from the towns of the border, the liquors made south of it were no more than names to Americans who had heard of them at all. But with whiskey declared so perilous that *it could only be legally served to invalids,* Gringos were ready to take on any drink with the spike of life in it. So over the boundary came distillations that were anything but spirits of grain. From grapes and sugarcane came aguardiente and habanero. From one variety of the century plant came tequila, so popular with Mexicans that smugglers as well as sellers of liquors were known as tequileros. From a botanical cousin came mescal. Those who found the prices of these too high settled for sotol, distilled from a member of the yucca tribe.

With the market wide and deep, the stakes were high. Inside the United States wholesale fencers of contraband stood ready to pay premium prices. South of the line were merchants who could make it worthwhile for smugglers to risk imprisonment or death. The only involved persons who could not make a profit were the American officers who obeyed orders by trying to stop the influx of Mexican spirits. They got no raise in pay when "dry" lunacy made their jobs a hundredfold more hazardous than they had been.

The Mounted Guards were formed for no such purpose as this, yet they were drafted to fight Volstead's War. While attending to their normal duties they had suffered no fatalities since being organized. The Wartime Prohibition Act had been in effect for less than half a year when two officers were slain within a month of the other. On April 16, 1919, Clarence M. Childress was gunned down near El Paso. Three weeks later Charles L. Hopkins shared that fate in Laredo's vicinity.

The Mounted Customs inspectors were even more inevitably involved than the Guards since blocking smugglers was their primary occupation. And the Texas Rangers were embroiled for two reasons. There was a state as well as a Federal law against bringing liquor over the line into Texas. Then the tequileros, or horsebackers as they were known to many Americans, often committed other crimes on the way back from depositing their contraband.

They owed the name "horsebacker" to methods of operation which in turn were due to the state of the border zone at the time. In 1920, seventy-five years after the Rio Grande portion of it officially became a part of the United States, most of it was thinly settled or complete wilderness. Outside of sea oriented San Diego and El Paso there were still no sizable towns on the American side, and they were the only ones tied to the rest of the country by highways.

Setting aside parts of the industrial Northeast, it can be said of the United States that it had railways before it had roads. This was triply true of the West. It had wagon trails which were seasonally unusable, for as they were without foundations, rains or melting snow turned them into quagmires. In desert stretches bogging down in sand was a likelihood for machines. Many roads were gnawed in two by flash floods.

By 1920 the horse was on its way out elsewhere in the country and multi-horsepower very much in. Yet in the West, and most particularly near the border, the old-fashioned hay burner, be it horse, mule or burro, remained the standard means of transportation.

Liquor from Mexico was brought in by pack animals that were sometimes the smugglers themselves. Generally it was loaded on trains of mules or donkeys, led by mounted and heavily armed tequileros. Safely across the boundary, they next had the problem of putting their contraband within reach of American bootleggers. Serving cities, these were car drivers who could only go as near to the border as the road system would permit. The situation at El Paso was different, for roads led in and out of that city over which drivers could steer machines with confidence, if not the comfort offered by paved highways. But from points farther down the Rio Grande it was necessary for horsebackers to follow trails leading deep into the interior.

Down in the river's Lower Valley, for example, a network of half a dozen trails ran through the chaparral of Zapata, Starr and Hidalgo counties to deposit points in Duval and Jim Wells, which it took loaded pack animals several days to reach. Other trail patterns served tequileros in the High Plains and Big Bend sections. The point where they delivered and were paid might be an old building near a road or the siding of a cooperative railway. These could lie inland 100 beeline miles and many more overland ones.

The Mounted Customs Inspectors made a practice of trying to intercept the Mexicans well inside Texas rather than at riverside posts. In a dry country satisfactory camping spots were none too common. Men who were working animals all day in the heat had to bring them to a water hole by night. And there had to be grazing available, too, or brisk pressing forward the next day would be out of the question.

So strategy often took the form of lurking near a guessed camping point until smugglers had unsaddled and were taking their ease. In the attack that followed the advantage was with the Customs men, reinforced at times by Texas Rangers. But the country was so big and the bandidos so wily that they often got through to where American bootleggers were waiting. For had not percentages been in their favor, the traffic would, of course, have come to a soon halt.

Also they took lives as well as lost them. Such a case was remembered in a modern Bureau organ, *Customs Today:* "One afternoon in 1922, on the road between Aguilares and Torrecillas down in Webb County, Texas, Mounted Customs Inspector Robert Stuart Rumsey was killed by three Mexican Whiskey smugglers."

Officers fared better the next year, according to a report published by the Hebbronville, Texas, *Enterprise:* On November 23, 1923 "Mounted Customs officers Jack Webb, Roy Hearn, Will Cotulla, Art Barter and Frank Smith trailed a bunch of horseback liquor smugglers from Jenning's Ranch in Zapata County to Bruin's pasture in Webb County, where they overtook them. There was a running gun fight in which one smuggler was killed. The officers seized 450 quarts of liquor, four horses, four riding saddles, three pack saddles, two Winchesters and 200 rounds of ammunition."

But as was implicit in such early names as the River Watchers and the River Riders, the Mounted Guards were policers of the line. "It was our business," Judge Rawls recalled, "to learn all the river crossings feasible for smugglers in the stretch of the border assigned to us. Acting on an informer's tip or a hunch we would wait by a trail leading away from such a crossing—all night, if need be—for men moving contraband to show up. Sometimes it was silver, jewels, textiles or leatherwork. More often it was cattle, sheep, or liquor."

In combination with former Guardsman Robert Sparks, Judge Rawls offered a description of the tequilero pack trains. The animals, which might be horses but were more commonly mules or burros, might number from six or eight to as many as twenty. Their herders might be two or three or twice that number. The liquor was not carried in anything breakable or hard to adjust to the beasts' pack saddles.

"The smugglers would bring in skin bags full of liquor—mescal, sotol or tequila—across the river by burro or mule trains," Sparks declared. "They used goatskins, with the hair on the inside. The hide of a big billy would hold about fourteen gallons. No, the smugglers didn't bother to clean them first."

Thus the man on watch by night for tequilero trains could detect their approach by two senses besides sight; first he could hear the liquor sloshing in the skins, and next he winced at the rank odor for which goats have been forever famous.

In 1921 Judge Rawls joined the Mounted Guards at Presidio, in whose vicinity he patrolled for several years. Interviewed at McAllen, he told of a time when he and his partner, one Cleve Hurst, devised a method of posting night watch along a path and getting some much needed shut-eye, too. The warning system they worked out was to stretch athwart a narrows in a hillside trail, a string of which one end was weighted by stone. A horse breasting the string would twitch it from the branch of a shrub and drop the rock on a tin mess plate.

This burglar alarm went off somewhere in the small hours. "I didn't hear it," the Judge said, "but Cleve and the Mexicans did. Knowing something was wrong, they were trying to turn around in a place we'd picked because the trail skirted an arroyo there, and the commotion and the swearing of the smugglers was what awoke me.

"Hurst and I grabbed the rifles we had handy and fired warning shots over the heads of the Mexicans to tell them we had the drop on them and yelled in Spanish for them to stay where they were and stick 'em high." Judge Rawls sipped his coffee with reminiscent satisfaction. "Well, the shots and our shouting panicked already nervous horses, which began squealing and rearing, keeping the smugglers too busy to shoot back, so they hollered they were surrendering and dropping their guns. The noise their weapons made crashing through the brush scared the horses worse than ever. Backing down the trail, a couple of them got tangled up with the mule train loaded with contraband, and a couple of mules rolled down into the arroyo. They were loaded with tequila, as it turned out, and so were the other four that the three smugglers we arrested had led into that tin pan trap."

Immigration problems were mounting at this period for men who had largely been turned into a Customs police. In 1921 Congress put the first real bar on the Open Door as far as Europeans were concerned. Taking a look at the census of 1910 rather than the less significant figures of the 1920 headcount, the national representatives noted that in the first decade of the century foreigners had swarmed into America's unbarred ports of entry at the rate of over 820,000 annually. Their corrective move was to cut the permitted total to 350,000 a year.

Three years later, by using the census of 1890 as a yardstick, an annual immigration total of 164,677 was arrived at. And what was called the National Origins Provision set up an immigration quota for each nationality, reckoned on the percentage of foreign-born immigrants from the respective countries resident in the United States as of 1920.

Now the remarkable thing about this essay in planned immigration was that it affected peoples of the Eastern Hemisphere only. Specified as "non-quota immigrants" were all comers from Canada, Mexico, Cuba, Haiti, San Domingo and the nations of Central and South America.

Congress recognized, however, that the clapping of quotas on immigration from Europe would multiply the problems stemming from the Chinese Exclusion Act and its successors. The sorts of people most affected were peasants who wouldn't scruple to enter America as trespassers. An emergency had been created, in a word, with which the few and loosely organized members of the Mounted Guards could not be expected to cope.

Thus the need for a sizable and formally organized immigration police was grasped and acted upon with unusual promptness. The United States Immigration Border Patrol was created May 8, 1924, by the Labor Department Appropriations Act. This specified that at least "$1,000,000 of this amount shall be expended for additional land-border patrol." If the Rio Grande was not technically a land boundary, it could be crossed with ease at enough points to make the shoe fit.

The Canadian Border was also to be patrolled, but it differed from that of Mexico in several important ways. The Great Lakes and their St. Lawrence River outlet were not shallows, easily forded by illegal aliens. West of the Lakes the boundary was difficult of access by Europeans and most of it was so skimpily settled as to offer neither operation bases for smugglers nor likely destinations for their clients. Along the eastern part of the Canadian line there was smuggling, to be sure, but it rarely involved the intrusion of foreigners. The rum being run across it was not in the main done by aliens but by American citizens, denying the immigration issue raised along the Mexican border.

3

THE
BORDER
GETS AND
INITIATES
ITS PATROL

History was so little regarded when the Border Patrol was formed that official recollections of the period today use such phrases as "about" and "it is thought that" when naming the number of officers assigned to particular posts. Some of the information that follows is therefore based on estimates rather than on accurately recorded data.

Originally the allowed muster was 450 officers. Some were Mounted Guard veterans; others were former Rangers, sheriffs or town marshals. Many came from a curious source. These were appointees culled from the Civil Service Register of qualified railway mail clerks. All except some of the latter hailed from border states. Most had been reared on ranches and owned all the arts of cowmen, including skill at tracking and the use of revolver and rifle.

El Paso was their organization point. Recruitment began in July 1924. How informal it was can be gathered from the reminiscences of Emmanuel A. "Dogie" Wright, who joined on September 18. A former Texas Ranger, he was in El Paso at the time for the excellent reason that he hadn't seen it before. While satisfying his curiosity, he met an acquaintance who told him of the Border Patrol and urged him to enlist. Slight of build, Wright fell short of the new force's physical requirements, yet his experience as a Ranger gave him points not scored by the burliest of railway clerks. Seeing this, the recruiting officer told him that if he could stretch himself up to the required five feet seven and come within ten pounds of the asked weight, he was in.

Bachelorhood was at first a requirement, and no obstacle in the as yet stag West. The other demanded qualifications were limited to the old Persian trio: skill at riding and shooting and a sound grip on verity. The members bunked in a military police barracks dating from World War I, where they trained without benefit of manuals, uniforms or any other government issue but badges. Like the Mounted Guards, their horses joined when they did, and the riders supplied their own firearms.

They adopted a slogan which, being men of the frontier, they didn't bury in Latin. "Honor first," it ran, but from there on their course had to be plotted by guesswork and experience. Beyond the two-man patrol teams of the Mounted Guard they were without precedent to look to. They knew no more of immigration and international law than did or does the average citizen. There was one thing they felt sure of, though. Not counting smugglers from below the line, they didn't expect to have trouble with Mexicans, so free to move into the United States on peaceful missions that only census takers kept any count of those who did.

After a mobilization period which lasted a few months, the approximately 450 officers were distributed to posts on the Canadian boundary as well. The Gulf Coast and Florida peninsular border wasn't created until 1925. Along the Mexican Border the Patrolmen were divided into three groups, each answerable to a different district immigration director. The California district, which included a post in Yuma, was supervised by a Los Angeles headquarters, and posts on the Lower Rio Grande Valley and the High Plains by a San Antonio one. Only in the El Paso district, which stretched from the Big Bend to the western Arizona desert, were the headquarters of the immigration director and the commander of the Patrol in the same place.

The designation of a district supervisor was Chief Patrol Inspector. Subordinate to him were one Deputy Chief and two Assistant Patrol

Inspectors. Outpost stations were headed by Senior Patrol Inspectors, at first appointed and later earned by merit in addition to seniority. All others were Patrol Inspector, usually referred to as PIs.

Before following them into action, the state of the border as of that time will be briefly presented. At its Pacific Coast end, San Ysidro wasn't a name big enough to make any but detailed maps, while Chula Vista on the American side and Tijuana on the Mexican were too insignificant for notice by encyclopaedias. The most significant development was in the Colorado Desert area. There irrigation farming had brought flourishing El Centro into being, and south of it, line-touching Calexico faced its opposite anagram. Not quite yet the metropolis of Baja California, Mexicali had been made its capital.

In Arizona now booming Yuma was doing anything but that and Mexico had no Colorado Valley offering. East along the line little Sonoyta looked across it at even smaller Lukeville. Farther on was twin-Nogales, neither bustling. Over toward the New Mexico boundary, the copper smelting town of Douglas was thriving on its lone specialty, but Agua Prieta, Sonora, was no more than a settlement. In New Mexico nobody since Villa had thought Columbus worth noticing, and other points were hardly more than railroad stops which served ranching districts along a line which Mexicans had likewise sparsely settled.

In Texas, El Paso was larger than rapidly growing Ciudad Juarez. Downstream from there, towns were developing on a much more modest scale but following the same pattern. In every case the American town was considerably larger than its Mexican competitor across the river. But the Spanish-speaking population on the United States side was even greater than is now the case. Irrigation farming had not then drawn many Anglos to parts which were hard to take before the advent of indoor cooling devices.

Inability to bear the climate was one cause for the soon resignation of some who had become Patrolmen by shining in tests designed to uncover capable railway mail clerks. Others quit when they found out the actual nature of their duties. "We hardly thought of ourselves as immigration officers until Prohibition was over," as Wright explained. "While it lasted we didn't have much time for aliens that weren't packing in liquor."

As earlier pointed out, the smugglers packed guns, and in consequence the Border Patrol's beginning years were fierce, explosive and bloody. But if the going was rough, what the force got out of training

34

under fire was an esprit de corps and a tradition of carrying assignments out at all costs that could not have been gained under the umbrella of peace. Some 25 percent of the original recruits thought the action too hot to be faced. The volunteers who took their places found themselves among men who had learned to trust each other when the heat was on and expected newcomers to be equally dependable.

Then there was a subtropical sun to be endured, and seasonally it could be snakeblood cold. Watch was kept not only every day but every minute of each and whether or not winter winds huffed out of snow-topped mountains.

An entire book could easily be devoted to that era. Here it will be sketched via the recollections of some who took part and albums of newspaper clippings, most of which were published in three newspapers of El Paso. Because of its size, its relation to also biggish Ciudad Juarez and its proximity to both desert and valley wilderness, this town was the centerpiece of the whole wild epoch.

An appraisal of how the Border Patrol comported itself in its initial two years was given in a 1926 International News Service feature issued from San Antonio. "W. A. Whalen, district immigration inspection director, is emphatic in his declaration that the border patrol, although only two years old, is the most effective law enforcement organization of its kind in the world . . . They must be able to ride, shoot and work singlehanded—at times in the wildest of country. They must be diplomatic and possess the instincts of a good detective. They must have good habits and stamina to withstand the rigors of border life."

Whalen also gave it as his opinion that the Border Patrol outshone the celebrated Mounties. "Canada's noted northwest mounted police, famed in song and story . . . apparently have a 'soft snap' when one considers the multifarious duties of the border patrol. About the most hazardous duties of the Canadian force is the suppression of smuggling along the United States border. Not so the border patrol . . . That vast hinterland that sweeps along the Rio Grande from the Gulf of Mexico to the New Mexico line must be guarded against the surreptitious entry of undesirable aliens; banditry must be suppressed, and along this particular stretch of the frontier, banditry seems to be the favorite occupation of hundreds . . .

"Gun running is a profitable source of income to many who reap a rich harvest from the smuggling of arms and ammunition into the strife torn republic south of the Rio Grande."

By the time of Whalen's remarks, five Patrolmen had died in the line of duty, of whom four were slain on the Mexican boundary. The first was James F. Mankin, shot at Laredo on September 9, 1924. On December 13 of the same year, Frank H. Clark got like treatment at El Paso. Two were killed at extremes of the Border in 1925: on August 2 Augustin De La Pena at Rio Grande City, Texas, and on October 22 Ross A. Gardiner at Elsinore, California.

De La Pena was thought to have been the victim of a Mexican crazed by marijuana. But most of the fatal operations as of 1926 and the succeeding Prohibition years involved liquor smuggling. And they can be followed in considerable detail, for in that year Mrs. Mary C. Cecil, now a radio operator for the Border Patrol at Laredo, began keeping a scrapbook of pertinent clippings. These were usually dated by the year only, but in some cases the month and day either precede the item or can be extracted from its contents.

Here is a 1926 Associated Press dispatch datelined Tucson, Arizona, which at that time was a wing of the El Paso district. "Tucson officers are hunting three mounted smugglers who ambushed a party of border patrol officers after the latter had seized a liquor pack train 75 miles northwest of Nogales, killing officer William Walker McKee. The party had seized the pack train and were returning in an automobile to Nogales after failing to find the smugglers when they were ambushed from both sides of the highway by three mounted men who fled as they fired into the automobile party. McKee jumped from the machine and charged toward the brush from which the shots came, but he fell, expiring soon afterwards."

The next Patrolman to fall was named in an AP dispatch from Tucson dated July 26, barely more than three months later. "That Lon Parker, United States border patrol officer who was killed Sunday afternoon by the bullets of an unknown assailant, may have been the victim of the same band of smugglers that killed William McKee, fellow officer of Parker's, in the Serrita mountains last April, was the opinion advanced this morning by Walter Miller, inspector in charge of the border patrol operations in this state.

"As Mr. Parker took an important part in unearthing evidence against the two men that were later arrested for Mr. McKee's murder . . . it is thought that they had an operative who had given Mr. Parker a false 'tip' on a train of contraband, and then shot him from ambush as he went alone to investigate."

Concurrently, as clippings testify, Patrolmen were doing their share of the straight shooting. "Two Mexicans, who were killed in a gun battle with border patrolmen near the smelter last night, were identified today as Gabino Godoy, 23, and José Perez, 37," a 1926 El Paso item declared.

"Godoy had been wanted for questioning in connection with the murder of Bob Trice, night watchman in Clint, about eight months ago. State rangers said a Mexican bandit gang has been terrorising Clint, Fabens and Tornillo residents. . .

"Three border patrolmen testified that they fired at the pair in self defense, when they refused to halt while crossing the border near monument No. 1.

"Godoy had a rifle and Perez was armed with a pistol, patrolmen said. The officers said the men fired after they were told to halt. About 30 shots were exchanged."

Another shooting in the same vicinity was related in the El Paso *Times*. "Augustin Avila, about 45, of Juarez, was killed at 8 o'clock last night in an exchange of shots with U. S. Border Patrolmen near monument 1, San Elizario island, about 35 miles east of El Paso.

"Avila was challenged by three patrolmen when he came across the border, Chief Patrol Inspector H. C. Horsley said. Instead of halting, the man opened fire on the officers . . . ."

If these were engagements out in the brush, a large number of articles show that smugglers also tried to bull contraband directly through downtown El Paso. On May 11, 1926, it was reported that, "Ysodor Lopez, 20, was fatally wounded by officers John G. Gillis and C. C. Mattox of the border patrol, in a gun battle at 9 o'clock last night at Fourth and Canal streets . . . . According to the story of the officers, Lopez was one of four men who were challenged by them after they had crossed the canal bridge with four sacks of liquor.

"Two of the men, according to the officers, dropped the sacks and fled, but Lopez and another man stopped and opened fire."

The shooting by smugglers toward a populous American town naturally imperiled its inhabitants. EL PASO CAFE HIT, a subheading of one news story announced. "Under protection of 12 gunmen lined in battle formation on the Mexican side of the river, two men smuggled a quantity of liquor across the river this afternoon. When two border patrolmen made a run after the smugglers the gunmen on the opposite bank of the river opened fire. . . .

"During the time of the battle a bullet crashed thru a window of the U & I Cafe at Oregon and San Antonio and fell on the floor."

Another item indicated that citizens of Ciudad Juarez would rather shoot at El Paso than be shot back at. "Protest against U. S. officers shooting across the Rio Grande was made by Mexican Federal officers today.

"The protest followed a gun battle about 6 A.M. between U. S. border patrolmen and gunmen protectors of liquor smugglers during which Angel Tarango, 26, of 427 Charles, El Paso, was killed on the Mexican side, and a horse was shot from beneath Horge L. Carillo, Mexican Customs guard. . . .

"Seventy-five shots were fired during the battle, which began when two patrolmen stepped out of hiding in the standpipes district to intercept two smugglers who were coming across the river with sacks on their shoulders . . .

"Immediately shots rang out on the Mexican side of the river, and someone in one of the adobe huts on the American side of the river also opened fire on the patrolmen, U.S. officials declared . . .

"Patrolmen say that every night for the past six months they have been fired on from the Mexican side of the river."

A couple of El Paso newspapers attacked patrolmen for shooting back at snipers from Juarez, drawing a letter to the El Paso *Times.* "Recently the Times and Herald have both printed editorials commenting on the gun fights between border patrolmen and Mexican smugglers. They criticize the American officers for careless shooting into Mexico.

"The Times editorial writer . . . failed to mention the fact that a bullet fired by a Mexican fiscal guard about ten or twelve days ago landed in El Paso and broke one of the plate glass windows out of one of the downtown cafes. He fails to mention the fact that in this same fight there were perhaps some seven or eight Mexican fiscal guards firing at the United States officers, and that the only reason these fiscal guards had for firing upon the American officers was to distract their attention so that a band of Mexican smugglers might bring their smuggled goods into the United States under cover of their fire. . . ."

The constant gunfire, as one newspaper feature writer noted, was changing the style of El Paso architecture. "New houses that have been built recently along the Rio Grande back of the gas works, known as the standpipes district, have blank walls on the river side. They were so constructed to prevent unexpected bullets from smashing thru windows and doors. For there is where the U.S. border patrol recently has been battling rum smuggling gunmen."

The feature likewise detailed common procedures on the part of contraband runners and their backers. "Between noon and 5 P.M. is the favorite crossing time. Smugglers assemble their liquor behind a dike on the Juarez side of the river in a sparsely settled section. A Mexican customs outpost is within a few feet.

"Ready for the dash, the smugglers throw their sacks of liquor over their backs. A spotter on the American side fires a signal if the coast is clear.

"Gunmen crawl upon a high bridge which overlooks the American side of the river. The bridge is within fifty feet of the Mexican customs block house. Then the smugglers make a dash for the north shore.

"Over the river, they climb the river road embankment, dash over the railroad tracks in five steps, plunge thru the Franklin irrigation canal on the run, and are inside the sheltering houses in two steps.

"If anyone who resembles an officer or hijacker shows his head above the railroad embankment the Mexican gunmen cut down on him. They fire directly into a thickly populated section of the city. House fronts are bullet marked."

According to former Patrolman Wright, there were houses of a particular sort in Ciudad Juarez which were also bullet marked, and concerning this a letter was written which was not designed for publication in any of El Paso's journals. The commander of Fort Bliss complained that officers firing toward Mexico were sending bullets into the redlight district of Juarez, thereby endangering the lives of American soldiers.

Yet in spite of acting as customs officers most of the time, the Patrolmen managed to attend to their proper duties of suppressing unlawful immigration. One 1926 case was humorously pathetic. "His fondness for wieners and sauerkraut caused the downfall of Emil Kieskott, German alien, who was arrested by border patrolmen yesterday. Kieskott, who had been in El Paso but two days, found a small El Paso restaurant which was more or less known for its canine delicacy and sauerkraut.

"The idea of enjoying some of his favorite food caused Kieskott to return to the cafe. Meanwhile patrolmen had been tipped off . . ."

The story is also interesting on the score of showing liaison with information sources—presumably immigration officials on the staffs of consuls—deep inside Mexico. "Kieskott's movements had been traced from Tampico, where he landed, to Mexico City and thence to Juarez, from where he crossed to this country."

There were also immigrants from the Asiatic Barred Zone and gun-handy smugglers of that sort of contraband. In September of 1926 an El Paso paper reported that, "G. C. Dennis, U. S. border patrol inspector with headquarters here, was wounded and narrowly escaped death, while Churoku Andow . . . was shot through the right thigh in a battle today between immigration officers and Japanese smugglers 25 miles from Valentine [Texas]. Andow, who is said to be an alien, was brought to the City-County hospital here.

"Dennis's forehead was grazed by a pistol bullet fired by Andow, it is charged.

"Inspectors were watching for four Japanese who were to be smuggled into the U.S. When a signal was given by two Japanese on this side of the line, Dennis closed in.

"Dennis grabbed Andow's arm, when the latter opened fire. Inspector Lester R. Dillon, who was down the river, rushed to his comrade's aid and shot Andow."

But most from the Eastern Hemisphere were white. "Sixteen Europeans have been apprehended by border patrolmen in December," a 1926 report affirmed. "A total of 118 aliens were caught, 102 of them being Mexican [smugglers]."

On the eighteenth of December the El Paso *Times* printed an article which shows that patrolmen also took part in posses searching for missing men. The item interestingly blends the flavor of the old West with the savagery of Prohibition gangsterism. It also speaks for a day when most men of parts had nicknames.

"The presumed victim [of a 'ride' by mobsters] was P. O. 'Denver Blackie' Burcham . . . Burcham has been missing since last week. The story of the kidnapping came out yesterday when officers questioned a youth known here only as 'The Blue Punk' who told him that a booze running gang had seized the restaurant owner and had taken him to an isolated spot where he was thrown into a water trough, bound with rope, fish line and barbed wire and left to die. Investigators found substantiation of the story at the trough but Burcham was gone . . . The Blue Punk told officers that the act was in revenge for the hijacking of a half million dollar cargo of liquor last Friday . . .

"Participating in the present search are . . . patrolmen Warren 'Tombstone' Smith and 'Del Rio' Earl Young."

4

VOLSTEAD'S
WILD
WEST
SHOW
CONTINUED

What was taking place at El Paso was being duplicated to a lesser extent at other places along the line. And the small but active force of Mounted Customs Inspectors were continuing their practice of riding away from the border to hunt tequileros in brush thickets to the north. In this, as an item published in the Hebbronville *Enterprise* on January 16, 1926 demonstrates, they were now being sided by patrolmen.

"U. S. Mounted Customs Inspectors Jack Webb, Frank Smith, Tom Brady, Will Cotulla, John Moore, and Border Patrolmen Charlie Wallis and Don Gilliland trailed a bunch of horsebackers from La Mota pasture in Zapata County, trailing them about forty-five miles into Duval County, where they found them camped on the Ball Ranch near Benavides, Texas. A gunfight followed in which one smuggler was killed and three others escaped with their horses and saddles. The officers seized 550 quarts of tequila, three Winchesters, one pistol, seven horses and six saddles."

But the horse-riding Customs Inspectors could not effectively cope with rum runners who sped in cars toward collection points in or near El Paso. For that purpose the auto-driving Customs Agent was the needed man. He was also, as a 1926 news bulletin proves, the shot-at man. "The five casualties in the battle between rum runners and customs officers Thursday night are:

"Unidentified rum runner, first name is Alexandro, was killed.

"U. S. Customs officer Leon L. Gemoets, 51, of 2400 San Diego, shot in the back, the bullet deflecting from eighth rib and lodging against spine. Danger of some paralytic condition. Probably recover.

"U. S. Customs Officer John Parrott, 48, of 3020 Cambridge, shot thru stomach. Probably recover unless peritonitis sets in. Condition critical.

"Francisco Rodriguez, with rum runner party, wound in side. Not serious.

"Vicente Ariola, rum runner, shot in shoulder. Not dangerous."

Gemoets did recover, as predicted, while the fears expressed for his partner were not an alarmist's cackle. "John W. Parrott, U. S. customs agent, shot in a liquor battle several days ago, died at Masonic hospital Friday night," a follow-up bulletin declared.

"Leon L. Gemoets, who was shot during the same battle, is improving . . .

"A touch of pneumonia was indirectly responsible for Parrot's death. Coughing aggravated the wound."

But most of the war of that border epoch was fought close to the line. It is noteworthy that unless patrolmen became casualties their specific actions were rarely reported. In particular, no officer was ever named as one whose bullet brought down a smuggler.

"We didn't want any of us to get the reputation of a killer," Dogie Wright explained. "Some of us were probably as good with a gun as a lot of the famous old timers whose strings of shootings everybody knew about, but we didn't want to be known that way. We shot a lot of men then, and we had to—for we ourselves had the highest casualty rate of any police force in the country—but none of us built up any reputation as a gunny, and that's how we liked it."

Wright also made it clear that the Mexicans whom patrolmen faced were expert gunmen. "Most of them had seen service in one or more revolutions before they became smugglers. They were tough, game and knew how to shoot."

Newspaper testimony of 1927 proves that Wright was correct on both counts. "Rum Runner Is Shot In Gun Fight," a February headline announced. "Francisco Loya, 22, is in the City-County hospital probably fatally wounded as the result of a battle between border patrolmen and smugglers near the river bank at San Elizario last night. Another Mexican, wounded, escaped in the underbrush. Three other Mexicans, said to have been lookouts for rum smugglers, are prisoners. . . .

"Following the shooting of Loya, an attempt was made to ambuscade border patrolmen, and about 40 rifle shots were fired at them from several houses nearby."

A time when the smugglers scored was recounted in the El Paso *Herald* of April 21. "Thad Pippin, 37, was killed and Egbert N. Crosett, 30, was wounded, when they were ambushed by Mexican liquor smugglers just south of the brick plant, opposite the Smelter, late last night.

"Pippin and Crosett, both members of the U.S. Border Patrol, had just arrested two Mexicans and seized two liquor-laden burros when pals of the arrested pair opened fire on them with sawed-off shotguns . . .

"Seven buckshot wounds were found in Pippin's body, three in the breast, three in the right shoulder and one in the face. Patrolmen said the shots were fired at close range.

"Crosett was wounded four times, four pistol wounds being found on him."

Scattered reports came in from other precincts. The Fort Worth *Star-Telegram*, for instance, published a dispatch from Brownsville dated April 28: "Search for the body of a liquor smuggler, drowned in the Rio Grande south of Hidalgo following a gun battle with border patrol officers Tuesday, has been unavailing . . . The smuggler went down when his boat overturned in midstream . . . The officers came upon the smugglers at Grangene, and when the smugglers opened fire a lively battle ensued. One of the party of liquor runners succeeded in making his escape, two were captured and the fourth went down while trying to reach a safe haven on the south bank of the Rio Grande."

There were also reports of a new smuggling angle. "Rum runners from Mexico," a United Press dispatch from Brownsville related, "bring much liquor into this country by airplane, according to J. F. Deloney, federal immigration patrolman here.

"It is almost impossible for the border patrolman to halt this type of rum runner . . ."

The Associated Press issued a concurring wire, datelined Tucson,

Arizona, Dec. 13: "United States border patrol officers said here last night that airplanes believed to be engaged in smuggling aliens and contraband are flying across the southwestern border between El Paso and Tucson without officials being able to check them.

"The declaration was made by Walter Miller of El Paso and Sam Gray, divisional heads of the border patrol.

"The information was based on reports from Ajo, an Arizona mining camp, which told of the activity of planes along the border."

Long to be without an air arm itself, the Patrol was having all it could do to deal with the invading ground troops. Most of the published reports were based on information obtained second hand; but Pete Haines of the El Paso *Post* appointed himself war correspondent and wrote a graphic description of a 1928 engagement.

"The battle . . . took place in the old river bed 20 miles from El Paso near San Elizario.

"Seven patrolmen had been assigned to the area . . . All were on the bank, hidden behind clumps of bushes.

"It was pitch dark. A horse snorted and a cavalcade moving up the river became visible. There was an advance guard, a center detachment and rear guard. There were a dozen in the party.

"The first two officers planned to let the entire cavalcade through . . . Their plans went for naught when a sharpeyed smuggler spied them . . . and the liquor runners fired a volley into the clump of bushes. They were using rifles, shotguns and revolvers.

"A hat of one of the officers was shot from his head. . . . Lead literally rained around them. Then they swung into action with their rifles at close range. . . .

"One of the invaders circled and opened fire from the rear. He was met with a barrage. The horse fell, regained its feet and with its rider, retreated. . . .

"Snipers from a haystack and houses on the opposite side of the river bed started a rat-tat-tat of rifle fire to protect the retreat of their confederates. . . .

"The determination of the smugglers to carry their cargo thru was shown by a survey of the field at daybreak. From the place where the first shots were fired the invaders advanced approximately 100 yards up the valley before they gave up.

"Liquor, most of it in sacks, was strewn along the line of battle . . . The farthest advanced sack, within a hundred feet of the paved highway, was bloodstained. A trail of blood led from it to the opposite bank of the valley and into the brush.

"One smuggler remained behind . . . He was shot thru the mouth, left side and right hip.

"Three blood trails leading from the valley were found . . . Shotgun shells, rifle and revolver cartridges were found scattered over the ground today. A smuggler's hat, pierced by a bullet, was found . . ."

Two advantages enjoyed by the Mexicans were mentioned by Wright when discussing such night encounters. "Being all Indians or just about that, they could see better in the dark than we could, and if the wind was right for them they could even smell us."

But if the scouts of the smugglers did pass the lurking place of the patrolmen, these could pretty well gauge the progress of the smugglers by the sounds of the oncoming burros or mules. "Sometimes we could tie the smugglers into knots by spooking the whole pack train," Wright remembered. "One of our men had a trick of throwing a blanket just as the train drew abreast of us that would scare the lead mule and they'd all scatter."

Animals traveling at night were not the only beings subject to startling surprises at that time and vicinity; so was a purveyor of bedding who fancied himself securely at rest. In describing an early morning exchange of gun fire between patrolmen and smugglers in downtown El Paso, the *Post* declared that, "One bullet crashed through a window on the eighth floor of the Paso del Norte into the room in which C. F. Thomas, blanket salesman, was sleeping. This was several blocks from the scene of the shooting."

One reason why bullets sometimes flew promiscuously about the city was that so many besides smugglers took to arms on the Mexican side of the border when an international affray began. In the previous chapter it was noticed that a letter writer to the *Times* charged Mexican officials with abetting contraband runners. The accusation was echoed by Chief Patrol Inspector Nick D. Collaer in a 1928 missive to the *Herald*. "For years it has been common knowledge that Mexican fiscal guards have assisted smugglers of contraband. This assistance has taken the form of directing such smugglers to the points of crossing, 'spotting' on the American officers, and protecting smugglers with rifle fire from the Mexican side of the Rio Grande . . . Patrol Inspectors have, through field glasses, seen smugglers pay off fiscal guards before said smugglers were permitted to enter this country. They have likewise seen fiscal guards fire upon them from Mexico . . ."

In another letter Collaer took note of what he defined as the regular bribery rate by which liquor could be moved from Juarez to El Paso. "That . . . the Mexican fiscal guards charge $2 per 4½ gallon can to permit smugglers to cross with liquor is as well known to the smugglers as is the wholesale price of liquor in Mexico."

The fiscal guards were not the only Mexican officials who took a kindly interest in the smugglers of Juarez. Chief among these was one Manuel Vasquez, who was subsequently jailed south of the river for some unrelated offense. Learning as much, Dogie Wright and a fellow patrolman decided to cross by bridge and look over an elusive enemy. He remained in that class, for when they reached the Juarez jusgado, they were told that Senor Vasquez was out at the moment and wasn't expected back until morning.

"The city bosses didn't want to interfere with his rum running," Wright chuckled.

Yet, as in 1926, the Patrol Inspectors of the Immigration Bureau found time now and again to do some of the work for which they had been primarily organized. "After a lull of two years," the *Post* announced in 1928, "Europeans are again attempting to sneak into the United States thru the 'back door,' as the frontier along the Mexican border is called.

"This is indicated by the fact that thirty-one Europeans were arrested last month by border patrolmen on charges of entering the United States without passports, federal agents said today.

"Immigration authorities say that a large number of the aliens who have been arrested are Russians who have lived in Mexico for comparatively long periods. Since September 21, border patrolmen have arrested 21 Russians . . .

"Immigration authorities say that for more than a year they have had information that aliens have been slipping over the border with smugglers in the desert west of El Paso and going north on freight trains at night."

Mexicans, considered as aliens separate from smugglers, were now occasionally a problem, too. Southwestern irrigation farming was luring to the American side of the line men who didn't wish to risk being turned back by immigrant inspectors because of bad records, illiteracy or inability to meet financial responsibility requirements. They therefore took the wetback route into the United States. Most were simple laborers who shrugged and accepted arrest when challenged, but hard case exceptions inevitably turned up.

Word of the first major violence involving a Mexican who was braced for his immigration credentials was broadcast by the Associated Press under the dateline, Calexico, California, February 12, 1929. "Jose Prado, identified as the Mexican who killed Norman G. Ross, American border patrol officer, near here Friday night, was shot and killed at a ranch two and a half miles from Mexicali, Mexico, by Alberto Garcia, chief of the Mexican rural police.

"Search was started for Prado after his brother, Julio Prado, was taken into custody. The automobile in which Ross was killed belonged to Julio Prado, a check revealed.

"Ross, with another immigration officer, W. L. Ferguson, arrested two Mexicans Friday near Calipatria, when they found one of them without a passport and the other carrying a pistol of Spanish make. Ross started to El Centro with the prisoners but never reached the county seat."

At the other end of the border the United Press told a story with a better ending on or about the same date. "Lupe Garcia, bad man of the border country, is dead. He was shot and killed near Santa Maria Friday in a gun duel with . . . [a] United States border patrolman. . . .

"Garcia became a very much wanted man in October, 1926, when he shot and killed 'Slim' Billings at the request of a rum running ring that had found Billings in their way. . . . He organized a dope and alien smuggling ring. Many times American officers surprised one of Garcia's convoys, but each time they were repulsed by the youthful bandit who covered his runners with machine gun fire."

Not often referred to during this period, dope was again in the news, not much later, this time at El Paso. "Approximately 50 pounds of marijuana, characterized as 'enough of the drug to hop up all Juarez,' and one of the largest . . . seizures to be made here in years, were seized with a quantity of liquor in a vacant room of a house near the stand pipes early Sunday morning by border patrolmen."

That fifty pound drop in a bathtub would make modern patrolmen smile. It was a portent of things to come, though, and meanwhile, all contraband wasn't being moved in one direction. A 1929 El Paso news story told of an effort to push a wondrous assortment of goods south across the line while birds were awake to watch.

"Pedro Pichardo, 25, Juarez, was wounded in a daylight gunfight between border patrolmen and a gang of men attempting to smuggle goods from the United States into Mexico . . . west of the Santa

Fe bridge at 6:30 A.M. Thursday. Another man, border patrolmen believe, was either killed or seriously wounded on the Mexican side of the border . . .

"Pichardo, patrolmen charge, is one of three men who dashed across the river a few minutes before 6:30 in answer to a spotter's signal from the United States side.

"As the three men approached . . . a car containing large bundles of goods drew along the canal bank. Three patrolmen, hiding a block away, arose to challenge the men crossing the river because their act constituted illegal entry.

"The men dropped their bundles in the water and two ran for Mexico and one for the United States. Simultaneously . . . two men opened fire on the patrolmen from Mexico, while a sniper fired on them from one of the houses . . . at their rear. The driver of the car ran into hiding."

As a result of all this excitement, "Patrolmen seized the goods and the car. Two hundred and fifty rounds of high calibre, soft-nosed expanding ammunition was in the catch . . . Bolts of rayon cloth, overalls, gloves, towels, silk stockings, a bridal dress and baby clothes are among the articles in the lot."

Smuggling into Mexico furnished more 1929 news. In March, a revolt against the administration of President Portes Gil was staged in the border states, and sundry American firms were trying to capitalize on the situation by running munitions over the line. To this situation a pair of photographs in the El Paso *Herald* bore witness. "Below," ran the caption, "is shown Border Patrolman Francis E. Scott . . . at William Beaumont Hospital, where Scott is recovering from wounds received in a gun battle with ammunition smugglers. Bottom picture shows August Steinburn, wounded border patrolman. Steinburn was also wounded by arms smugglers."

Apparently some of this battlefield-type ammunition got into the hands of other than revolutionaries, for it was no common six-gun bullet which felled Patrol Inspector Benjamin T. Hill on Memorial Day. A trail favored by liquor smugglers led through what is still known as "the Hole in the Wall." A break in the cliffs hanging above the Rio Grande's Mexican bank, it lies 20 miles downstream from El Paso. Patrolling his own side of the river in this landmark's vicinity, Hill was assassinated by a man who loosed at his back "a .38 calibre lead bullet of the 'dum dum' type."

Not quite two months later a fellow of Hill's was gunned down at almost the same spot. This, however, was not the work of a sniper from ambush; it took place in an affray "said to have been the most furious and desperate ever fought between United States peace officers and Mexican bandits along the boundary," according to the *Herald.*

Actually two engagements between patrolmen and tequileros were fought on July 20. Ivan Scotten survived the first of these. In the opinion of the *Herald*'s reporter, it "was not too serious . . . 40 rounds of ammunition being fired before the first of the two slain Mexicans dropped from his horse. His body was never recovered, but it is thought that his companions carried the body back across the river while Scotten and his two companions went for assistance."

With three more to side them, the patrolmen promptly returned to a spot where they found smugglers who had been much more successful in gaining reinforcements. Because a downpour was dimming such light as early dawn afforded, the officers could not see what they were driving into until they were trapped.

"Six border patrolmen took part in the second battle. They were ambushed from each side of the narrow road and their front was raked with withering fire from men hiding behind a canal bank and from others concealed in brush in Mexico."

Swinging aside, the patrolmen "drove their automobile into a bank and sought refuge in the dense foliage along the roadside." As Scotten sprang from the car, gun in hand, he was struck with bullets that downed him instanter. Certain he was dead, his comrades surged to make a stand in a copse only to find themselves outmaneuvered. "As they entered the brush they came in close contact with one group of the Mexican desperadoes and saved their lives by rushing into a small cotton patch, closely pursued by other Mexicans who confiscated their automobile for breastworks."

The bandits wanted to seize Scotten's corpse, but this was something his fellows were determined not to allow. "His companions," the *Times* said, "were forced to fight their way back to recover his body and in so doing drove the last of their opponents into Mexico . . . More than 200 shots were fired before the charging inspectors forced the gunmen [estimated to number 20 at the outset] to flee across the Rio Grande. . . .

"Scotten was shot twice while getting out of the patrol automobile when it was ambushed and caught between a cross fire from three sides. Scotten dropped to the ground dead with a bullet wound in his head and another through his body as his five companions fought for more than thirty minutes to save their own lives and to regain possession of their fallen comrade."

The tequileros suffered casualties in the second as well as the first affray, as the *Times* reported in a follow-up story. "Two men, known to United States immigration border patrol officers as Mexican rum runners and 'killers' are believed to have paid with their lives for the fatal shooting of Inspector Ivan E. Scotten, 26, early yesterday morning."

Reported by the *Post* to have been 25, Scotten was a young man with a bright, engaging face. He was El Paso's own, having shone there as a high school athlete in several sports. The town took his snuffing out hard, and its newspapers gave him coverage accordingly. This was of value, because the spotlight was turned upon a previously unnoticed battlefield factor—from the date of organization the officers of the corps were strictly forbidden to shoot unless first fired upon.

Actually in Scotten's case it would seemingly have made no difference, for he could not have secured an even break with men who were already in firing position when he sprang from his car. But passion, if here illogical, fingered a point which undoubtedly had mortally handicapped other patrolmen. "Further investigation," as the *Herald* affirmed, "revealed that Scotten was killed while carrying out orders from Washington preventing an immigration border patrolman from opening fire until he is positive his life is in danger."

"The killing of Ivan E. Scotten, immigration border patrolman, by smugglers," the *Post* complained editorially, "is another sacrifice to duty by members of a brave and loyal band. He is the second patrolman to be killed within a few weeks and the tenth within the past three . . .

"It is another example of the dangers run nightly by the immigration border patrol. They deal with desperate men and not a week passes without their being shot at from ambush.

"In the present case the little band of men with Mr. Scotten was ambushed from two sides during the darkness. Following the rule of the service they did not fire until first fired on. Once in action they drove off their attackers, for the patrol can shoot fast and straight.

"But it was too late to save the life of the brave and popular El Pasoan."

"A dispatch from Washington," the *Times* groused, "says that a recent tour by Commissioner [of Immigration] Hull indicated that the situation is acute and additional forces are needed there as well as along the northern border.

"'Acute' is a mild way of stating that about three times a week vigorous efforts are made to kill the patrolmen, sometimes by direct fire from across the river, sometimes by ambuscades and sometimes by rifle shots from houses on this side."

The pulpit had its say as well as the editor's typewriter. "It is cold-blooded murder," the Reverend H. D. Tucker told his Asbury Methodist flock, "to send border patrolmen out to protect our national borders against smuggling under present rulings. . . . We are not giving those boys or their families a fair deal, for it is almost certain death to tell a man to wait until he is fired upon before he opens fire. . . .

"I don't know whose business it is, but there should be some agitation started to have this ruling changed. Personally, I believe these brave and gallant men should be instructed to fire upon any person they see trying to cross the international boundary at night, except when crossing at a recognized port of entry."

As the United States Government was unmoved by that call from the church militant, the rule continued to stand and men who abided by it continued to fall. On September 9, 1929, Senior Patrol Inspector Miles J. Scannell was killed near Polvo, Texas. This tiny town in the Big Bend region stands across the river from La Mulato, whose place in the Patrol's history will later be explained.

The passing of Scannell wound up the list of 1929 fatalities, but in 1930 the numbers were up for three more patrolman. East toward the Gulf, William D. McCalib was slain at Alice, Texas, on January 7. West along the Pacific, a bullet found Harry E. Vincent on March 23 near Oceanside, California. On July 2 the Laredo *Times* carried a picture of a rugged young man above this caption: "Known as one of the most fearless members of the United States border patrol and slain by ambushed rum smugglers at Laredo, June 25, W. R. (Red) Kelsay, former Denton High School and Denton Teachers College football star."

Yet men with guns were not the only deadly hazards faced by patrolmen in 1930. One of them, while lying in wait by a frequented smugglers' trail, was jumped by a rabid animal, described by the El Paso *Post*. "Sneaking up to Border Patrolman J. W. Metcalf, as he lay on the snow covered ground near the Santa Fe Bridge, a thirty-pound coyote sprang at the officer at 6 P.M. Tuesday.

"Startled as the animal's teeth clicked over his head, Metcalf struck the coyote a blow on the head with his pistol, stunning it. Several other blows and a bullet were necessary to kill the animal."

In 1930, too, the Chinese were back in the news, but this time as fugitives rather than invaders. The background of this movement was an abrupt Mexican effort to reverse a trend. For many years the Chinese had been allowed to dig in south of the border, where they tended to prosper more than the natives. Belatedly discovering as much, Mexico adopted an ouster and confiscation policy with results described in a 1930 issue of the Tucson *Arizona Star*.

"Chinese who are fleeing to the United States by the hundreds because of present conditions in Sonora . . . are doing so to avoid paying their own way back to China, according to statements made today by various U.S. officials who are handling the matter of illegal entry into the United States.

"The Chinese are found frequently straggling along on the street, or they boldly come to police stations and 'hang around' until they are placed in a cell and given food and shelter. Many have money but are sending it home and pushing themselves on the American government. . . ."

Bret Harte's Truthful James would not have been astonished by this brazen swindle on the part of the "Heathen Chinee." Others were not prepared for it, though, and the expensive nuisance continued for a couple of years. But a Tucson judge finally lost his charitable cool, as the *Arizona Star* noted in 1932. "On the theory that if they are sent to jail now, others of their ilk will not be so anxious to illegally enter the United States and thereby gain free passage back to China, 25 Celestials were given seven months in jail by Judge Albert M. Sames, federal jurist, Saturday . . ."

In that year as well as the one before, there had been a falling off of smuggling which can easily be accounted for. The depression resultant from the great stock market crash of 1929 did not immediately trouble the West. By 1931, though, the buying power of the region was so sharply curtailed that the pinch was passed on to even the underworld. If drink was still available, to be sure, it mostly took the form of stuff distilled from who knew what by American moonshiners. Few could afford to pay for foreign contraband, its price ballooned by the costs of smuggling.

The gain to the patrolmen was that in 1931 and '32 none was lost to gunfire. But following the turn of 1933, the economy of the region began to pick up and so did the running of rum across the line. On

March 7 this increase proved fatal to Patrol Inspector Philip D. Strobridge at Fallbrook, California.

Prohibition was then about to end, for the Federal administration which took control three days before Strobridge's death had a mandate to abolish Volsteadism. The official burial hour, nationally, was midnight September 15, but its ghost continued to haunt the border for reasons besides the fact that Texas did not promptly repeal its state dry law. Legal purveyors of liquor by the bottle and drink had first to obtain licenses and second to receive stock from a slowly reviving distilling industry. As thirsts in the Southwest were among the last in the nation to be lawfully assuaged, the liquor smugglers of Mexico had several months of freedom to carry on. A consequence was the publication in *The New York Times* of the following 1933 article.

> El Paso, Texas, Dec. 7—Guns blazed at . . . points along the Texas-Mexico border today as officers surprised smugglers attempting to run liquor into Texas, which is still dry, and the toll was counted tonight at three known dead and one wounded . . .
>
> A Federal border patrol exchanged volleys of shots with a band of sixteen men in the Rio Grande River at the foot of Park street here. One patrolman and two of the rum smuggling band were killed. They were Dorne C. Melton, 31, formerly of Conyers, Ga., United States patrolman; Francisco Gonzalez and Higinto Perez, both of Juarez, a Mexican city across the river.
>
> Francisco Mosqueda, 19, a former high school student here, was shot twice and is in critical condition.
>
> The patrolmen said they saw two men fall in the water and disappear as the smugglers fled toward the Mexican side. Belief was expressed that the two lost their lives. . . .

A day short of three weeks later, Bert G. Walthall was slain just after he and another patrolman had stopped three known smugglers in downtown El Paso. The following account is taken from some reminiscences of Nick D. Collaer. He did not name Walthall's companion, but in another account he is referred to as Smith, perhaps the "Tombstone" Smith who helped search for the missing Denver "Blackie" Burcham in 1926. In any case, Collaer quoted an eye-witness as follows.

"Bert never had a chance. As I pulled the car up beside where they [the tequileros] had stopped, and as Bert was stepping out, he got it through the head—the bullet striking immediately above the center of the car door. Jose Estrada (they called him 'Firpo') was driving and Fidel Ortega (who claimed to be an Oklahoma Indian) sat with 'Firpo' on the front seat. We learned later that Jose leaned forward while Fidel laid his carbine across his back and shot Bert. I did not see the rifle protrude from the car and I'm sure Bert didn't either. I fell out on the opposite side and stepped around the back from where I could 'pour the soup' to them as they drove down Piedras. I did not know until later that one of my shots had gone through Fidel's head but did not kill him and that others sprinkled Ramon Rico (who was in the back seat with the liquor) with fragments from the car body. He thought he had been shot with bird-shot and sure looked it."

As far as reported action is concerned, the border's gory Prohibition epoch closed on that fierce note. In 1934 Texas repealed its dry edict, and the Patrol, for the first time in its ten years of existence, was free to pay major attention to the purpose for which it was created.

PART

II

THE
FIRST
GREAT
WETBACK
INVASION

5

THE
EVOLUTION
OF
PEACETIME
OPERATIONS

When the border patrol truly began functioning as a corps opposing illegal immigration, it had survived both a threat of extinction and a decimating attack from Washington. Both of these events were outcomes of Franklin Roosevelt's assumption of the Presidency.

His choice as Secretary of Labor was Mrs. Frances Perkins. Not unnaturally, in view of what the Patrol had mostly been doing, she saw it as an anti-contraband force which was no part of the Labor Department's business. She was, therefore, ready to pass the customs buck back to the Treasury Department and spend the money allotted her on other things. The crisis passed when she was made to see that she had the responsibility for enforcing laws against unsanctioned immigration. If the Patrol was abolished, some replacing police would have to be organized, so she kept the hand she had. Unluckily for the border's special officers, they were involved in a departmental shakeup.

By an executive order of June 10, 1933, the previously separate bureaus of Immigration and Naturalization were combined as the Immigration and Naturalization Service. This entailed a review of the operation by the inevitable board of accredited owls. In this instance according to Dogie Wright, they were, "a bunch of eggheads from Princeton, Yale and so on, but we called 'em the Benzine Board."

In due course this array of dignitaries sat in judgment on the Patrol—probably one of the most incongruous confrontations in the history of the United States. The ovoid gentlemen were full of theories about police work, which were an ill match for the first-hand knowledge of frontiersmen who had bullet scars to show for it plus the memories of slain comrades. Of these actualities the reviewers took no notice. Their concern, like that of certain modern jurists, was for the safety of the breaker of the law rather than for the well-being of its upholders. They tapped newspaper clippings which told that many smugglers had been planted or damaged and took this for evidence—expressly denied by newspapermen acquainted with the case's facts—that the Patrol was irresponsibly pistol-quick. They were particularly pained by headlines which announced that "Mexican youths" had been shot.

"Youths!" Wright snorted in comment. "Billy the Kid was a youth, and so are a lot of the toughest soldiers in any army."

But the Benzine Board put a stock question to patrolmen, individually interviewed so the black hats could be weeded out, leaving only those with white headgear. "Suppose your partner had been killed by a Mexican," this touchstone was worded, "and you saw him coming across the border again. What would you do?"

This was a trap reserved for honest men only, and some fell into it. The real answer, as Dogie Wright pointed out, was "Why I'd shoot the son of a bitch, of course, and if his spook showed up, I'd bag that, too."

Their worst fears realized, the eggs of head would purse their lips and scratch names from the roster. But the odd fact was that only the first few called before the dry cleaning board at any particular time were bloodhungry. The washed out frank ones warned the rest that candor wasn't wanted. So when the crucial question was asked, the answer would be "Well, I'd warn him he'd be subject to arrest if he didn't turn back," or some variant of that theme.

Incidentally, two who were kept by the Benzine Board for sidling around truth in the fall of 1933 died of quick Mexican trigger fingers before the year was out. As declared in the last chapter, these were Melton and Walthall. In the case of the second it was editorially lamented that death was due to the Patrol practice of never starting gunplay.

Not all the discharged officers were replaced, and those who were allowed to carry on took a cut in salary. They had by this time long had uniforms, khaki ones topped with a slouch hat. They still carried what arms each thought best, but the Government now provided mounts. Horseback patrolling remained the daily routine for most. In and around El Paso, as has been demonstrated, automobiles were much in use. They were also employed to a limited degree in California, Arizona's Santa Cruz Valley and the Lower Rio Grande. But the border's fragmentary road system made machines generally impractical.

Such cars as the Patrolmen did have were a scratch assortment of heaps from used car lots. Yet they were supposed to challenge better-equipped suspects and give chase in their rattletrap antiques if a signal to halt went unheeded. One such pursuit was summed up in the reminiscences of Nick Collaer. "We took after the Cadillac in our old Model T, hoping against hope that he would run out of gas, and believe it or not, he did!"

But it was mostly horseback work in areas where poor or missing roads weren't the only communication lacks. Away from the larger towns, telephones were scarce. If a pair of patrolling partners rode off to points 100 or so miles from headquarters, they might be out of touch with their command post for weeks. How they might be employed in the meantime may now seem quaint, though the thinking behind it was sound. Scratch every other Patrol Inspector of that day and you found a cowhand. Patrolmen fraternized with ranchers when they were covering their beats, because they were of the same ilk. Cattlemen, therefore, helped the officers by furnishing tips and sometimes more solid help.

"So at roundup time, if we weren't on somebody's trail, we'd pitch in and help," Dogie Wright explained. "My orders transferring me from El Paso to Sierra Blanca had been lying around a week before I turned up, but I'd been out on the range punching cows and nobody knew where to find me."

Wright also told an anecdote which shows why helping cowmen was considered good business. When he and another PI were assigned to a New Mexico point on the line for a while, they were ordered to go by train and to apply for mounts to a certain rancher. Although they reached the home of this stranger at the godless hour of 3 A.M., he uncomplainingly gave them what they asked for.

By the standards of the border, incidentally, they were there not out of touch with headquarters. "It wasn't a regular railroad stop," Wright remarked, "but they'd throw our mail off, and we'd come around and pick it up, when we had time to."

When on outpost duty that might stretch from weeks into months, a pair camped, sometimes with the simplest of equipment. Wright, for instance, was later on duty in western Arizona. "As it never rained in that part of the desert, you didn't have to bother with a tent," he said. "You just picked out a likely piece of sky and moved in under it."

Although there were sometimes airplanes in the border's skies, none yet served the Patrol. The nearest any of its members got to air observation was via towers, wooden ones mostly, from which boundary crossing points could be checked through field glasses.

They were not wary of being fired upon when thus exposed. Goods were still being pushed across the line, but by small-time operators. The traffic in narcotics was as yet trifling. No longer supported by the profits from rum running, the tough smuggling gangs fell apart. It took a while for people on both sides to become accustomed to the fact, but with the passing of Volstead's madness, the temper of the border underwent gentling. The sniping and rifle fire died away. The bold frontal attacks gave way to furtive infiltration. If found, smugglers fled rather than fought, since the profits from minor articles of contraband weren't worth the risk of blood.

But it was now not smugglers that Immigration Patrol Inspectors looked for or mostly encountered. They were on watch for illegal aliens, including Mexicans in search of employment. Among them were many who had been lawfully settled in the United States but had returned to Mexico during the Depression. Finding things even worse there, they wished to return to America but could not satisfy entry requirements such as financial responsibility.

The majority, however, had never attempted legal entrance because the thinking behind America's immigration laws was totally beyond their grasp. Not knowing a visa from a vestibule, they saw no sense in paying to pass through a port of entry when one could sneak across the line for nothing. They couldn't state how long they expected to remain; as long as they felt like it. As for financial responsibility, they wouldn't have been loco enough to seek stoop labor jobs on foreign farms, if they had had that. And of course they had no prearranged employment, they couldn't imagine a way of life in which things came that easily.

The wetback had replaced the fast-shooting tequilero as the Border Patrol's number one problem. Because of his determination to enter the United States lawlessly, he had to be caught and sent back to his country. But he wasn't necessarily violently engaged and the methods used to repress dangerous invaders weren't applicable. Here were not challengers, but men as anxious to escape notice as a garden-raiding rabbit. Called for in dealing with them were all the qualities and attitudes which had been difficult to develop under Volsteadism's deadly reign. These were: a cool implacability in pursuit and arrest, a calmly brisk shakedown for weapons, firm but temperate quizzing, and hauling to detention with as little handling as the situation allowed.

But as the frontier proverb put it, "if you want buckskin, you ought to first nail a buck." The border was wide, the patrolmen few, the points of crossing limitless and the wetbacks wily. What had to be worked out, then, were methods by which all these handicaps could be minimized.

The starting point was a craft which American pioneers of all periods had picked up from Indians. Forgotten in other parts of the nation by the 1930s, tracking—or "sign cutting," as it was regionally called—was still practiced in the West. Ranchers found it an indispensable skill, needed for finding cattle scattered over vast ranges, as well as following prints of horses ridden by rustlers, or hunting down animal predators. Now Patrol Inspectors who had been taught to read sign as boys put their learning to the uses of tracing the course of human strays.

On hard ground the sign might be no more than a tiny patch leveled by the weight of a passing man or a pebble seen to be newly out of place. Where grass and brush were a mingle, the sign might be fallen leaves that a shoe had scuffed or flattened, or tufts pressed a little out of line. The sign need not have been made by a foot at all. It might consist of a rump-print, where a wetback had rested. It might consist of human waste or casual refuse—tortilla crumbs, a shed button or a thread plucked from a man's shirt by thorny brush.

There were means by which new sign could be told from that too old to be worth following. In soft or sandy ground the schooled PI could gauge the age of a print by the degree of sharpness in its outline, whether wind had drifted sand or vegetable matter into it, and whether passing creatures had scuffed it or left deposits. In hard ground the degree of glazing by the sun could determine age, and the cavity left by a misplaced rock could be tested by the same means.

Once so much as a full toe or heel print was located, the sign became an individual thing which could be recognized as clearly as a man's signature when encountered miles away and hours or days later. The shape, the depth, nail marks, worn spots, cracks, bulges and uneven wearing caused by habits of distributing weight while walking went on file in the sign cutter's mind. If an entire track was found, the PI knew the make of the heel and whether his quarry toed out or in. And even from two consecutive indistinct marks on hard earth, he knew the length of the wetback's stride. Picking up a Mexican's trail farther on, the cutter would know just how far ahead of one sign to peer for the next.

The craft of sign cutting made the Patrol many times as effective as the corps would otherwise have been. What it meant was that a wetback didn't have to be intercepted right at the line. If watched trails proved barren, unwatched ones would preserve the record that one or more wetbacks had used them as border crossing points. The majority of illegal aliens preferred the cover of darkness when sneaking across the line. When going off duty, the night shift, working out of a Patrol divisional headquarters, would report developments to the relieving day shift, whose members would then know where, and where not, it was worthwhile to check for sign.

Assuming tracks found the next morning indicated that a pair of wetbacks had entered the United States at a given location during the night, patrolmen could both trail and move to intercept them. Riders, and where feasible, drivers of cars would race to points ahead through which the invaders would probably have to pass on their way to find employment. Or such riders or drivers would make for a known stretch where tracking was easy. If sand or soft dirt showed that the Mexicans in question had already passed, pursuit could begin at that point, with the advantage of miles made up and a surer knowledge of the fugitives' destination.

To keep natural traps for sign useful, they were brushed over once or twice every twenty-four hours. A shift scouting for footprints would thus know that they were made not later than a certain time, so no minutes had to be spent on calculations as to whether they were recent enough to deserve further attention.

The next step was the creation of traps which might be miles long. Called drag-roads, these were soft dirt runways parallel to the border, over which any wetbacks who jumped the line in that vicinity would have to pass. Cars trailing big brooms kept them serviceable for sign cutters by periodically erasing all old shoe or huarache prints.

In the absence of airplanes and electrical developments of the future, this was as far as the Patrol was able to proceed in the way of hunting human game. Meanwhile thought was given to the problem of what to do with the quarry when bagged.

The Mexican illegal alien raised procedural questions that other types did not. Asians and Europeans were turned over to Federal authorities who funneled them into ships bound for their respective continents. The process was a lengthy one involving determination in court that each invader was guilty of illegal entry. Assuming such immigrants were deported, they were put where repeating would be an expensive and time-eating business.

But where invaders from other nations might be arrested by dozens, the Mexican catch was running to hundreds annually at some points and thousands at others. If each individual wetback were to be tried, it would swamp the Federal courts of the border states, while nothing would be accomplished. Deported, the wetback might or might not trouble to move to another part of the border before scooting north again.

As there was no corrective of that nuisance for many years, steps had to be taken to keep from impossibly crowding courts and jails. The prisons of unpopulous counties had not been designed for many tenants and they could not hold, pending trial, a tenth of the arrested wetbacks.

The only possible answer to this puzzle was the voluntary deportation system which emerged. If wetbacks caught by PIs would admit illegal entry and express willingness to be deported rather than endure imprisonment and trial, they could be turned over to other immigration officers, authorized to repatriate them without more than one further check. This concerned their criminal records, including the count of having been seized as illegal entrants before. Although any with criminal pasts would either be held in the United States or turned over to Mexican police, the shad run were shipped back to Mexico in jig time.

Sometimes, arrested Mexicans insisted they were United States citizens even though unable to speak more than a word or two of English. This was perfectly possible, since many border communities on the American side remained totally Hispanic, and numerous children had been born to Mexican refugees temporarily in the United

States. These people had to be given fair hearings and sorted out from pretenders.

Another reason for careful questioning on the part of patrolmen was that it was of use to them in making further arrests. By assessing the responses of a number, favorite points of entry could be learned. Or where smuggling of aliens was involved, which it was then in comparatively few cases, new methods of conveyance and concealment might be ascertained.

But as prisoners would not cooperate if they got angry or turned sullen, the PIs had to be diplomatic as well as firm. For some of the veterans that was too much to expect, because of viewpoints acquired during years when every Mexican crosser of the line was potentially a deadly foe.

None of the corps had been trained as immigration officers, but this began to be undertaken in 1935. In that year the Patrol was brought back to pre-Benzine Board strength and pay scale. The force besides was awarded its own officers' training school, the first non-military one for Federal employees.

Opening shop in El Paso, it held sessions lasting eight weeks. During this period candidates were instructed in immigration laws, pertinent phases of international law, how to interview arrested aliens and how to present evidence in court. But as not all wetbacks were agreeable fellows, and no smugglers could be so classed, methods of keeping the upper hand were also stressed. So school graduates had to qualify as good pistol and rifle shots.

Applicants first had to pass Civil Service tests designed with the needs of the Patrol in mind. The day of the railway mail clerk approach was left behind. All who passed examinations were not admitted to the school, however. No matter how high the score registered, success only entitled a candidate to a screening by Patrol seniors who had learned what kinds of men they could profitably do without. Hotheads, grandstanders and bullies were no more wanted than the over-cautious, the hypersensitive, the sour, the buck passer and the goldbrick.

The applicants who made a good impression were then assigned to divisional headquarters for four months of field training. If approved by the PIs with whom they worked, the school's door was open, but graduation at the top of the class meant no more than that; a year as a working Probationer lay ahead. Only when he had passed this exacting field test was he placed on the roster as a Patrol Inspector, entitled to tenure and promotion when earned.

6

OF
WARS
AND
HARVESTERS

After a pair of practice aggressions, Hitler's Germany started World War II in earnest with the invasion of Poland on September 3, 1939. A wave of European immigration to the United States followed a rape which Stalin's Russia was happy to join. But next came what was tantamount to the capture of western Europe by the Nazis, cutting off the means of escape for most objectors midway in 1940.

For the Patrol that was the year in which an important Federal decision was reached with respect to it. The Nazis and their supporters in Mussolini's Italy wished above all to keep the United States neutral or, failing that, militarily impotent. Propagandists, saboteurs and similar agents of these nations were free to try to infiltrate America via the border, even if most other Europeans were not. Recognizing as much, Franklin Roosevelt's administration came to understand something else.

Viewing immigration as a threat to national security changed official thinking about it. For many decades this had been conditioned by the Industrial Age's need for more hands than could be supplied by the native birth rate. That attitude found expression when the old Bureau of Immigration was made a subdivision of the Department of Labor. As naturalization was thought of as a sort of graduate school of immigration, the bureau governing it had likewise been lumped with Labor, although never properly so.

What immigration and naturalization had in common, was not labor but law, international as well as home grown. As this point was at length grasped, the Immigration and Naturalization Service was transferred to the Department of Justice in 1940. With that shift, the Border Patrol was at last under a governmental branch which understood its functions, if not necessarily the techniques by which these could best be forwarded.

Of those who wished to take refuge or make trouble in America, many were desperate or ruthless. So seven years after Prohibition, guarding the border again became a perilous occupation. On January 17, 1940, Patrolman William L. Sills was killed near McAllen on the Rio Grande, and on December 12, PI George E. Pringle was shot down along the Colorado near Parker, Arizona.

By then the United States mail was hefty with "Greetings" from the nation's President, a faint whiff of battle smoke was already in the air, and the men who received those presidential salutes were packed off to military training centers such as El Paso's Fort Bliss, the last of the cavalry posts.

The Border Patrol was still largely a mounted outfit, too, but the war commenced to change that. An important byproduct of the conflict was that it brought the West the skein of improved roads it never had before. The current demand for supplies and raw materials was insatiable. Utilized to capacity, America's great railway system was inadequate. Unlimited supplemental trucking was the only way in which the yawning holds of war-bound ships could be filled, factories kept running, and troops in training fed and equipped. So blacktop and cement wound through mountains and straight-awayed over plains and deserts which had previously known only wagon traces. Improved state or county roads crossed or fanned out from national highways, and along the line it began to be feasible to tool automobiles at many new points.

The war's other gifts to the Patrol embraced equipment and non-highway communications. In 1941 the corps got the air arm plugged for as long ago as 1927. It wasn't a very extensive one, consisting as it did of a lone plane, but its pilot could spot hiding aliens invisible to ground crews and signal their whereabouts.

To meet battlefield needs, cars designed to scurry cross-country taking brush and ditches in stride, came into being. In particular, the "scout and command car," known to all but its builders as the "jeep," commenced rolling off assembly lines. High slung as a straddle bug, it could charge over obstacles that would stop orthodox machines. Muscled with four-wheel drive, it could churn through slop, bull through sand and skin over ridges that would stall two-wheel power.

The Patrol didn't get many at that time, but some officers let their saddles gather dust inside while they collected it outside, tearing through the wilderness as jeep pilots or passengers. And while doing this, they could be hearing from headquarters. For if two-way radio communication had not been perfected by 1941, a man with ear phones could pick up voices, even though not able to talk back. That was still a thing of the future when the United States entered World War II at the year's end.

Since some PIs chose military service, the remaining veterans carried on with the aid of raw newcomers. Men able to stand the border gaff were so scarce that recruiting through Civil Service examinations had to be bagged. No reviewing boards asked searching questions, and the training school lapsed. Candidates who looked possible were buttonholed on the street and put afield with a minimum of coaching.

Meanwhile, Mexicans who aspired to be farm laborers were not being forced out of the United States but coaxed to come in. Between the demands for fighters and factory workers, the Southwest had been drained of seeders, weeders and harvesters. Peons from south of the line found immigration qualifications waived in part; and provided for as to the rest. If they were illiterate, for example, they yet had assured employment in places whither transportation was supplied.

There were still Mexicans to be watched for, though. The labor groups contracted for by the Government in Mexico were checked for good health and criminal records. But there were those who'd rather not be noticed on either count, as well as smugglers and subversives. Then aside from boundary policing, the Patrol had special duties during the war. It was the Patrol that rounded up numerous members of the Japanese fishing fleet on the West Coast and took them by train for internment in the interior.

It was patrolmen who held the Japanese ambassador and members of his official family in protective custody at a Southwestern dude ranch during the first six months of 1942. Still operating, the ranch is the Triangle-T, three miles east of Benson, Arizona. And one who languished there at the time had been the Japanese consul general in Hawaii, described by Dogie Wright, who was himself on guard at the Triangle-T, as "the fellow who pulled the trigger at Pearl Harbor."

Patrolmen staked Fritz Kuhn, the head of New York City's Nazi Bund, out in the Southwest. Not given ambassadorial treatment, Kuhn was interned at Fort Stanton, the New Mexico post from which General Pershing had launched his drive into Mexico in pursuit of Villa.

German prisoners of war were also interned at a fort where their neighbors were Mescalero Apaches. These factors produced a notable Patrol coup, described in an undated official release. After stating that the "Border Patrol had custody of some 500 German internees . . . in the rugged mountains at Fort Stanton," it proceeds as follows:

> It was some time before suitable fences could be constructed and because of manpower conditions, only a small portion of the Border Patrol could be spared to operate the camp. During the first two or three months of operation several escape attempts were made. Then the fence was constructed and the officers relaxed . . . but the morning role call of the internees showed three were missing. The camp was searched and it was found that the trio had dug a tunnel from a shed housing work tools, the tunnel going under the fence and coming up behind a horse corral, a distance of about 74 feet. Sign cutters were immediately called in from El Paso to assist in tracking and apprehending the aliens. While waiting for the sign cutters to arrive, it was decided that the Apache Indian Reservation be asked to furnish trackers . . .
>
> The Indian trackers were on the job one hour before the Border Patrol sign cutters arrived. The patrolmen picked up the trail of the escapees and, after thirty-six hours of continuous tracking through the rugged mountainous area, took the aliens into custody. They reported they had seen nothing of the

three Indian trackers so a check was made of the Reservation, and the Indians had not returned. The Border Patrol sign cutters then went on another tracking expedition and followed the trail of the three Indians. On this assignment only twelve hours were expended and the officers found three sad, hungry Indians wandering aimlessly through the woods completely lost and about three miles from the trail left by the German aliens.

These, incidentally, were said to have known what they were about, for they were officers versed in astronomical navigation and thus capable of finding their way to Mexico through unfamiliar country.

In addition to hostile aliens, the Patrol also had custody for a time of potential allies. These were soldiers and officials seized by Russians when that tribe and the Nazis had whacked Poland up in 1939. Sent to Siberia, the captives had been subjected to bestial cruelties which had reduced the survivors to blind stagger madness.

But Russia and Germany were no longer partners when the trigger pulled at Pearl Harbor rocketed the United States into World War II. Needing men for one of the many fronts it was fighting on, England had conceived the idea of forming a Polish legion; so through the joint intercession of London and Washington, Moscow let go of the mice it had been playing cat with. Passed over the Pacific, the Poles were met on the Coast by patrolmen. But the freed prisoners were still in such crazed shock from what they had endured that they could not understand that they were now with men who wished them well. They could hardly understand anything, in fact.

"We were trying to break them down into groups, so they could be entrained," Wright remembered, "but every time one bunch was told to move to a given spot, the whole gang would come stumbling after. They were just like spooked cattle that will stampede, if you try to drive 'em anywhere. When I realized that, I advised the train commander to do what's done with steers in that shape, which is to let them quiet down and sort themselves out.

"That's what these Poles did. In Siberia they had been caged by groups. The men in their chain gangs had come to be the only familiar thing in the world to them, and when they were separated, they panicked. Well, we let them all find the groups they were used to, and then we were able to get them aboard and take them to a rehabilitation camp. And when they were in good shape again, they went over to England, as planned, and were organized as a Polish fighting force."

Patrolmen found enemies, during the war years, without leaving the line. On February 26, 1942, Ralph W. Ramsey was killed at Columbus, New Mexico, and on June 23, 1945, Earl F. Fleckiger was slain at Calexico, California. Then in that year flying along the Border proved a perilous trade. The war had been left astern as of November 18, 1945, but that didn't keep Ned D. Henderson from crashing near Sullivan City, Texas, his plane being an autogyro or helicopter.

A consequence of the war that was slow in being noticed was the amnesty granted the wetback, for Mexican contract laborers were needed in many parts of the United States, leaving the Southwest short. Other Mexicans moved in to take their places, and nobody asked how they came to be available.

Always short-handed and more and more involved with national security problems, the Patrol eventually didn't try to hold the line against any but probable trouble makers. So peons in search of work splashed through the Rio Grande or slogged across dry portions of the boundary in ever-mounting numbers.

In other years they had come as stags. Now they straggled over as families, setting up their homes in any place to squat. An abandoned shed would do, or square of canvas perched on sticks or a cave dug out of a river bank. They not only lived in such places, they were fecund in them. Diseased, ill fed and taught nothing, children swarmed about such nests and burrows.

By 1946, the wetback had for so long been considered a necessity of war that few could see him as a peace-time evil. He was considered part of the Southwest's husbandry. What had come to America, indeed, was a horde of people so unassimilable that they could be looked at and not seen as humans. They were a phase of nature, to be ignored except when work was required of those old enough to exploit.

The problem created for the Patrol was not one which could be solved by the means at hand. Both the numbers and the equipment of the force remained utterly inadequate. Its muster was not increased. Its vehicles, where horses didn't still prevail, were largely as yet a scrub lot. If important electrical advances had been lately made, the corps benefited by them only minimally. And poor communications were aggravated by a bad organizational setup. The Patrol was neither autonomous nor unified. Its three divisions were each responsible to separate district immigration heads and had no direct liaison with one another.

The trouble confronting the officers was meanwhile getting more unmanageable with every passing week. When normal policing of the border was resumed after the war, entering the United States at any convenient point along it had become such an accepted practice that wetbacks saw no reason to be furtive. They came over the line by droves in daylight. The fact that some were stopped did not daunt others, perhaps in plain view of PIs too busy with the arrest of one group to attempt halting another.

There were other difficulties. The Patrol was geared to arrest and detain for questioning only male peons. What was an officer to do who caught up with a man who had a wife and a flock of youngsters? He could and did shoo families back across the wet or dry line, but as soon as he proceeded to other sections of his beat, the Mexicans would wade or trudge into the United States again.

They thronged wherever irrigation or natural moisture made large-scale farming possible in the southern parts of border states. They dug in like termites along the Lower Rio Grande, up river in western Texas and New Mexico, in some of the valleys of Arizona and California's Imperial one. And for long nobody but the undermanned and hobbled Patrol tried to quash the menace. One reason was that most citizens of the affected states had no idea of what was going on. Few but residents visited the border, which had lost its one popular attraction with the passing of Prohibition. State political figures were not troubled because they received no complaints from officers of the counties involved. And county politicos said nothing, because the farmers and ranchers who paid most of the taxes were satisfied with the situation. For the wetback families formed a labor pool that knocked wages down to within spitting distance of the vanishing point.

With all its terrible facets, it was the biggest story in the United States, yet none of the nation's great news media got hold of it. Even the professional scolds that make a career out of inventing bad American smells missed the biggest genuine stink of the day. This was due to the relationship which the Southwest then bore to the rest of the country. It was a region of which the people in the country's main population centers remained unconscious. As the great "western tilt" stampede had not yet begun, ignorance about

71

the West was a standard feature of American education. California was known about, as movies were made there, and Texas had been discovered on account of oil. But neither of these commodities focused attention on the border.

Nor did the Federal Government appear aware of a grave and steadily worsening matter. Administrative officials had once been concerned because Border Patrolmen were shooting back at armed smugglers. No Benzine Board, however, showed up to explore a many-sided social mess.

Economically the condition bore hardest upon American citizens of Hispanic standing. Before the war they had formed the core of the border's labor legion. Drafted for one of the services or called to work in war-supply factories during the conflict, they had returned to find wetbacks wanted while they were not. Their undesirable quality was expecting to be paid wages they could live on. Their protests went unheard, for they had no organ of complaint. Like the county officials of the region, its newspapers sided with the ranchers and farmers who were their principal subscribers as well as the chief customers of their advertisers.

The papers in question were not long in finding a villain to denounce. This was the Patrol, as the only body engaged in trying to rock a perfectly sweet boat. They found the ranchers to be not stingy exploiters of wetbacks, but benevolent distributors of employment to needy foreigners. In ugly contrast stood cruel patrolmen, who would stop at nothing in order to keep poor Mexicans from earning enough to feed their families. Some journals editorially invited the good citizens of an outraged community to notify them of Patrol atrocities. Of these it rapidly developed that subscribers had been told of numberless ones, even if no writers signed statements that they themselves had witnessed dark and bloody PI deeds.

Forgotten amidst a mixture of vindication and smear were the native Latin Americans. And their plight grew grimmer as the number of squatting wetbacks passed the one hundred thousand mark and then the two hundred thousand one. Once families of them were settled in their pitiful dens, there seemed no way of unseating them. No rent or tax collector braced them for default of funds, so no sheriff or U.S. Marshal did. Nor did any truant officer threaten them with proceedings because their children didn't attend school. No enjoyer of diplomatic immunity was farther out of reach of law than they.

Once entrenched, groups of them were even indifferent to the approach of a patrolman. They knew he was helpless since he could not separate men from their families or require women and children to follow him afoot. Effective action could be taken only when a motorized detachment closed in.

The Patrol's area of responsibility was meanwhile increasing. For as the boundary became more connected with the national highway network, roads inland were patrolled to an ever greater depth. Two years after the war Patrol Inspectors John Fouquette and Anthony L. Oneto were on duty as far away from the line as the vicinity of Indio, California. On March 11, 1947, they stopped the car of a suspected Mexican. Searching him for weapons and finding none, they told him to get back in his machine and precede them to their station for questioning. "He had seemed so cooperative," Fouquette recalled, "that when he stopped after he had gone a ways, it didn't occur to us that he had a pistol stashed in his car. We figured he had run out of gas and thought that was what he meant to tell us when he got out of his job and came toward us. It was only a couple of steps to where we had stopped, so we didn't guess he was armed until he yelled he was going to fix us and fired. What saved me was that I was the driver, and I had just bent forward so I could look around Oneto and ask the fellow what he wanted. So the shot meant for me went over my head, but he killed Oneto, though I didn't know that, being busy jumping out of the car so I could use my own gun. But by the time I was on the ground and had run to where I could fire at the Mexican, he was back in his heap. Pistols didn't have the long range that some of them do now. I slung a couple of shots after him, but in no time at all he was long gone, and I couldn't follow, because then's when I found that my partner had got it."

Firearms were not the only dangerous weapons used on patrolmen; witness the ensuing official release.

On December 18, 1950, Patrol Inspector Richard D. Clark was stabbed to death by an alien who had been taken into custody at El Paso, Texas. The alien, Eulalio Corgero, was held by the grand jury.

The incident began as a routine immigration procedure, Inspector Clark questioning the Mexican alien upon a street in El Paso . . . First claiming to be an American citizen, Corgero admitted he was an alien illegally in the United States. He was being transported in a patrol car when he took a knife that had been previously taken from him and stabbed, in the heart, Inspector Clark, killing him instantly.

The year 1950 was the one in which the Patrol returned to pre-war normalcy in the matter of recruiting. Once again applicants had to pass a special Civil Service examination and go through a full course of training at the force's academy. The men who graduated from it, though, were no longer necessarily horsemen. By 1949 improvements in the border's road system had permitted the corps to become dominantly motorized, and the disuse of mounts entirely being then but ten years in the offing.

7

THE
WETBACK
SCANDAL
GETS
UNVEILED

In July of 1952 a bulletin announced that "Patrol Inspector Edwin H. Wheeler was killed in the line of duty near Mathis, Texas. On the night of July 6, 1952, Inspector Wheeler had been performing patrol duties alone when he was shot to death. His murderer is unknown."

When Wheeler was replaced, approximately 700 officers were again patroling the 2,000 miles of boundary in the depth represented by the geographical point where a bullet found him. For Mathis was 150 miles due north of the Rio Grande. Stretched thus thin, the force was yet contending with a steadily worsening immigration problem.

But something had at last been done about it, even though the Patrol wasn't able to realize it in 1952. Action had begun a year earlier, as a matter of fact, taking the form of a Government report which enjoyed popular notice no more than most such reading matter. Nor did the sponsoring Labor Department adopt any follow-up course of procedure. The publication was useful, though, because of presenting figures which could be pointed to by those who wished something done about trespassers from Mexico. Here are some quotes from *Migratory Labor in American Agriculture*, published in 1951:

"The magnitude of the wetback traffic has reached entirely new levels in the past seven years . . . In its newly developed proportions it is virtually an invasion. It is estimated that at least 400 thousand of our migratory labor force of one million in 1949 were wetbacks . . . Wetbacks often bring or acquire families. . . . It must be noted, moreover, that a child born in the United States, though of Mexican illegal alien parents, is a citizen of the United States. . . .

"A comparison of more than incidental interest is the volume of the wetback traffic as contrasted to our admissions of displaced persons from Europe. In 1949, when we admitted 119,600 displaced Europeans, our apprehended wetback traffic was almost 300,000; in 1950, when we admitted 85,600 displaced Europeans, our known wetback traffic was between 500,000 and 600,000."

The pamphlet then took up the deplorable results of the invasion. "Foremost among these consequences is the severe and adverse pressure on wages in the areas nearest the border. A second consequence of the wetback is competition for employment and displacement of American workers . . . Furthermore, there are other developments which, although not directly and entirely consequences of the wetback influx, are nevertheless inevitably associated with it. These include the astoundingly high disease and death rates of the counties lying next to the border."

The above attracted no immediate attention, nor was the contents of the pamphlet first brought to light by any news or political agent of a border state. But somehow Congressman John Rooney of New York had run across *Migratory Labor in American Agriculture* and had been sufficiently moved by the part of it dealing with the border to make a pilgrimage to the Lower Rio Grande Valley. In June of 1952 he undertook to voice findings that had shocked him on the floor of the House. These were repudiated with vehemence by the Texas Congressional delegation in both chambers. No action was therefore planned by the incumbent Democratic administration, but the smell had at last been let out of its local box. It was not forgotten by at least one prominent Republican, and in 1952 his party won the Presidential election.

The man referred to was a lawyer named Herbert Brownell, Jr., whom President Dwight Eisenhower made Attorney General of the United States. He could not, of course, begin to function until 1953. In the meantime an effort to do something about the border's abominations was being attempted locally.

The sponsoring organization was the American G. I. Forum of Texas, many of whose members were Latin Americans who had gone off to war, only to find themselves unwanted as workmen when they returned. Their counteraction took the form of the illustrated exposé titled *What Price Wetbacks?* Its editor was a member of a prominent Latin American newspaper family named Eduardo Idar, Jr. The photographer was Andrew C. McClellan, a Scotch businessman who had reached the border by way of Canada and identified himself with its affairs.

What they set out to do late in 1952 was to produce a document which no politicians or newspapermen could dismiss as an unfounded smear. Where the Labor Department's investigators had generalized, they were specific. They named wetbacks and cited the exact parsimonious wages on which they were forced to exist. They took pictures of foul boxes and holes in the ground, complete with inmates of both sexes. They told exactly what canals were used both as latrines and sources of drinking. They named children photographed sleeping in filth and covered with flies. They told just how many pregnant women were lying under a lean-to in a precisely located community, waiting for their babies to arrive in a compound bejeweled with piles of human excrement.

What Price Wetbacks? also told how peonage was enforced by blackmail. For it noted that the wretches living as described and pictured were "at the mercy of employers who can—and will—turn them over to the Border Patrol if they complain about working conditions or wages."

These were complainable. A wetback who was required to work twelve hours in order to make $3.00 a day was comparatively in the upper pay brackets. Many made but $12.50 a week, sometimes with a very poor class of "found" and sometimes without it. Rooney testified that he had seen wetbacks paid as little as $5.00 per week, and the findings of Idar and McClellan supported him. They encountered one woman who said she had received $10.00 plus food for two weeks of cotton picking. Youngsters, naturally, could not expect such wages. One fifteen-year-old boy was paid $4.50 weekly for putting in fifteen hours a day at a grocery shop.

The health statistics offered in *What Price Wetbacks?* make parlous grim reading. As to tuberculosis, bacillary as well as amoebic dysentery, gonorrhea and syphilis, the index for the border counties of Texas far exceeded that of the state as a whole. The index for amoebic dysentery, for instance, was 6.5 for all Texas as compared with 37.8 for all eleven border counties and 74.3 for the Lower Rio Grande counties of Hidalgo and Cameron.

The infant mortality rate was terrible wherever wetbacks were prevalent. In 1949 among the English-speaking people of Hidalgo County the rate of deaths from birth to the age of four years was 11.5 percent, while the rate for the Spanish-speaking population was 59.5 percent.

There was a great discrepancy, at the same time and place, in the death rates for the old, too. Among the Anglos 52.3 percent lived to be sixty-five or over. Of those of Spanish speech but 12 percent lived as long.

Turning to crime, the pamphlet made it clear that although the rate was appalling in counties overrun by wetbacks, the invaders were as much the victims as the perpetrators. Although it was not so presented by Idar and his associate, the invasion was in part composed of the savage bandido ilk. These had not come into the United States to work but rather to prey on the long-suffering peon farm laborers. But of course such gangsters did not exclusively assault and rob their own countrymen; they were a general menace.

What Price Wetbacks? furthermore put the finger on the politicians and pressure groups responsible for preserving this atrocious state of affairs. It began with Washington, pointing out that on August 20, 1952, ". . . the Truman administration presented a law providing penalties for employment of illegal immigrants. It was defeated in Congress."

After declaring that the national legislature had been dissuaded from backing Truman by border representatives, the work went on to remark that "these same Congressmen were notoriously active" in efforts to cripple the Patrol by the withdrawal of operating funds. The politicians in question were cited as having the support of the Lower Rio Grande Valley Farm Bureau and similar organizations. "These groups have consistently—and successfully—opposed every effort to increase the strength of the Border Patrol." This charge was supported by a quotation from a Mexico City newspaperman: "While Mexican officials have not made any public statement, they let it be known that on June 26, 1952, both Texas senators, then Johnson and Connally, as well as McFarland (D-Ariz.) voted against a measure to grant more funds" for Border Patrol personnel and equipment.

What the Patrol was accomplishing in the face of handicaps and attack from all directions was also told in figures. In 1946 patrolmen arrested 100,200 wetbacks; and in 1947, 198,000. In 1948 there had been a slight recession, reported in a catch of but 197,500. But after that came the wetback deluge. In 1949 detentions for deportation totaled 293,000; 480,000 in 1950; 513,815 in 1951; 543,538 in 1952; and 875,318 in 1953.

Politicians were this while plumping for an open border, over which all comers could swarm at will. And propaganda against the Patrol had been so successful that thwarting its collective efforts and insulting its individual members were alike reckoned marks of good citizenship.

Perhaps as a means of arousing public sentiment in parts away from the boundary, one immigration official expressed his intention of abandoning it to invaders and holding the line elsewhere. *What Price Wetbacks?* included a photostat of a 1953 Associated Press dispatch, datelined San Antonio, July 1, worded as follows:

> District immigration chief John W. Holland, San Antonio, will pull his patrolmen back 80 miles from the border in the face of an onslaught of illegal migration from Mexico.
>
> The move was described as a strategic withdrawal from the [Lower] Rio Grande Valley where the tide of 'wetbacks' invading the country has passed the 800 daily mark.
>
> Holland said a shortage of manpower forced him to redeploy his border patrolmen along a line from Hebbronville east to Falfurias and Riviera, south of Kingsbury. He said the withdrawal will keep illegal entrants from spreading forth to other parts of the United States.

On the Pacific coast an alarm had been sounded a couple of months earlier. For on May 9 the *New York Times* Service had broadcast from Los Angeles this message:

> Illegal immigration from Mexico into the Southwestern United States, on the increase since World War II, has reached such

overwhelming proportions that officers of the United States Immigration Service admit candidly, if unofficially, that there is nothing to stop the whole nation of Mexico moving into the United States, if it wants to.

The numerical equivalent of more than 10 percent of the population of Mexico has come in already.

A record total of 87,416 border jumpers was caught last month. . . .

But help was at hand for the Patrol because of two appointments made by President Eisenhower. As already noted, he had made Herbert Brownell, Jr., his Attorney General. Then as Commissioner of Immigration and Naturalization he appointed a World War II comrade in arms named General Joseph M. Swing. With entire appointive organizations to rebuild and set in motion, neither could give the Mexican boundary immediate attention, but by the time *What Price Wetbacks?* went to press in the fall of 1953 they were both in action. As the Immigration and Naturalization Service was a part of the Department of Justice, theirs were cooperative efforts.

On August 16 Brownell announced in the course of a speech made at San Francisco that the Eisenhower administration had no intention of allowing the open portal for immigration that peonage fanciers had been demanding. According to an Associated Press wire out of Denver dated August 17, the Attorney General followed up by reporting to the President that the "United States Border Patrol, hampered by manpower shortage, is powerless to halt the illegal entry of thousands of wetbacks into California" among other states along the line. The next message on the subject which the AP broadcast stated that "President Eisenhower Monday authorized Attorney General Herbert Brownell, Jr., to use all resources of the Federal Government to stem the ever increasing tide of 'wetbacks' entering this country illegally from Mexico."

About then General Swing sent his ace of clubs to the border to look the situation over and take action about it. A dateless dispatch from Russeltown, Texas, carried by the San Antonio *Express*, reported this news of him:

A "task force" of seventy-five border patrolmen directed by plane-to-car radio, apprehended an estimated 2,500 illegal aliens in this area Wednesday in a five hour period, the largest one-day haul of the season in the Valley. . . . Assistant United States Commissioner of Immigration Willard S. Kelley of Washington, D.C., came to the Rio Grande Valley personally to direct the huge roundup.

The aliens were collected at this small settlement, midway between Brownsville and San Benito, for voluntary departure to Mexico. The aliens included men, women, children and babes in arms. . . . Some . . . were living in shacks, some in tents, some under trees and tarpaulins and some of the men were sleeping in cotton rows, using partly filled sacks as mattresses.

Up river at McAllen, as an approximately concurrent item in the San Antonio *Express* recounted, there was action of the same sort. "The United States Border Patrol, using a 'task force' of about 50 men, rounded up an estimated 2,000 illegal aliens Friday in the area from McAllen to Weslaco and so to the river, Patrol Chief Fletcher L. Rawls of McAllen reported."

The magnitude of these operations can be contrasted with one made earlier in 1953, before Brownell had assessed the situation and urged a massive crackdown. Not drawn from newspaper coverage, this was described in *What Price Wetbacks?* from direct observation. "The Task Force consisted of eight patrolmen, a truck, a passenger bus and two cars. . . ." The small detachment had proved unequal to the prompt envelopment of a large group of Mexicans encamped by the Rio Grande. Only about a hundred of a guessed half thousand had been trapped. The rest had ducked into the brush or skipped across a river bottom which was dry at that point. Arrived south of the line they lounged in full sight of the PIs, "laughing, joking and gesticulating . . . Some climbed trees . . . scouting the situation and preparing to give a signal [for immediate return to their camp] on the departure of the patrolmen." This had been anticipated by abandoned children who "showed no fear of the Border Patrol and stated that their parents would be back just as soon as the Task Force left."

But by the end of the following August the Patrol was ceasing to be a joke to illegal aliens, while it aggravated lawlessly disposed Americans more than ever. The express will of the White House notwithstanding, the corps' Anglo enemies didn't give up a lost game without a struggle. The ranchers who had wanted to have work done for next to nothing were inconsolable at efforts to deny them their pet luxury. As their political spokesmen and newspapers took up the cry of outrage, a mass tantrum was thrown. No child ever howled more bitterly over the loss of candy that was sure to make it sick.

Some border journalists sought to have the emphasis shifted from the acute wetback problem by making it but one element of a program aimed at all illegal immigrants. Typical of this was an editorial complaint in the Laredo *Times* headed "Why the Mexicans?":

> President Eisenhower has seen fit to take official notice of Attorney General Brownell's alarm over the Mexican "wetback" situation and has instructed the Department of Justice to use all the resources of the federal government to stem the "ever increasing tide of wetbacks entering this country from Mexico." . . . This newspaper fails to see why Attorney General Brownell and President Eisenhower should confine themselves to Mexican "wetbacks!"

After remarking that there were illegal aliens, from all sorts of countries, in many eastern cities, the editorial trotted out the sanctity of a good old local practice.

> For many, many years laborers crossed the Rio Grande . . . That was the accepted custom and nothing was said or thought about it. . . .
> The *Times* resents the singling out of Mexican aliens and turning all the resources of the federal government into stopping and rounding them up. In many cases the Mexican aliens are much more acceptable than the aliens here from some other parts of the world.

By this pose the protesters assumed the guise of defenders of the people whose pitiless exploitation they wished to continue. A couple of the meaner fashions have not yet been mentioned. Sometimes whole families were employed, including children of both sexes as young as six years old who worked all day at stoop labor. There was the company store angle of peonage, with ranchers getting an undue share of trifling wages back for poor provender. To insure the return of a wetback for another tour of labor, there was often a withholding from small pay at the close of a given harvest. Through this combination of foresight and frugality a man never got paid in full.

But practicers of these extortions were heroes in many parts of the border where people who considered themselves worthy citizens were furious at opposers. Men who had been cronies of patrolmen before the era of peonage set in, now cut them. Tradesmen refused them business. Restaurants flaunted signs that read "Dogs and Border Patrolmen not allowed." The feud was carried over to their families, too. Wives were ostracized or insulted by formerly cordial neighbors. Children were snubbed by playmates at school and picked on by teachers.

Notwithstanding the fact that the PIs were Federal officers, there were overt efforts to keep them from carrying out their orders. Ranch roads were padlocked to prevent officers from driving to fields where wetbacks were known or suspected to be at work. Some ranchers even set up communications systems which would enable them to warn foremen of the approach of patrolmen, so that these lieutenants could order wetbacks to scatter until summoned back by a gong or some such signal. There were even threats to shoot PIs, but it is not on record that any of the force died of those growls.

More hurtful was a campaign of vilification. Although members of the corps now seldom had occasion to aim the guns they carried, they were portrayed by gossip as a mob of professional killers roving in search of wetbacks to gun down on sight.

The outfit didn't have much to smile at during this phase of its history, but the sun finally found a slit in the clouds at one spot. At the height of the "down with the Border Patrol" frenzy, an accident furnished the force's enemies wit ha choice bit of grist. Planes searching for wetback encampments or sign indicative of their whereabouts have to fly as low as a hundred or half that number of feet from the ground. That's hazardous flying anywhere because of the abrupt down drafts that may be encountered. They are particularly apt to lurk in mountainous country, of which the line has more than its share.

A Patrol Airpilot stationed at a certain headquarters got entangled in one such gust at a point where he was just above a man jogging along on a mule. When the bottom fell out of the sky, he was powerless to do anything besides work to pull his plane out of its plummeting. In this, by a miracle of skill and luck, he succeeded. While the plane was still a runaway, though, a wing had sheared off the rider's head. It chanced that the man who then fell from his mule in two pieces was a wetback going about some ranching chore. As patrolmen were avouched to delight in the slaying of wetbacks, all the local citizenry hopped to the conclusion that here was an undoubted, if unique, assassination.

The pilot was cleared in court of achieving murder on the fly, but the public remained so furiously convinced of his guilt that he had to be transferred. Unappeased, the people of the town where the headquarters was located stepped up their campaign of ostracism, making things so unpleasant for the families of patrolmen as well as the officers themselves that a request to have said headquarters moved to a neighboring burg was made by its chief.

The Patrol's chief at Washington had not had time to act on that petition, when local emotions faced about with startling speed. Threatened with the absence of people they had been treating as public foes, the fathers of the town recalled that patrolmen drew its largest payroll. Collectively they were the biggest spenders thereabouts. They paid the most taxes, and they had children for which Federal school funds, based on the daily attendance record, had been annually forthcoming. They operated vehicles, too, ranging from pickups to airplanes, for which local services supplied fuel, tires and repair parts.

With the realization of what would be lost should the headquarters be moved, all remembrance of the beheaded mule rider vanished So did the scorn and prejudice built up over the years. Second thought found the local representatives to be anything but logical targets for cold shouldering. At work they performed well and tirelessly in the service of their country. Off duty they were good and agreeable citizens, married to wives of a like nature with disciplined, intelligent children.

Yet while seeing all this, the business leaders of the community also saw that some bridge had to be built between the new attitude and the old one. And it had to be done pronto, to keep tireless public servants fine citizens and all the rest of it from stampeding out of town and taking its best payroll with them. Grasping the problem, the Chamber of Commerce didn't flinch. It plastered public spots with notices that a soon calendar event would be "Honor the Border Patrol Day."

Even outside of that reformed community, the climate began to be less chilly for patrolmen. A helping event was the publication late in 1953 of Idar's and McClellan's illustrated pamphlet. If dealing with Texas, it was applicable to all the border states and was distributed in them. The spotlight had at last been turned on. Some of the farmers still thought they had the constitutional right to maintain a vicious nuisance, but the facts put on raw display led many of their followers and echoers to fade out and pipe down.

8

THE
BORDER
GETS A
SCRUBBING

The importance to the Patrol of having a military commander as Commissioner of Immigration was demonstrated in 1954. Previous commissioners, or those since the corps's organization at least, had been professional or business leaders. Men of cities and cognizant of international affairs on normal levels, they had grasped and taken an interest in such matters as seaport immigration, exceptions to quotas made in favor of special abilities and the intake of displaced European personnel. Qualified to move in such matters, they had not been schooled to envision the problems of men ranging rural or wild country to thwart a primitive horde.

For a man who had been a combat general, on the other hand, the activities of the Patrol could be seen as more familiar than any other phase of the Immigration and Naturalization Service. After thirty years of subordination to commissioners who were uncomprehending, nonsympathetic or both, the corps found itself under a man who viewed its concerns with interest and understanding. Better yet, General Swing had a gift for organization and a knack for getting things done.

During the summer of 1953 he had experimented with the described task forces directed by his assistant. These had both shown Swing their worth in theory and their inadequacy when measured against the huge number of wetbacks to be dealt with. The Patrol did not have the manpower and equipment for the large scale maneuvers demanded. Nor could funds to provide for them be gained by fiat. Congress had to be persuaded to vote the money needed, and before this could be done, a plan of campaign and the exact number of implementing men, vehicles and supplies had to be presented. Accomplished, all of this took time, and actually obtaining more officers and equipment an additional period.

Another thing that the Commissioner worked out was what to do with the wetbacks when arrested en masse. What had long been apparent to patrolmen was that simply conveying Mexicans south over the border was useless as a means of discouraging illegal immigration. As indifferent as ants to the fact that they weren't wanted, they would submit to deportation with fatalistic or even amused shrugs. For they knew they would be right back.

Patrolmen divided these Mexican boundary jumpers into two classes. The more enterprising as well as tougher ones were called *pachucos*. Farm work was not for these descendants of bandidos. Some wanted to shake the border and make their way to American cities to the north of it. Those that stayed near the line were the hard cases responsible for 75 percent of the crimes committed in the border counties of California as well as Texas. They were a minority, though. Typically the *espaldas mojadas*, or wetbacks, were meek, hard-working field hands known collectively to the line's Anglos as "Guanajuato Joe."

Guanajuato is not one of Mexico's border states. Centrally located, it is far closer to Mexico City than to any point along the Rio Grande. Characteristically, the wetback came from the populous states of central Mexico then. Some of these were to a considerable extent industrialized by the 1950s, but Guanajuato Joe knew no occupation but farming. As practiced by himself and other Indians of communities that had once been ecomienda villages, it was not productive enough to meet conditions described in *Migratory Labor in American Agriculture*. "Of first importance among 'push' forces in Mexico is population pressure in relation to resource development. . . ."

87

The pamphlet went on to point out that the population of Mexico grew from 16.5 million in 1930 to 25.5 million in 1950. The peons had at last been given land but not the knowledge or means to develop it. Soil primitively tilled could not support the multiplying appetites of rustic communities. Somebody had to leave, so Guanajuato Joe and family did.

A wetback was willing to stay in America in spite of frightful living conditions, because no matter how little penurious farmers north of the line might pay, it was still a lot more than peons could hope for at home. For in Mexico the per capita yearly income was $114. Only people used to making do on such incomes could have done what was ascribed to Guanajuato Joe, considered as a stag. Out of salaries that might be no more than $12 or $15 a week, male wetbacks were able to send or take more than half their earnings home.

Home in the sense of local provenance was where General Swing had decided to send trespassers from central Mexico, thereby taking the profit out of border jumping. The Patrol always saw to it that the aliens it arrested got all the pay coming to them. That money wasn't much dented and could soon be added to if a wetback was no more than sent across the boundary. But shipped back to Guanajuato, Joe had the choice of staying there or of investing all that he had netted in the United States in another trip to the line.

This economic check was the crux of the general's scheme. The cooperation of Mexican officials had to be obtained, of course. But this was forthcoming since Mexico City was opposed to a mass exodus of its nationals. What then remained was to work out the logistics of a bipartisan transportation effort.

For most of the first half of 1954 meanwhile, Mexicans continued to swarm across the boundary. Pending readiness for a great drive, the Patrol made no more partial ones but carried on as usual until Operation Wetback was abruptly launched.

What happened during the initial phase was described in the next annual report of the Immigration and Naturalization Service. "During the fiscal year ending June 30, 1954," this document affirmed, "the Border Patrol apprehended 1,035,282 aliens, an increase of 190,000 over the year previous. . . . Nine-tenths of the arrests were 'wetbacks' from Southern California, Arizona and the Lower Rio Grande Valley. In addition to the 'wetbacks' who have been apprehended along or adjacent to the Mexican Border, 37,413 Mexican nationals were apprehended working in industries."

After pointing out the utter undesirability of the invaders, the report proceeds with an item headed Operation Wetback: "In order to gain control over a situation which had assumed such alarming proportions, the Attorney General . . . announced that the Border Patrol would begin an operation on June 17 to rid Southern California and Western Arizona of 'wetbacks.' Simultaneously with the Attorney General's announcement, a band of road and railroad blocks was established and manned some distance from the Border to prevent the escape of those who might flee toward the North unheeded. During the week prior to June 17, 10,917 aliens were apprehended at these points."

A description of the tactics employed follows:

> On June 17 a special force of approximately 800 officers from all Border Patrol Sectors was assembled at El Centro and Chula Vista, California. The operation was divided into two task forces which, in turn, were divided into command units consisting of 12 men headed by a Senior Patrol Inspector and equipped with trucks, jeeps, and automobiles. Radio-equipped vehicles formed a communications link between the unit and Patrol aircraft and the task force headquarters. The aircraft pilot and observer were used to locate alien groups and direct ground units to them.
>
> When the task forces went into action they used a system of blocking off an area and mopping it up. Gradually they enlarged the operation until it embraced the industrial and agricultural areas of the entire State of California. . . . The peak in apprehensions was reached during the first week of operations when a daily average of 1,727 was apprehended.

The daily catch would have been much greater had not word of what was going on caused a wetback stampede for home.

> As news of the operation of the Special Force spread, unknown thousands left the country voluntarily to avoid arrest and transfer to the interior of Mexico . . . These voluntary departures, an important factor in the overall planning, were given impetus when the Commissioner, during the week preceding the drive, announced over the radio and through the press that the 'wetback' population was to be removed.

The deportation process was also dealt with in the report.

> When the number of apprehensions warranted it, a daily com-
> mercial bus service was inaugurated from the staging areas in
> California to Nogales, Arizona. Only males who were without
> families were expelled through the staging areas; all others were
> allowed to depart through the ports of Mexicali and Tijuana.
> Provision was made for feeding and shelter at the staging areas
> and each alien was provided with adequate food while traveling
> to his point of repatriation. By arrangement with the Mexican
> government, Mexican officials were responsible for placing these
> deportees on special trains at Nogales, destined to the interior
> of Mexico. . . .
> The Patrol unit at Nogales, Arizona, was augmented in antici-
> pation of the attempted return of any of the deportees. How-
> ever, largely as the result of the excellent cooperation of the
> Mexican officials, very few were able to escape the trip to the
> interior. Only 23 of the 23,222 aliens deported through the area
> had attempted to return to the United States and had been appre-
> hended by the Nogales Patrol Unit up to the end of June.

As of that date Operation Wetback was by no means through
sweeping out California. By the end of July though, it had expelled
or chased wetbacks from all other border areas and was mopping up
the section near the Gulf of Mexico. This part of the maneuver
was ably dealt with in a series of articles contributed to the San
Antonio *Express* by a staff feature writer named Clarence J. La-
Roche. As a native of the eastern end of the border, he was well
informed about the region's background. He also knew just who
was doing what in a vain effort to have Operation Wetback called
off in southeastern Texas. LaRoche led off on July 28, 1954.

> U. S. Immigration and Naturalization Service is on the move
> in the Rio Grande Valley to bring an end to an era of Colonial
> Economy. The howls are heard all the way to Washington.
> People just don't give up something cheap and useful like
> wetbacks without a last-ditch fight. . . .
> Latest howl being raised in the Valley against the U.S. Border
> Patrol . . . is one of brutality.

90

This charge has been built up to the extent that the Valley Farm Bureau is now demanding a Congressional investigation through a resolution passed in Mercedes Tuesday.

The San Antonio *Express* carried that story, too. It must be said for the embattled farmers of Mercedes that they were no small game hunters. Included in a telegram sent to Washington was "a demand for a Congressional investigation of the Justice Dept. in connection with the conduct of the drive.

"C. B. Ray, executive manager of the farm bureau, sent this telegram to Senators Lyndon Johnson and Price Daniel and Representatives Lloyd M. Bentsen, Jr., and Sam Rayburn . . .

" 'Recent acts of misconduct, attributed to the border patrol by reputable persons, leave little doubt that the situation is deplorable. Allegations have been made of aliens being struck and kicked, of entry into homes and to threats of violence to both citizens and aliens.' "

LaRoche's comments reduced these charges to piffle. "During the opening phases of the current wetback drive, I rode and flew with patrolmen; I went out on my own, and I checked around the Valley area and did not turn up any report of mistreatment.

"I covered many hundreds of square miles by air—and what patrolmen were doing on the ground is no secret to someone watching them from the air—and saw no signs of brutality.

"On the ground, during those first few days, I saw thousands of aliens rounded up. I never saw one act of violence on the part of patrolmen."

The embittered men of Mercedes wanted the Department of Justice carpeted on another serious charge. "Citizens of the area are demanding," their wire read, "that the Dept. of Justice return any and all monies taken from illegal aliens when apprehended."

As to this count, LaRoche also had comments. "I've personally seen patrolmen get together, pool their 'pocket change' and buy a small mound of supplies that their arrested wetbacks could take back across the Rio Grande with them.

"I've known of patrolmen who summoned doctors—at the patrolman's personal expense—to look after a sick infant or child; I've seen these patrolmen go out and buy milk for these kids . . ."

The Executive Manager of the Valley Farm Bureau said his organization "is encouraging eyewitnesses to reduce to writing accounts of misconduct by border patrolmen." LaRoche reduced to writing facts that added up to indictments of members of the Farm Bureau on counts of larceny and conspiracy as well as extreme cruelty.

> Wages? The wetback gets what he can. Sometimes it is as little as 15 cents an hour and I have talked to wetbacks who were getting only meager meals.
> "The patron tells us the tomato market is bad right now. We're still picking, but all he can give us is our meals and this shelter," a wetback once told me. His meals consisted mainly of frijoles, tomatoes and flour tortillas. [As opposed to the far more substantial cornmeal ones . . .]
> He is kept on the farm, and on his meager wage in many instances because he is threatened with "la patrulla"—being turned over to the Border Patrol, if he complains of his lot.

The last of LaRoche's articles on Operation Wetback appeared July 31, 1954. As Congress had not responded to urgings from Mercedes, the Border Patrol's drive continued for some weeks. At its conclusion the pestilential camps stood untenanted. Only the nearby groves of crosses, most of them marking the graves of infants, remained to tell that the human cycle had been carried out in such filthy surroundings. Flies no longer buzzed greedily about lairs in the chaparral. Families and single males had ceased to creep in and out of mud huts, brush hutches and hollows scooped out of a stream or canal bank.

In accomplishing this, Operation Wetback had deported or scared into voluntary absence 1,300,000 passportless Mexicans. That total was in addition to the hundreds of thousands of arrests made in the course of normal operations earlier in 1954. Then the figure differed from previous ones in a significant respect. They had included hordes of repeaters, caught several times a year. Only a few were counted twice in Operation Wetback. Conveyed to distant Mexican points— thousands by ships which took them as far south as Vera Cruz—most of those nabbed by General Swing's task forces did not feel like trying to jump the American boundary soon again.

Some did, inevitably, and wetbacks who hadn't been burned in 1954 were willing to give life in the United States a try. Yet the traffic across the line was only a fraction of what it had been. The next annual report of the Immigration and Naturalization Service furnished the details. "Deportations and voluntary departures totaled less than 250,000 in 1955 compared with more than 1,100,000 in the preceding year." But the service's reports covered fiscal and not calendar years; the periods dealt with ran from July 1 of one year to June 30 of the next, that is to say. Such being the case, apprehensions in the last half of 1954 were included, and the actuality was that by 1955 the wetback traffic was much smaller than the offered figures suggest.

No longer swamped, the Patrol was able to operate more efficiently for other reasons. Under Eisenhower's administration its importance had been recognized for the first time since the days of their battles with liquor smugglers. General Swing was, therefore, able to arrange for the Patrol to receive all the equipment it needed. He also increased the force to 1,400 men. These worked out of well maintained and supplied headquarters, in place of shacks in need of paint and furnishings which had done nothing to help morale.

The change of front was reported by Ed Castillo in the San Antonio *Light*'s issue of October 9, 1955. He, as he explained, had last visited the border in 1953, when the wetback invasion had seemed hopelessly out of control. Castillo wrote of McAllen revisited:

> Even before entering the headquarters building, we noticed the change. Buildings had been renovated. Shops, and quarters housing an armory, radio transmitter, squad room and training center, had been added. There were numerous patrol cars, mostly late model, also jeeps, trucks and buses. . . .
>
> Even the uniforms were different. Where, for years, patrolmen stationed in the Texas area had been accustomed to wearing casual khakis and soft-brimmed Stetsons, they were now garbed in snappy forest-green uniforms of a worsted material, black shoes and hard-brimmed "patrol Stetsons." A Sam Browne belt and regulation pistol complete the outfit.

Another novelty was the esteem in which the corps was locally held, for reasons now to be explored. At the height of their dudgeon the Lower Rio Grande Valley's farmers had never complained that they would have been without harvest help, should the wetbacks be denied them, for there were two other available labor pools. One was made up of native Latin Americans. The other was composed of Mexican contract laborers, usually called *braceros*.

The low wages paid wetbacks had become standard wherever the invaders were prevalent. In consequence Latin American farm hands joined migratory labor groups ranging other parts of the United States. From Texas alone it was estimated that 100,000 men annually migrated to other sections each spring returning to their homes only after all harvesting was done. Some traveled alone, but most of the married men took their families with them.

The braceros were a continuation of the wartime emergency program cited earlier. They were seasonally imported laborers who entered without families and ideally returned to them at a stint's specified close. In *What Price Wetbacks?* it was declared that as of 1951, over 100,000 braceros had been found missing when it was time for them to go back to Mexico. But they were arranged for and processed on a bi-national basis. Criminals and disease-bearers were not recruited, and those that were seem to have been satisfactorily industrious workmen. What they were promised in the United States was far better wages than they could make at home, plus reasonably good food and living conditions. Though theory wasn't always put into practice, it was on the whole a very good deal for the workers and important to the Mexican nation. In 1953 it was officially reported in Mexico City that the money sent below the border by the braceros of 1952 made the program the third most profitable Mexican industry for that year. Topping it as peso winners were only mining and the tourist trade.

Braceros worked all over the United States, but they were available in border ones, just as Latin Americans were. The difference to the line states is implicit in the gains for Mexico realized by braceros. The wetback, in so far as he could, drained America's economy by spending elsewhere what he earned here. The bracero was even more of a bloodsucker. Fed, housed, and better paid, he spent not only more but a higher percentage of his pay below the boundary. Mexico's third most profitable 1952 industry stood for a lot of dollars dropped through a hole in Uncle Sam's pocket.

Conversely, wherever the Latin American was allowed work in his own border bailiwick, retail sales rose sharply. Although some communities thus profited, others remained hampered through the hiring of the cheaper braceros. But if these spent little locally, they were still a vast improvement on wetbacks.

Not spending half his time on the dodge or under arrest, a bracero could work more efficiently, if for fewer hours, and did not have to be constantly replaced. Whether or not he had a family, he did not create social problems by bringing them with him. Now that they were gone, the border's people were glad to be rid of wetback hives and their miserable inhabitants. The crime rate dropped—at some points as much as 75 percent—for the Patrol now had the wherewithal as well as the time to keep the pachucos where they belonged. The entire temper of life along the boundary had been sweetened by Operation Wetback, and the participating officers were given due credit.

The Patrol's directors had made reconciliation easier by shifting crews from towns where they were known to ones where they ranked as newcomers. People who had been furious at some officers could start fresh with strangers and buddy up without self-consciousness.

As for the wetbacks, they had shot their mass invasion bolt, as of that era, in the first half of 1955. By the fall of that year the news of captures and deportations had so discouraged candidates that line jumpers were hard to find. "Patrolmen literally have to beat the bushes these days to catch one," as the *Light*'s Castillo put it. "They no longer walk across in plain daylight the way they used to do. Not even in Brownsville, where they used to saunter across the riverbed in sight of the immigration building. We know this, because we went to Brownsville, too."

With its energies not absorbed in rounding up wetbacks in job lots, the Patrol settled down to tightening its control of the boundary by improved procedures. The most important of these were described in the Immigration Service's annual report for 1955:

> An integral part of the border security program is an intelligence organization, established during the year to collect, evaluate and disseminate information concerning smuggling and other illegal activities. During the last two weeks of the fiscal year, 251 illegal aliens and eight smugglers were apprehended in the Southwest region alone through information obtained by this organization. . . . Officers assigned to intelligence duties also watch for developments in the use of fraudulent documents to gain entry to the United States or any other violations of immigration laws.
>
> The intelligence units furnish strategic intelligence for use in planning future operations. This includes information on labor supply and demand, numbers and intentions of potential illegal entrants . . . crop conditions and forecasts, and public opinion samplings.

Watch on the border was given a further new dimension when a method of keeping tabs on boundary-crossing airplanes was adopted. "A new air intelligence center was . . . set up at El Centro, California, to collect and disseminate information relating to illegal aircraft entries across the Mexican Border."

The 1955 report also showed that the line was here and there being barricaded. "It has been the experience of the Service that a substantial fence will, to a great degree, discourage the illegal entry of aliens, especially women and children who attempt to enter near some of our largest cities. Fences had been completed at five locations totaling 11.6 miles; 7.1 miles of additional fencing is under construction at two other places and plans are being made to extend the program. By diverting the flow of aliens away from city boundaries to sections where apprehensions can be more easily accomplished, the areas can be controlled with a minimum force, thereby freeing officers for duty elsewhere."

The Patrol did not expect to keep wetbacks from leaping the international line. But it thought it had cut the flow down to manageable proportions, preventing the invasion from ever again being a serious American problem. That this confidence warmed hearts in Washington as well was shown by a dispatch which the Associated Press issued from the capital on January 17, 1956. "Uncle Sam's stake-out against 'wetbacks'—aliens crossing the Mexican border into this country illegally—apparently is curtailing the influx."

General Swing's report on the Patrol's achievements on almost the same date offered figures in confirmation. According to the Corpus Christi *Caller* of January 16, "He said the flow of illegal wetbacks across the border in 1955 was decreased more than 90 percent from 1954." The Commissioner said, too, that before Operation Wetback, arrests had mounted to 3,000 daily and that by the end of 1955 the total had been shaved to 200 a day.

PART

III

*EVENTS
PENDING
A SECOND
BUILDUP*

9

INTERIM
OPERATIONS

The one disservice afflicted on the Patrol by General Swing is that he is one of the reasons why the corps's records are so defective. Although there never seems to have been any official central deposit for information and case histories, the files of the El Paso headquarters and, to a lesser extent, some of the others, had accumulated much beside routine correspondence. But when the general revamped the organization, he ordered all papers that weren't pertinent to business of the moment junked, and with that ukase many a particle of history at its roughest and quaintest went up the flue.

But everything else that he did for the force was right. Some of them were recounted by Ed Castillo of the San Antonio *Light*. Others will now be presented.

Swing's chief benefaction was to give the Border Patrol the unity and autonomy that had before been lacking. Along the Mexican boundary the situation had been impossibly awkward. It was all very well for the Immigration and Naturalization Service in the Southwest to be divided into three districts with headquarters respectively at San Antonio, El Paso and metropolitan Los Angeles, for these could maintain liaison with one another or communicate directly with Washington. But because its necessities had never been intelligently examined in the past, the Border Patrol in the Southwest had been considered portions of three separate Immigration Service detachments rather than as belonging to one police force.

General Swing made it that by separating it administratively from the Immigration and Naturalization Service proper. In place of the old setup, he supplied the Border Patrol Chief in Washington with field deputies, each in a regional headquarters. Jointly these supervised the patrolling of an entire national boundary.

Stationed at San Pedro, on the Pacific Coast, the deputy chief in the Southwest was handed authority that didn't stop short of the Gulf of Mexico. All subdivisions of the Patrol on the Mexican line then belonged to one team. Liaison and cooperation between its various units became matters of course. Fluidity was achieved, too, because the man in charge at San Pedro could shift men and equipment in response to the changing needs indicated by his local commanders.

These were in charge of regional divisions called sectors. The Mexican boundary was divided into ten such parts, named for the towns chosen as headquarters seats. Reading from west to east, there were Chula Vista and El Centro in California; Yuma and Tucson in Arizona; El Paso, Marfa, Del Rio, Laredo, McAllen and Brownsville in Texas. Each of these has a number of regularly manned outposts known as stations. Not all sector headquarters towns were right on the border, Tucson lying sixty odd miles north of it and Marfa a dozen more. But they were strategically located with respect to the traffic lanes, primitive or civilized, by which wetbacks and other illegal entrants infiltrated the United States.

The boundary frontage of the various sectors was not uniform. The controlling factor was traffic patterns. Some sectors were therefore relatively narrow and deep, others broader in terms of border mileage but reaching not as far inland. All were huge areas of responsibility, made manageable by improved equipment.

Here the greatest aid was a radio network amplified by repeaters. A sector was "salted," that is to say, by towers on commanding heights that picked up voice-laden electric waves and flung them to one another across wilderness. Patrolmen in vehicles equipped with F-M devices could utilize the huge party lines in any part of a given sector, barking such information as they had picked up and receiving orders or news in turn. Previously, keeping touch by radio had only been possible when vehicles were quite close together, and then only when no ridge humped its back between them. Now head-quarters could hear from and direct PIs on distant missions, and the motorized men of any team could swap ideas over rugged terrain and pass information to an airpilot cruising in a different county.

Sign cutting had meanwhile graduated from a ground activity to one which embraced the sky as well. That had been so in the lim-ited sense that planes might hover and relay findings to ground crews scouting the vicinity. But with radio repeaters ballooning the area in which teamwork was possible, a pilot could find sign and summon ground crews that were many leagues from the point of discovery.

On behalf of those who haven't witnessed vehicular tracking, the methods of trailing by a team of jeep-borne patrolmen must first be put on view. For if patrolling is customarily done by separately engaged vehicles, once sign has been discovered, effective following demands two cars. Assuming a PI has found a track which he has ascertained to be fresh enough to warrant action, he gives the air the news, either by talking to a specific officer whom he knows to be in the general area or telling the headquarters radio operator that he has something hot and needs help with it. Due to the practice of regularly checking in by all on field duty, the radio operator knows approxi-mately where all officers are and buzzes the one in the best position to hasten to the action scene.

The first man has in the meantime been following sign afoot to determine the direction of the aliens. The arriving officer may or may not pause to confer; a signal may suffice to speed him ahead a half mile, say, toward some spot along the indicated azimuth where finding sign is easy. When he picks up the trail, a blast on his vehicle's horn or a call over walkie-talkie alerts the PI afoot. He lunges for his scout car and races past the second patrolman, who now in turn be-comes the pedestrian tracker. By this process, known as "leapfrog-ging," a pair of sign cutters can cover perhaps five miles while a peon is trudging one. In a couple of hours officers can thus pare away all the advantage of a headstart gained by jumping the line at some point during the night before.

Sometimes a leapfrogging officer will find no sign. He will then let his partner know that the quarry is somewhere between them,

101

resting or aware of pursuit and holing up. The PI behind will then continue to track while the one ahead closes in along the logical line of flight, should the game break cover.

But with the addition of air observation, the range and speed of sign cutting can be greatly extended. For while two cutters are covering ground in the manner described, a summoned airpilot can cruise miles in advance of them and pick out tracks which he knows to be the ones they are following. Notifying the ground crew, he circles above the discovered sign until the men in scout cars reach it and determine the fugitive's next line of march by the leapfrog method. In this way a team of sign cutters can sweep over country with the speed of a prairie fire with a gale behind it.

In many cases, of course, scouting airpilots are the original discoverers of tracks. In such instances the flyer notifies the headquarters radio operator and either hovers in the vicinity or sets his plane down and waits for scout cars or pickups to dust nearby. The four-seaters might ask something as formal in the way of a landing strip as a dirt road. The two-seater mosquito planes are planked down on the desert at any vaguely level point where shrubs and rocks are not too numerous.

As sign cutters pilots are especially effective during the early morning hours and late afternoon, when the sun's rays meet the earth at a sharp and searching angle. Then a man in a plane can see what was undiscernible to a man afoot or in a car. Where desert sand has been pressed by the shoe or boot of a walker, a level of particles can be created, smooth and coherent enough to act as a reflector of beams that slap it from a slant. The pilot's line of vision, also being oblique with respect to the track as he flies toward rather than directly over it, can then see what old Sol does.

A pilot might also spy into lurking places which ground crews could only find by lucky chance. The doggo wetback might break into the open and be easily caught. Or if he depended on the hope that the man in the sky had missed him, jeeps or pickups could be called to a sitting duck's vain hideaway.

And planes likewise made it difficult for wetbacks to get out of the Patrol's reach by the once popular method of hopping freight trains. By day or with the favor of the moon, pilots could spot men flattened out on the roof of a boxcar or sprawled in an open gondola.

To return to sign cutting, it did not stop when daylight did. Aided by spotlights and specially adjusted headlights, patrolmen could follow tracks rapidly through benighted sand, grass or hardpan. Some-times it would be necessary to alight and search; at others sign would be traced for long stretches by PIs hustling along in vehicles they were at once driving and leaning out of. By flashlight signals as well as radio, a team of jeepsters could comb a brush-dotted expanse and come out with the fox they were after.

There were other schemes and devices to get the better of darkness. One was an electric eye focused across the roadbed of a railway line known to be favored by wetbacks slinking in at night. When the walker passed this orb, it sprang an alarm at headquarters, where the officer in charge could then direct a patrol team to the spot.

In areas where there were a number of border crossing points close together, trip lights came into use. A wetback who stole from brush or cane fringing the Rio Grande, would hit a wire that would flash a warning beam to lurking PIs. By this means one pair of officers could stand guard over a half dozen infiltration trails.

Drag trails, the roads athwart paths across the line which were especially designed to catch footprints, were regularly prowled by patrolmen in cars. Some of these traps ran along the miles of ten-foot cyclone fences by which technicians unacquainted with wet-backs had set great store. They might as well have tried to thus contain so many monkeys. Still, the tall barriers were useful with regard to drag trails, for the invaders that scrambled over and dropped from the top of them left tracks which offered PIs sharp footgear prints, complete with the makes of rubber heels, say, and any wear and tear on them or the soles.

Basic line watch, or lying in wait by crossing points where modern devices were of no avail, remained an after-dark routine. Yet now as much time was devoted to patrolling city streets and paved highways of a zone which was responding to three enlarging factors: One was the great westward population surge whose particular ter-minus was the Southwest. To that general condition were added two local ones. Expanding irrigation projects and the profits to be made by farmers with capital and know-how were attracting people to the border, at a time when the greatest obstacle to its settlement by Anglos was being removed through the availability of refrigeration for offices and stores as well as homes.

The highway systems of developing sections were policed in part by checks of cars and trucks passing a shifting series of points. In town all public conveyances were regularly sifted. Included were car rental establishments and taxi servies. The first were usually found innocent of serving wetbacks and/or smugglers; the second were forever apt to be taking anybody's pay.

By way of coping with air traffic across the line, the Patrol had established a private plane index at its El Centro headquarters in 1955. Through the cooperation of the Federal Air Administration, the course of every privately owned plane in the country could be charted. In common with seaports, commercial airfields were manned by personnel that kept records of all incoming and outgoing craft. The patrolman in charge of the index at El Centro was posted, accordingly, about the American points of departure and destinations of all such planes. He knew which ones regularly flew across the line, commuting between landing fields in Mexico's interior and commercial or community fields north of the border.

Any pilot who didn't give straight information about his American destinations could soon be known and become suspect. For airships have one drawback, as far as those who wish to operate secretly are concerned, not shared by seacraft. They are not selfsustaining for any considerable length of time but have to be refueled daily if not oftener. Unlike the drivers of automobiles, pilots cannot roll up anonymously to service stations where no questions are asked. The only places they can obtain what they need are airfields, where planes and their operators must be identified by radio reports before landing strips are assigned.

Exceptions were the planes of ranchers who might have their own private gasoline pumps. But their facilities could only be used by lawbreakers in the rare cases where smugglers and farmers or stock raisers colluded. And the man who so avoided checking into a regular airfield left a question in his wake. Absent from both his base airfield and any other where a register was kept, he asked to be investigated.

So the Patrol's aircraft index was effective wherever American writ ran. But it could not follow the course of a private plane south of the boundary. To some degree, though, this could be managed through a Patrol department which also began functioning in 1955. This was a fact-finding corps composed of officers who shed uniforms in the interest of being able to operate on both sides of the line.

The new rank of Intelligence Officer had a representative in each sector headquarters. His purpose was to evaluate all the data dredged from international channels of information. Much of it was pumped out of wetbacks by the Patrol Inspectors who captured and quizzed them. Some of it was obtained from Mexican officials; establishing a good footing with those across the boundary from his sector was one of the primary duties of an Intelligence Officer. Then there was the matter turned up by PIs on detached duty with the "anti-smuggling section" of every headquarters.

The number of these in each sector depended on the incidence of wetback smuggling in a given part of the border. This tended to be large where sizable towns faced each other across the line, and negligible in rural areas. For if the trail of human contraband runners had often cut uninhabited regions in horseback days, the triumph of the automobile had narrowed the world for non-airborne smugglers. Instead of trying to travel where they wouldn't be seen, they tended to place their trust in good roads and the speed that high-powered cars could make over them.

But those overt dashes through the United States were preceded by bargaining and solicitations, implied in a paragraph of *Migratory Labor in American Agriculture*. "The hub of the wetback traffic is in the plazas of the Mexican towns and cities immediately below the border . . . The principal topic of conversation in the plazas of the Mexican border towns for several months of the year is how to get into the United States and what crops and jobs promise employment once there. His (the wetback's) urgent need of food and money makes him an easy mark for the smuggler. . . ."

It was, therefore, in the towns south of the line that the anti-smuggling officers mainly worked. No more in uniform than Intelligence Officers, their mission was to make friends in Mexico who could give them accurate tips. Not all this amiability was on an amateur basis, however. Each officer was given instructions to build up a stable of informers.

At times the Mexican stool pigeons were paid in cash. In other cases they were rewarded by chances to work in the United States, their places of employment being ones where espionage was needed. But their effective tours of duty were never long, for as Patrolman Leslie Bell of the Laredo anti-smuggling section phrased it, "Informers burn themselves out." They lose their nerve, he went on to explain, and either quit or become unreliable.

What was expected of the spy while he remained useful was to frequent the drinking dens and whorehouses where smugglers commonly got in touch with men anxious to be guided north of the boundary and past the Patrol's watchmen. From the chat in such places the informer could gather when and by how many the line was cracked on a given date. From some would-be wetback in his cups the name of the smuggler as well as the method of jumping the border might be ascertained. And meanwhile a lot of incidental underworld gossip—possibly pertaining to the operators of boundary crossing private planes—might be gathered by the stool pigeon and passed on to his PI patron.

Anything thought to be of general Patrol interest was reported to the local Intelligence Officer, who bundled it with any supporting data that had been picked up and relayed it to border headquarters at San Pedro. From there the word went out to every subordinate headquarters, so that the latest thing in criminal procedures could be watched for by PIs, however assigned.

But while attending to its enlarged 1955 duties, the reorganized Patrol often pitched in on behalf of other law enforcement agencies. By winning a reputation for never turning a request for help down, the corps also served its own purposes, to be sure. State, county and town officers that knew where to look for siding when they needed it were glad to come back by offering patrolmen tips, manpower and equipment upon requests for them.

Cooperation with other Federal services which could and did act in kind, was another corps activity. "Bond Jumper Nabbed Here," the Laredo *Times* announced on January 14, 1958. "Augustin Permui, 54, a Cuban citizen wanted for jumping bond in a federal theft from mail charge in Chicago on December 6, 1954, has been turned over by the Border Patrol to the FBI in Laredo.

"At a hearing before U.S. Commissioner Frank Y. Hill Monday the man waived removal proceedings and he is held in jail in lieu of $10,000 bond. He was taken in custody by the Border Patrol Sunday."

Because of the Patrol's known specialty of sign cutting, it would take over from some other law enforcement agency the assignment of tracking down jail breakers. On one notable occasion the Laredo sector so served the FBI as well as officers of Webb County.

PATROL NABS FUGITIVES, a streamer across the front page of the *Times* shouted on February 19, 1956. Who was nabbed and why, was set forth in a story with Tom Green's by-line:

> U.S. Immigration Border Patrolmen recaptured early Saturday four of seven prisoners who staged a break at 12:05 A.M. from the Webb County jail. . . .

The F.B.I. Saturday filed new charges against the four recaptured men for escaping from custody . . . The four men reapprehended after fleeing from jail went to Gateway Chevrolet Company's lot and stole a 1955 Oldsmobile.

They then headed out north, but the car stalled near KVOZ radio station. Then they took off through the brush to the north. . . .

Two men got away when the four recaptured were first spotted in the brush by a team of border patrolmen who were tracking them in the brush north of Laredo, east of U.S. Highway 81 . . . Caught there were Charles Waymire, 20, of Tulsa, Oklahoma, and Ralph Victor Gordon, 42, of San Mateo, California. The other two, Richard Bernard, 25, and William J. Lee, 21, both of Tulsa, broke and ran.

At the ranch of Watt Casey they stole a 1953 Studebaker . . . The escapees crashed through a ranch gate in the car out into the highway. Other patrolmen were notified by radio and the Border Patrol airplanes got into the chase.

At the alien check point maintained by the Patrol 14 miles north of Laredo, the escapees ran through without stopping. Patrolmen there then gave chase.

Patrolmen in the tracking party were Leslie Bell, Norman Bedlington, Oscar Doyle Stevens and John Jackson. Men at the check station who jumped in the car and went after the escapees were George Bradbury and Rodney C. King. In the plane were Charlie Henderson, pilot, and James F. Gray, observer.

The combination was too much for the runaways. They had learned the rough way that there was no hiding place in the brush that expert sign cutters couldn't find, so they didn't try running again when boxed by machines. "With border patrolmen pursuing in a car behind them, and a border patrol plane surveilling them from the air, the unarmed escapees finally pulled to the side of the road and gave up at 1:30 P.M. eighteen miles from the junction of U.S. Highways 81 and 83, on U.S. 83 toward Eagle Pass."

The Patrol, furthermore, helped states far removed from the border. One such instance was narrated in the *Times* of January 19, 1958. "Three Iowa officers left Laredo at 6:40 A.M. Saturday to return a prisoner, Jack Hendricks Hoskins, 30, who is charged with the murder of his estranged wife at Rock Rapids, Iowa, on January 5. . . .

"Hoskins, who is charged with having shot his wife to death in the pastor's study of a church in Rock Rapids, following baptism of their two-month-old son in the church, was apprehended by border patrolmen in South Laredo the night of January 11."

As the 1950s drew to a close, then, the Patrolmen had the border in its fist. They had the men and equipment to handle their own assignments without undue strain and could help keep the peace in other respects. They worked hard but were not often called upon for lengthy overtime. Nothing like the grueling years that preceded Operation Wetback was viewed as possible for five years after that cleansing.

10

SOME
FRONTAGES
AND
DEPTHS

The descriptions of separate Patrol activities, offered in earlier chapters, give only a partial idea of the corps's operational scope. With a view to bringing that into clearer focus, the anatomy of several Border sectors will be here sketched.

For one thing, developments of the 1960s have increased, by hundreds of thousands of square miles, the force's area of responsibility. Improved communications and the trend of wetbacks to strike inland in search of employment, have combined to give the policed boundary a depth which wasn't imaginable at the time of the Patrol's founding.

The Tucson Sector is the most obvious case in point. Originally headquarters was located at the border town of Nogales, Arizona. But Nogales straddles only one north and south bound highway; to the east and west it is hemmed in by mountains which can be crossed in a hurry solely by airplanes. Sixty-six miles from the line, Tucson is the hub of a first-class, compass-boxing road system, so it is from that city that Chief Patrol Inspector James P. Kelly and his staff currently direct proceedings.

Subordinate are seven stations, each with a specific responsibility area. One of these is the Tucson station, housed at headquarters. Of the others, only the Nogales and Douglas stations hug the border. About as far from the line as Tucson is the eastward lying one at Willcox. To westward, those at Casa Grande and Gila Bend are some forty miles farther north. The one at Phoenix is around 160 wild geese miles from the boundary.

Yet that indicates less than half of the sector's scope. Stretching north to the Utah line, over 200 miles from Arizona's capital, it has a maximum depth of 370 miles. Its border frontage runs from New Mexico to Yuma County, Arizona. The total area is 76,440 square miles. Comprehended in them are deserts high and low, plateaus many leagues wide and mountain ranges scaling up to 12,000 feet above sea level. There are large irrigated areas, huge grazing belts and yet huger forests. There are Indian reservations—bigger than several Eastern states in one instance—and one of the two largest metropolitan areas that clock by Mountain Time. That, of course, is Phoenix and its satellites, while the Tucson cluster is likewise large.

The sector is crossed by two railroad systems and several highways teeming with transcontinental traffic. Included are the coaches of two great and numerous smaller bus lines. Air traffic abounds in the sector. Lines great and small criss-cross its skies, and every town with any municipal pretensions has a flyers' field used by private planes at least.

So much for the sector's dimensions and complexities. To patrol a diversified area almost exactly the size of New England with New Jersey added, the corps allots in the neighborhood of a hundred men. The number is presented indefinitely because of the fluidity of the Patrol's policy. According to an official statement "the authorized force is 1,185 Border Patrolmen for the Southwest Region . . ." but "the number of Border Patrolmen on duty . . . varies considerably from day to day and week to week." What is true of the whole is true of its parts. As PIs are constantly being moved from point to point as emergencies bulge here and flatten there, the sector forces wax or wane accordingly.

In the Tucson Sector the two largest detachments are those assigned to the Douglas and Nogales stations. With some help from nature—parts of barren mountain ranges in the ten thousand foot class are nothing that even a wetback would care to thread without equipment—they divide the policing of 270 miles. In the vicinity of the respective station towns, the PIs keep line watch on a twenty-four hour basis, driving endlessly along a pattern of roads designed to cross all known paths of ingress. Some of these are drag-roads. Swept night and morning so that they will register foot prints, they may lie as much as eight miles north of the line.

In Nogales, which confronts the much larger city of Nogales, Sonora, there's an international bus line to be checked daily. In both Douglas and Nogales the freight trains of the Southern Pacific are regularly examined. Electric eyes report to the station the passage of any wetbacks who use the tracks as walk-ways by night.

Electric eyes also keep watch in two flood-control tunnels that unite the line-divided towns of twin-Nogales. In Douglas, which is not boxed by mountains, the terrain of the Sulphur Springs Valley makes tower watching feasible. In both American cities, street patrol is maintained.

To east and west of the port of entry gates of both towns extend cyclone fences of heavy wire and ten feet high. At Douglas, where the country is more open than by hill-hemmed Nogales, the tall fencing stretches seven and three-quarter miles eastward and eight and seven-tenths miles toward the Pacific. It is checked not only for footprints leading away from them but for damage done by wire cutters or filers which must be reported to the International Boundary Commission.

On either side of the cyclone fences the line is protected by no more than barbed wire strands which smugglers sometimes buck through in trucks. Most of the wetbacks who skirt the heavy fencing are afoot, though. Three valleys—the Santa Cruz container of Nogales, the San Pedro where the husk of Tombstone mellows and the cited Sulphur Springs encircler of Douglas—invite pedestrian line jumpers to strike inland, slogging more or less due north. If they do so within the scope of cyclone fences, they are bound to cross one or more parts of the drag-road system. Should found tracks be fresh, a team of sign cutting PIs rolls out in scout cars, confident that no more than ground pursuit will be necessary. If the footprints indicate that the wetback has a long start, a call is put in for the Cessna four-seater at Tucson or the Piper Cub attached to the Douglas Station.

Soaring back and forth over the grass, brush, washes, gulches, canyons, knobs and buttes of a wide cattle range, the pilot has in mind an exact description of tracks found near town by the patroller of a drag-road. By the time the ground crew reaches the scene of his maneuvers, he is often able to tell its members where they can find the trail of the one or more wetbacks in question. Or he may have found the man or men himself. If they are in the open, he pins them down by the hazardous but effective means of standing his plane on one wing very close to the ground and describing a small circle that keeps his quarry from knowing which way to break. This is the more daunting because of a curiosity of optics. Gazing upward through Arizona's searing sunlight, it is very difficult for a man on the ground to descry a small plane of whose nearness he can yet be convinced by the roar of its motor.

When not engaged in sign cutting operations, the pilots of the Tucson sector scout the mountainous reaches of the border which frame three named valleys. Or they fly west by north from Nogales over desert sharps and flats as far as the Yuma Sector. In these flights they are looking for more than indications that trudgers of rough country have recently crossed the line; the planes of smugglers and their secret landing strips are also watched for.

A great many illegal immigrants are whizzed into the United States by planes, yet the Patrol has never been given the equipment to deal with this branch of the boundary-hopping traffic. "We haven't got any pursuit planes, just observation types," air-pilot Harry Aitkens explained. "Our fastest is a Cessna that can do a hundred and seventy-five miles an hour—or could when it was younger—and smugglers have kinds that can make three hundred or better. The best we can do, as the score stands, is try to figure out an operation pattern, so we'll have some idea of where to look for 'em after they land."

There is smuggling by automobile, too, naturally, especially at twin-Nogales. There the heavy tourist flow is an aid to smugglers, whose cars mingle with those of visitors on their way back from the border. The Patrol counters by traffic checks which, however, are held irregularly. Like the rest of the sector, the Nogales station is insufficiently manned for thoroughness in this and divers other respects. There are too many rings in its circus for any one to get the attention PIs would like to apply.

So it is understood that many wetbacks are carried through or hike around the Douglas and Nogales front lines. Assuming that a lone

Mexican does so, he then becomes the responsibility of one of the back-up stations. The small ones at Willcox, Casa Grande and Gila Bend are staffed by only a few men. How they function was described by William C. Joyner, one of the Tucson Sector's two Assistant Chief Patrol Inspectors.

"The wets who make for the vicinities of those stations are all farm laborers or ranch hands." He thumbed through the sector's portfolio. "The Casa Grande area is 4,912 square miles—about the size of Connecticut—but still it's smaller than the others. It has the most farms, though—790 as compared with Willcox's 550 and Gila Bend's 230.

"Well, the Patrol Inspectors at those stations have to know what's grown seasonally on all the farms and how many wetback laborers each can employ. The same thing goes for stock ranches in the various areas. It's up to the PIs to keep tabs—sometimes by asking for planes and finding out from air inspection—where a farmer or rancher has wetbacks staked out in camps they'd just as soon we didn't see."

Joyner also dealt with the patrolling of some of the huge blocs of territory piled up north of some of the stations. "Now, the Willcox area includes 33,000 square miles, which is just about the size of Maine. I don't say it's done very often in some cases, but all the points in it where wets might logically find employment are visited in the course of every year."

That holds good for the 23,400 square miles of the Phoenix station's area. As is true of the smaller Tucson Station's domain, operations are rural as well as urban. If the Phoenix metropolitan area houses a population of over 900,000, there are 920 farms on its outskirts, and farther out sprawl 315 cattle, sheep and goat ranches.

Although a great many wetbacks are picked up in the cities of Phoenix and Tucson, most of them are on their way to California or points east. So far the nature of Arizona's industries has made demands—union membership being one of them, in spite of the fact that it's not a closed shop state—that have kept Mexican invaders from getting much of a foothold. In mining and the building trades, for example, the casual vagrant hasn't a chance; and immigration from the East has created a situation in which only veteran knowhow can make its way. The industrialization of Phoenix and Tucson, as the sector portfolio notes, has attracted a "substantial pool of skilled labor sufficient to fill the needs of all the present industry," hence the opportunities for wetbacks are very limited.

In El Paso, on the other hand, they have been found in about all industries from which unionization doesn't exclude them. The chief problem here is the practice of granting border crossing cards on a wholesale basis to the residents of Ciudad Juarez. Holders of these cards are in the same position as the Americans that daily stream over the Mexican line without benefit of any sort of a pass. They have the unchecked freedom of a city they are supposedly entering for the purposes of shopping, seeking entertainment or calling on friends.

The difference is that the American who crosses the border without luggage is, in fact, a tourist, there to find amusement and sure to spend money in the course of doing so. He is not asked to show any documents, because he is an asset to a community he is certain to leave when short of cash. But, by the thousands, Mexicans with visitors' permits are something quite different. They are nothing more than licensed wetbacks, operating on a daily basis and without hindrance of Border Patrol opposition.

Owning authentic port of entry permits, they stroll over the bridge linking Juarez to El Paso, and so to work. Like wetbacks hired by farmers, they are welcomed by American employers because of being cheaper. Worse than the out and out wetbacks from America's monetary viewpoint, they do not have to invest in the United States so much as the cost of meals. If they bring a lunch across the Rio Grande with them, together with their own smokes and chewing gum, they need not spend a penny in the land they are looting before it's time to saunter back to Mexico with their pay.

El Paso is also plagued with the standard variety of unlicensed Mexican invaders who may be seen perched like buzzards on one of the border's curious features. This is owing to the fact that the Treaty of Guadalupe-Hidalgo authorized the Rio Grande to determine the whereabouts of the international boundary. It followed that when the river shifted its channel, as all but conservative estuaries will now and then, the border moved with it.

The one place where this fluvial flightiness has so far caused difficulty is at El Paso, where the Rio Grande so threw its weight about as to leave strips of Mexico in the United States and parts of El Paso south of the border. Referred to as "islands" but not perceptibly so, one was known as Chamizal. For some years the Border Patrol was in the equivocal position of maintaining a sector headquarters south of a line it was supposed to keep people from violating by taking a stand to its north. But the international court at Geneva, in the deliberate way of such tribunals, at last got around to adjudicating the case. As of 1967 President Lyndon Johnson ceded Chamizal to Mexico and got back a matching piece of that country.

But in order to keep the Rio Grande from playing such a trick again, the El Paso section of its channel was furnished with a concrete-walled straitjacket. It is on the south wall of this conduit that prospective wetbacks begin to assemble hours before darkness makes leaping the line feasible.

"Yet there are some who don't wait for night," Assistant Chief Roger A. Stout observed. "They'll watch for a day shift Patrol car to pass and make a break for it. They can drop down from perches on the Mexican side, splash across, skin up the American wall and find cover in a matter of minutes."

But for men afoot to try to work their way north of El Paso is hard scrabble. A large metropolitan area, its outskirts give way to peculiarly forbidding wilderness. Introductory is a spread of shrub-dotted dust the size of a golf course fittingly known as "the sand traps." By the time a group of wetbacks have tramped through this heavy going, they've left identification marks behind that are all a sign cutter desires.

"We never give up on 'em," PI Ben Parker said, after radioing the details of several sets of tracks to Airpilot Noel Williams. "If we don't find these farther out, it means the wets have holed up somewhere and will push on later. When I go off shift, I'll tell my relief just what to look for; and if it hasn't been found when it's my turn to take over again tomorrow, I'll keep that in mind along with new sign that *I* may have been told about by the man I'm relieving. Sometimes it takes two or three days, but if they're traveling through, instead of making connections with some rancher around here, we'll get 'em by following sign—maybe a hundred miles from where we first cut it."

A wetback has to traipse farther than that in order to get clear of the El Paso sector's manhunters. "Our area of responsibility includes the three westernmost counties of Texas and all of New Mexico south of Highway 66," Deputy Chief Robert E. Gardner pointed out. "We have a hundred and eighty and eight-tenths miles of land boundary to police and a hundred and sixty-one and two-tenths of Rio Grande mileage; three hundred and forty-two miles of frontage in all; 71,742 square miles of sector in back of that frontage; and most of them are rugged square miles."

One hundred and thirty-two officers, on the average, man this sector where the wetback traffic is second only to that of Chula Vista. El Paso is no longer the site of the Patrol's academy, which was moved to a disused Naval gunnery station at Port Isabel, Texas, in 1966. Located there, though, is one of the border's three detention centers where arrested aliens are held pending voluntary deportation or the outcome of trials for those who insist they have a right to remain in the United States.

El Paso is also the scene of disruptive activities by invaders whom the Patrol would like to somehow suppress, but its members are unable to take strong controlling steps because of the age of those involved. The matter is summed up in the sector's portfolio: "Unemployment, prostitution, other vices and the substandard level of living in Juarez, Chihuahua, Mexico, have produced hundreds of illegitimate and unwanted waifs. Those from five to fifteen years create one of the major operational problems in the El Paso sector."

"We can't hold anybody under the age of sixteen, even if we wanted to," Intelligence Officer James F. Gray explained, "and there's no Mexican agency for controlling juvenile delinquency to which we can turn the poor youngsters over. But those kids aren't small change as criminals. It isn't only the shop-lifting, burglaries and purse-snatching you'd expect from homeless little savages. Gangs of them are capable of major property damage: turning cars over, rolling five hundred pound bales of cotton into the Rio Grande—things like that. A copper ingot weighing seven hundred pounds turned up in the river after one of their raids, and they even managed to derail a diesel switch engine."

Gray shrugged and spread out his hands. "All we can do if we catch them at anything criminal is to send them back over the line— or wait for them to be sixteen."

Aside from the unusual problems created by the Rio Grande's concrete banks, the El Paso sector is policed much as is the described Tucson one. Allowing for geographical variations, that is true of the other sectors as well. Chula Vista is conditioned by the handsome but canyon-gouged Coast Range; El Centro by the Colorado Desert; Yuma by even bleaker barrens; Del Rio and to a lesser extent Laredo, by high plains country; McAllen by the subtropical Lower Rio Grande; Port Isabel by the same plus Laguna Madre, an arm of the Gulf of Mexico.

That last sector stages the Patrol's only sea operation. Port Isabel is home harbor of the largest fleet of shrimp trawlers in the United States. As it cruises down along the coast of Mexico and recruits crew members in that country, it is capable of bringing back men who wish to jump ship in America, and who may have been taken aboard with that understanding. Or the fleet may also pick up wetbacks who have crossed the border in the Brownsville area, with a view to carrying them to points farther north. To meet either contingency, the Patrol keeps a power cruiser at Port Isabel with which incoming and outgoing trawlers are checked.

Not so far mentioned in this chapter is the Marfa Sector which deserves special mention as it is the most remote from civilization. Many of its details, indeed, are on no map save one drawn to careful scale by Intelligence Officer Riley M. Barlow.

Taking in the Big Bend country, the Marfa Sector, with its area of 87,967 square miles, is something larger than the combined states of Pennsylvania and Ohio. It is policed by an average of seventy-three men with enormous liaison problems. Marfa itself is a pleasant but small dab of civilization in the midst of high grazing country with mountains looking on. From headquarters to its farthest station at Amarillo is 420 miles by road, though only 335 miles for those who prefer shortcuts. From Marfa to Presidio on the Rio Grande is seventy miles the way crows do it and another ten by highway.

The sector has 365 miles of border river front, broken by three canyons which deprive the Rio Grande of patrollable shores. The largest of these gashes in solid rock is Santa Helena Canyon, fourteen miles long. It can be seasonally negotiated in rubber rafts.

At this point the river courses past the great wilderness preserve known as the Big Bend National Park. But most of the entire Big Bend area qualifies as wilderness, in which 300 years of settlement have made but trifling dents. The metropolis is Presidio. First colonized by the Spanish about when El Paso was, or towards the close of the seventeenth century, it has, according to Barlow's 1968 census, a population of 1,168, some of whom have shares in twentieth-century America.

That is not true at all of towns up and down stream from it. Their inhabitants do not realize they are a part of today's United States; they might as well be inhabitants of Mexico before the Treaty of Guadalupe-Hidalgo lopped off the northern frontier of Chihuahua

117

and presented it to Texas. They live in adobe houses, dress as do their neighbors across the river, follow inherited Hispanic customs and speak nothing but a regional Spanish patois.

It is doubtful if even the Internal Revenue Service has discovered this exclave of the nation, and it is probable that the Texas tax collectors find it wiser to ignore its inhabitants. Little could be squeezed from tillers of small parcels of land by primitive methods.

To the extent that they have a political system, it is Hispanic rather than American. The head of a community is "el presidente," who seems to be a tribal patriarch rather than a regularly elected officer. In any case he exercises judicial as well as executive authority.

Outside of Presidio, the people of the Big Bend country are as remote from the American penal system as Marfa is from Mars. On a knoll below the Candelaria Rim there is a rusty contrivance suggestive, in its every aspect, of a great bird cage. It is tall enough for a man to stand in and long enough for him to lie down in, if temporarily in no shape to be homo erectus. In summer its iron ribs amplify the caloric Texas sun. In winter they offer no shield against the winds that whoop past a spot, some 2,400 feet above sea level. This is the local house of correction.

West of Soviet slave camps there is probably not as barbarous a prison in any civilized country, but there's one along the border. It bothered Riley Barlow until he felt constrained to remonstrate with the chieftain of that particular village. El Presidente came up with a not unreasonable answer. "Senor," he said, "we do not expect people to enjoy being in jail."

As a matter of fact, the grim cage on the knoll achieves the effect aimed at by all penal systems: it discourages malfeasance beforehand, instead of going to the expenses of arresting, convicting and caring for an imprisoned wrongdoer. "There is," Barlow mused, "a very small incidence of crime here."

Being unincorporated, with the exception of Presidio, the river communities of the Big Bend aren't given population listings or, in most cases, positions on even detailed maps. Because of Barlow's particularity, it is possible to locate and cite the populations of all of them. The relative posts and the head counts of only a few will be given here, though.

Upstream toward the boundary of the El Paso Sector is Porvenir, with fifteen people in the original settlement and twenty in a new development hard to tell from the old, farther north. Old Porvenir

der to get beyond commonly patr
here's much in the way of employmer
riding with airpilots can usually pi
ch in cover for men on the move. O
ith hiding places for those who choose
at night. Caves, ledges and old mining
vhich to foil air pursuit until darkness
se who don't worry about the vicinity's
wetbacks are daunted no more by the
ountains they must negotiate. They are
the intervening network of patrolled
center.

her regions, there are also smugglers
try. Presidio isn't favored by them, for
from it feed through a headquarters
lankets it. What the runners of human
ates prefer as a base is a parking lot on
ed abaft the Ranger Station at Cata-
Park. Sheltered by trees at the Casta-
horseless carriages of smugglers await
ty of nights.

them in the shade by the Rio Grande
ril 27, 1969. Intelligence Officer Riley
then glanced back up the road. "The
any minute to make sure that we're
y trouble," he remarked.

tains, 100 miles away, in o
roads and reach zones where

If tried by day, spotters
peons out of a region not ri
the other hand, it abounds v
to hole up by day and traips
shafts form fine hatches in
makes travel feasible—for tho
high rattlesnake count. Most
pit vipers than by the wild m
much more concerned about
roads, of which Marfa is the

Although fewer than in o
of aliens in the Big Bend coun
the two roads running north
town so small that the Patrol b
contraband into the United St
Federal property. This is loca
lon in the Big Bend National
lon Class B port of entry, the
by day the call to desperate du

There were about a dozen of
on the afternoon of Sunday, Ap
Barlow looked them over, and
Ranger will be coming down
not giving his smuggler pets an

He proved an apt prophet.

11

***

FLANK
ATTACKS
AND
SABOTEURS

The reason for a Federal Ranger's solicitude for breakers of Federal laws was bifocal. Individually he was limned by Barlow as a brotherhood of man Cyclops, who could grasp the plight of a needy foreign invader but not the damage inflicted by such on his own people. Stationed in the Big Bend National Park, he doubtless shared viewpoints and prejudices stemming from that reservation's founding.

As the function of the park was to preserve a wilderness area complete with all its native fauna, it was logical that visitors should be denied the right to bring in firearms. Illogical, though, was a serious effort to extend the restriction to Patrolmen on the trail of wetbacks flitting through. For if PIs use guns infrequently and then only under extreme provocation, they may need them to save their own lives or those of comrades. At other times, furthermore, the fact that they carry pistols and are known to be skilled in their use is a cooler of situations that might else get ugly.

Hence the Patrol continued to go heeled when tracking wetbacks through the preserve, to the grave chagrin of its first director. "He wanted us to set the tourists a good example," Barlow remembered. "We never could get him to understand that some of the people we arrested didn't like us."

Actually the park's supervisor wanted the border officers to set a good example for wetbacks, with whom he wished to come to specific, if unpublished, terms. The director knew, in a word, that primitive invaders were the potential poachers that the patrolmen were not; and by making the park an Eden through which illegal aliens could pass as peacefully as mountain lions and wolves, he trusted to buy safety for less fearsome and more edible game.

"We saw his point, but we never could make him see that we had our own responsibilities. We're on better terms with most of the people here since that old dreamer stepped down, but it still rankles some that we don't play Park Service ball." Barlow waved toward the pool of smugglers' cars nestling in trees bright with April's new greenery. "And those still try to get a better deal for cottontails and quail by making things easier for wetbacks."

If that's a local case of Federal officers taking sides against the Patrol, the force is badgered and bedeviled by orders issued from Washington by assorted governmental departments. It is also the victim of contradictory laws, arbitrary regional rulings and judicial decisions straight out of a not very witty comic strip.

Under a number of national administrations the worst enemy of the Patrol has been the very division—the Department of Justice—of which it is a limb. Since becoming that in 1940, as a matter of fact, the outfit has flourished only under the aegis of President Eisenhower. It is perhaps too soon to judge how the corps will fare under President Nixon, but as of this writing the facts are these: Since Eisenhower's departure from the White House in 1961, the situation of an able and crucially needed body of men has become increasingly deplorable. Personnel has not been stepped up to meet demands that are now of emergency proportions. At a time when more is asked of patrolmen, their pay level has steadily lagged while that of other Federal law enforcement bodies has advanced. Much of their equipment has been allowed to become so superannuated as to spend as much time in repair shops as in service.

The loss of efficiency is only part of the story. After certain mileage points, rolling stock and airplanes become dangerous to operate.

During the 1960s the corps's scout cars and pickups piled up fantastic mileages, most of them logged on rough trails and in trek across country—180,000; 200,000; 225,000 miles and still not retired from pursuit service. Sedans used for highway patrolling were also wrecks that had traveled most or all the distance to the moon, though still on the active list. Airplanes that should have been scrapped as unsafe were kept and flown on what would have been hazardous missions even for new machines.

To take up wheeled vehicles again, the sedans of patrolling PIs were at any time apt to be impressed into high-speed highway chases of known or suspected smugglers who didn't have to wait for Washington to authorize the acquirement of vehicles in good shape. Patrolmen trying to match the paces of much newer cars than the ones they were stuck with had to force frazzled heaps to the limit to keep from being outdistanced. So, in poor risks, they were taking the great ones of breaking highway speed limits by thirty or forty miles an hour.

Sticking to the subject of vehicles, the ruling re those belonging to smugglers seized by PIs is a piece of governmental tomfoolery to stagger even Jonathan Swift. When cars are used to transport any other form of contraband, they are very properly confiscated by the Customs Bureau, promptly and without any appeal. The Bureau, again very properly, has the prerogative of selling the captured rolling stock and turning over to the Treasury Department the cash so acquired. Funds so gained are not scored to the account of the Customs Bureau in any banking sense, but it marks the service as a money-earning agency, and therefore one which has an easier time getting pay raises than a force without such a history.

One of the reasons why the Border Patrol finds it hard to gain salary recognition of its works is that it adds no cash to Uncle Sam's account, although it easily could but for discriminatory idiocy. A fellow who tries to run a few tropical birds north of the line is penalized by the loss of his car, but the felon who is caught driving however many wetbacks into the United States has his vehicle returned to him. This not only robs the Government of revenue and the Patrol of credit assets but cuts down on the smugglers' overhead. As soon as he's out on bail or out of jail, he has the means to be in business again, faithfully put at his command by the very nation he wars upon.

In other ways the Customs Bureau justly gets credit for its excellent services while the collaborating Border Patrol unfairly does not. Since 1955 patrolmen have been ex-officio Customs agents and annually pick up contraband of all sorts. If much is destroyed as soon as it is used as evidence in a conviction (narcotics fall into this class), other items are salable revenue producers. But the Patrol is here again denied entries in black ink, because all the contraband it seizes is lumped with the take of the Customs Bureau.

Neither does the corps get credit for its part in the border war upon narcotics, often reflected in glittering financial figures. On May 14, 1969, a thousand pounds of marijuana were found by PIs in a disused building near Tucson. At current prices a half ton of "hay" ain't hay, as the contradictory saying goes, but it won't be credited to the account of the Patrol—as it should be—in the books kept in Washington. All the force has to show for its around-the-clock efforts are the numbers of men it has apprehended, and as these aren't dressed up with dollar signs and decimal points, they don't impress politicos unacquainted with the enormous values they represent.

While seizing and holding said men, patrolmen are required by Governmental decree to spout nonsense to them in Spanish, on pain of having defended the United States in vain. A wet back, it should be borne in mind, is not an American citizen but a foreign criminal. He is entitled to the protection of the U.S. Constitution no more than a foreign soldier captured in a combat zone. Thirdly he is invariably ignorant of the subtleties of the Anglo-American legal system. Let those truths rest. At the moment of contact, which perhaps takes the form of a football tackle, he must be assured of the sacred rights conferred on him by Coke, Littleton, Magna Carta & Company.

What it is like to prattle English legalities in Spanish to a fighting Mexican invader was recounted by Senior Patrol Inspector Albert Taylor, of the Chula Vista Sector. "The other day a couple of us grabbed a big, husky smuggler's guide that didn't want to be under the protection of American law at all. While I was sitting on him and nearly breaking my own arms trying to get him in position for snapping on handcuffs, I was telling him about all the rights he had and that he was free to say nothing—which was too late, as he was already saying things the Constitution never asked him to. I never felt such a fool in my life."

But if breathless balderdash hadn't accompanied a wrestle to subdue a violent criminal, his arrest would have been nullified in court, and he free to trot back to Mexico, there to promote new trespasses against America. This is justice turned buffoon. Where the fact of the crime is less important than thoroughly silly ceremony, due process of law becomes mere court-room clowning.

The modern bent for juridical farce also besets the Patrol when engaged in trying to stop the flow of narcotics from south to north of the line. Court edicts reduce efforts to halt a grave menace to the nation's whole society to a charade with a Victorian code of etiquette. In this game the car of a suspected smuggler is regarded as a woman that male officers are privileged to search to only a discreet degree. They can look in her purse and observe as much of her person as her costume displays, but they may not probe below it.

The analogy is unbelievably apt. Patrolmen may peer into an automobile's certified containers, such as the trunk and door and dashboard pockets, but they may not elsewhere examine a vehicle unless they can prove in court that they had a specific reason for believing that contraband drugs were hidden precisely where they were found. The fact of finding narcotics under the seat of a car, say, is not in itself considered grounds for holding and charging the smuggler. If a PI was only playing a hunch when prying into an unorthodox container, he is faulted for having a low, suspicious mind; and a particularly obnoxious species of felon is released with the court's apology on the count that his rights had been trampled on.

Judicial zeal to shelter scoundrels caught with poison to peddle can attain even loftier heights of absurdity. One such case was related by Assistant Chief Patrol Inspector Allon C. Owen of the El Centro Sector. "In March of 1962, California Customs Agents got information which led them to notify the Border Patrol—and California state and county peace officers, of course—that a certain fellow was running narcotics over the line. The boy and his wagon were described so carefully that everybody knew just what to look for; and his favorite route was named, too.

"No more than a week later the man's heap was spotted by a PI, who found the driver matched the description put out by the Customs gents; and he likewise found a load of dope in the car." Owen cocked a pale, sardonic eye at his auditor. "It might as well have been homemade fudge or paper dolls. The smuggler went free, and the PI got chewed out for bothering a fellow he had no right to suspect. The evidence—the narcotics—was right there in the Los Angeles District Court, and nobody tried to pretend that the guy wasn't found carrying it. But what saved him was the ruling that a week

125

after the Customs Agents got the word around was too long to keep on suspecting a man—who might have reformed in the meantime, I suppose. And it didn't make any difference that proof was turned up that he hadn't. At any rate the judge said that the information leading to the arrest was so old that *search was unreasonable*, and by God! a man nabbed with the goods was sprung on that account."

Turning to the matter of liquor, there are baffling border installations, owned by the Federal Government, which can serve no purpose but to make patrol of the line more difficult. These are bonded warehouses, chockablock with cases of whiskey dispensed under rules that are quaint indeed. Spirits desired for consumption in the United States cannot be purchased at any price. But whiskey whose destination is Mexico can be bought in large quantities, duty-free.

In the whole bizarre history of government versus spirits there was never elsewhere the equal of this situation. Supposing it to be exploited by honest people only, the net is still lunacy. This is not the same thing as a free port where, to foster general trade, it is found profitable to sell to all comers certain tariff-free luxury items. Here the citizens of the supporting government are discriminated against and the citizens of, or visitors to, but one foreign nation are the legal beneficiaries.

Why should whiskey be obtainable by Mexicans at far below American market prices, on the condition that they do not stay in this country? Why should United States' citizens be able to obtain cases of whiskey at a tremendous mark-down only if they depart, to invest in a foreign country the costs of living while the liquor is being consumed? Those are hard questions to answer, but the one that bothers the officers of the Border Patrol is, where does the whiskey actually find consumers?

The easily ascertainable fact is that wherever these bonded warehouses are found, planes loaded with cases of whiskey take off from nearby airfields. Until lost to the eyes of observers they fly dutifully south, and so across the line into Mexico. Some no doubt keep on and sell their bargain counter spirits to Mexican bars and clubs. Others, as logic contends, swing north across the border at remote points or under cover of darkness and make an even bigger killing by peddling Government-supplied contraband in America.

As has been remarked in another connection, the Patrol has not the equipment to keep track of smugglers by air; the corps's single-engine planes are soon outdistanced by the better powered birds of

126

lawbreakers. And in this particular respect the Customs Agents are even worse off than the PIs. To watch for airborne contraband along two thousand Gulf to Pacific miles these officers have one plane, itself not celebrated as the bullet of the border.

"But those Customs fellows shouldn't beef about it; they have the privilege of hiring planes in any emergency." Assistant Chief Patrol Inspector William Toney of the Del Rio Sector waved toward a stretch of emptiness somewhere between Del Rio and Eagle Pass. "You'd think planes were lined up along the border like taxis in front of a city hotel and all you had to do was to jump in one and yelp, 'Follow that guy!' "

This the Patrol cannot now hope to do, even though furnished with twenty planes to the Customs Bureau's one. The most that air-pilots can achieve re flyers who are customers of the bonded ware-houses is to make a note of where whiskey-loaded planes take off and are next found. When flight patterns have been worked out over a period of some months, seizures of contraband may occasionally be made on either out of the way municipal air fields or makeshift ones out in the desert. Saddled with an extra duty because of ad-ministrative craziness that they were never party to, PIs dig in with what they have and hope for the mechanical makings of a chance to do a better job.

Working counter to them, in the meantime, and playing fast and loose with the taxpayers' money while so doing, are officials of sundry Federal welfare programs. These were not set up to benefit foreign invaders, but in their haste to squander dollars which are not their own, some bureaucrats shell out to all applicants.

The original, or farmhand wetback, was never so rewarded for law breakage. But the illegal urban laborer sometimes discovers how to get money leaking from ill-kept agencies. Employment Security offices were set up for the temporary relief of American citizens and foreign nationals legally entitled to earn wages in the United States, not to further the careers of criminals. But illegal aliens, out of work because a factory has shut down, say, have learned to milk the Employ-ment Security cow.

Not many wetbacks get jobs which entail Social Security cards; one of the reasons American employers favor them is that payment for this program can generally be avoided when Mexican peons are taken on. Fewer wetbacks still have so far remained in the United States long enough to collect this Federal pension. It does happen, though; in fact one happily retired illegal Mexican immigrant was found near the border recently.

He was soon to be made even happier, for the fact that he was deported did not stop the regular flow of Federal payments to him. Rather he got to spend them in Mexico where their buying power was much greater.

His case so rankles the corps that a visitor who spends a day or so with officers of any Border Patrol sector is bound to hear about it in more or less these terms: "Look, he was an illegal alien; he was tried in an American court which ordered him deported as a criminal, and *he gets a paycheck every month for it!*"

Some of the state welfare agencies are just as silly. But this chapter will leave the subject of public saboteurs of the Patrol's work and take notice of private ones. These are both rustic and metropolitan; corporate as well as individual.

As earlier stated, the success of the bracero program had helped heal the breach between the corps and farmers or stock raisers before Operation Wetback. At the end of 1964, however, this program was canceled by Secretary of the Interior Stewart Udall. His purpose was the essentially sound one of opening more jobs for Americans, but the pay scale established was aimed at attracting youngsters of high school and junior college age rather than professional farm laborers with families to support.

Perhaps Udall's plan would have been more successful had it been implemented a generation earlier when the majority of youths in the Southwest grew up on farms and were accustomed to field chores. But the majority of the people in Southern California, Arizona and Texas are urban and their automobile-cradled children have scarcely mastered the art of walking on terra firma, let alone engaging in hard work while doing so. The idea appalled most youngsters, and most of those who tried to earn money in this fashion simply did not have the stamina to perform stoop labor in the temperatures registered out of the shade by the Southwest's sun.

Many crops went unharvested in 1965, because the boys weren't on hand in sufficient quantities and the men among farm laborers— the great majority of them Latin Americans—tended to work in parts of the country where the pay was more adequate. The bracero program was scrapped; in a word, the planned substitute was a bust, and the adjustments which the Government might have made were not. There was a hole in the Southwest's labor pool accordingly, and the farmers and ranchers reached for the wetback.

That's when history began repeating itself. Since the Patrol still followed orders to seek out and apprehend wetbacks wherever found, and as farmers were more and more pleased with illegal aliens they were paying less and less, buried frictions came to life. So did buried fictions, for tales of the Patrol's dark doings once more became a feature of border gossip.

In its mildest form, hostility consists of padlocking ranch roads, forcing the PI to leave his vehicle and demand a duplicate key. But after a couple of weeks this proves of no use, because the property owner has bought a new lock. The only check for this childish spitefulness is to obtain a government-issued padlock and give the farmer a key.

Now again, as in the small '50s, numberless spreads are the sites of secret camps, camouflaged to avoid detection from the air. In these hideaways wetbacks spend all their off-duty hours, whatever they need being delivered by a farmer's foreman. If a plane swoops near a field where harvesters are at work, or if a lookout reports that a Patrol jeep is nearing, the wetbacks make for rehearsed concealment. Left behind is an owner or his ramrod, who hasn't seen anybody.

A good few are not content with being silently obstructive or angrily abusive. There isn't a veteran patrolman of the border who hasn't had to face down the threat of a resort to arms or contend with the actuality of a cocked weapon. "Not since the days of the wetback era in the early 1950s," to quote the 1967 annual *Immigration and Naturalization Service* report, "have Service officers met with so much harassment and physical resistance in administering the immigration and nationality laws and in bringing violators to justice. The defiance has ranged from verbal threats and assaults to physical violence culminating in death. . . ."

After citing a couple of illustrative incidents, the report goes on as follows: "In another case, a patrol inspector, while performing farm and ranch check in search of illegal aliens near Modesto, California, was threatened by a farmer who pulled a shotgun from his pickup truck and swung it around into position in line with the officer. The officer, acting quickly in self-defense, grabbed the shotgun, pulled his revolver, fired, and wounded the attacker in the shoulder, forcing him to release his shotgun."

Industrial employers of wetbacks have so far not become as violent as their country cousins, but a good many have come to share their hard-nosed determination to employ criminals, plus their resentment of officers who try to rid society of them. Their methods take such shapes as demanding a search warrant if officers attempt to check premises for wetbacks, and refusing to let employee rosters be examined without court orders.

Speaking for both town and rural enemies of the corps are some of the border's newspapers, particularly those of the Lower Rio Grande Valley. Or sometimes they refuse to speak, which was the case in an anecdote related by John Eager, recently retired director of the Patrol's academy at Port Isabel, Texas. "A couple of years ago a reporter came to the academy who said he wished to write a feature article about it. So I gave him permission to look in on any activities he wanted to, asking only that he show what he'd written so I could check it for accuracy. He turned out to be a capable man and came up with a good article; but it was never published. A few months later I happened to run across the reporter and asked him what happened to his story. 'Oh,' he said, 'I found out it's the policy of the paper never to print anything favorable about the Border Patrol.'"

Abroad in the land, too, are today's perverse sentimentalists, who think that an advanced civilization has no right to protect itself against engulfment by backward hordes. The very things that make the wetback undesirable as a resident endear him to these cranks, some of them operative as instructors. According to an official Immigration Service report, "unfavorable reference was made to the Border Patrol" . . . in "the National Education Television Network production 'Human Cargo' telecast May 12, 1969 on 162 NET stations.

"The film was produced by a crew from KLRN TV Channel 9, San Antonio, Texas, apparently under auspices of the Southwest Texas educational television council." Patrolmen who audited this excursion into romance were amazed—and perhaps a little flattered as well—to find themselves classed as gunnies in the best and bloodiest tradition of the Western desperado.

It wasn't long before this piece of educational matter was being passed on as incontrovertible fact. At mention of the Patrol, people met far from the border were soon responding as though from positive personal knowledge. "Oh, that bunch of killers."

12

A
CROSS
SECTION
OF
ACTUALITY

The attitude of some current news media toward the Patrol is in sharp contrast to expressions about them offered before the wetback became a contention bone. An editorial which views PIs from a different angle was published in the El Paso *Herald* in 1930:

> Again the border patrol lived up to its high standards of courage and humanity, when Patrolman Frank A. Finnegan refused to return fire from a smuggler lest he hit children playing back of his assailant.
>
> The account of the affair says: "The smuggler opened fire on the officer while within 10 feet of him. The officer, after seeing small children playing behind the smuggler, refused to return the fire. The smuggler emptied his gun at Finnegan, but because of poor marksmanship, the officer was not hit. . . ."
>
> The impulse which led Finnegan to hold his fire and run

great danger of being killed is deserving of the highest credit.

It was following the custom of the border patrol. There is not a night they do not face danger of death and wounds. Yet one of the imperative rules of the organization is that they must not fire except in self-defense . . .

Service in the patrol along this border is more dangerous than with the much advertised Northwest Mounted or the New York and Pennsylvania constabulary.

These are splendid organizations, but down this way those familiar with the work of the border patrol thinks it ranks as high, perhaps a bit higher.

That was by no means the sole such laudation; others of the period were included in prior chapters. The discrepancy between them and the policy of papers which will print nothing favorable to the force makes it reasonable to ask, just what are patrolmen singly and collectively like? The answer that follows is by one who was without bias one way or the other before the necessities of this book enjoined a study of the subject.

The members of the Border Patrol share certain characteristics and interests, of course. As is true of other professions, those who elected to join were moved by native impulses which made the choice logical; and since belonging they have been shaped in certain general directions by the nature of their duties.

In view of the work done by PIs, physical fitness is an understood qualification. They have to like the outdoors and the challenges it proffers their hardihood at all points on the clock and the calendar; and they have to have swift reflexes.

By the time they have gone through the Border Patrol Academy ——whose sessions have now been extended to fourteen weeks——they have points of education in common. They have to be fluent in Spanish. They must pass examinations in immigration law, nationality law and statutory authority, and be versed in criminal law, constitutional rights and court procedure. Then they must be good marksmen, able in self-defense without weapons, ready at first aid, and know how to interrogate prisoners as well as type reports.

These and such subjects as Latin American Culture, finger-printing and sign cutting round out the course. Trainees may be admitted to the academy at twenty-one. Because of the rigorous physical demands of the corps's work, the mandatory retirement age is sixty-two.

Emotionally there is an effort to achieve unity by excluding the irritable and the irritating. "The fellow we try to spot before it's too late," Chief John Williams of the Laredo Sector affirmed, "is the man who'll bully prisoners if no one is watching. An officer like that can do us more harm than all the lies told about us by wetback-hiring farmers and ranchers. You see, the only reason why we've had so comparatively little trouble with the wetbacks themselves—the story's different when it comes to smugglers—is that the word has been spread all over Mexico that they'll be treated decently when arrested. That's why so few of them carry weapons, and that's why most of them don't make any trouble when apprehended. Now if they were afraid of being shoved around by PIs, a lot of them would cross the border armed and ready to fight; and we'd have to act accordingly."

While speaking to much the same effect, Chief Thomas Ball of the McAllen Sector identified a second undesirable. "There's the griper, who's usually the same man that's so afraid he'll work harder than others that he doesn't do his share. A sector headquarters team is a pretty small family, and one sour member can put everybody in a bad humor. On the whole we do a good job of screening out trouble-makers, but every now and then we get stuck with a fellow we can't use and can't easily get rid of, as he's under Civil Service."

No doubt such damaging mistakes are made, but it must be with singular infrequency. The observer who spends any considerable time with the Patrol cannot but be struck by the general good humor applied to exacting duties and the ready cooperation among all hands.

Morale is very high, without any pretense of an ideal camaraderie. The force's fabric, being human, is made up of a great many diversities, and a truth about it was summed up by Carl Philips, Senior Patrol Inspector of the El Centro Sector. He has had a better opportunity to judge than most, being a second generation patrolman. His father, Thomas Philips, joined the corps in 1928.

"Oh, of course, we have our squabbles and feuds and jealousies," the Patrol's current Philips said. "But when it's a matter of getting the job done, that comes first, and we all pitch in."

Through a sense of obligation and self-control a unified facade is shown the public. It becomes more remarkable when its individual parts are scrutinized. In matters of taste the one universal meeting ground is that they like strenuous activity in the open. But they are men picked for mental alertness, too. On duty their minds are concerned with the importance of their work and how best to forward it. Off duty, their thoughts ride a wide range of different trails.

For brains capable of weighing the border's wealth, there is much to stimulate study. Some PIs are students of Latin American folklore, others of Southwestern history and literature, Mexican history and Indian antiquities. Others again are fascinated by their region's multiplex reptiles, scarcely less fearsome plant life and rare assortment of birds.

There are patrolmen whose interests are less regional: students of sociology, penology, anthropology, English or Spanish letters or literature in general. Not a few are amateur musicians or artists. Some are free lance writers; others, radio hams, and so forth.

But people of these separate bents converge, when on the job, wearing on their left shoulders the round, blue patch with gold letters spelling "U.S. Border Patrol." They like their work and are sold on its importance. Somewhere in the course of their training—provided these virtues weren't theirs before joining the force—they have acquired excellent manners, punctuality in keeping appointments and doggedness in carrying out assignments. They have also absorbed the Patrol's attitude toward wetbacks which is paternalistic. "We couldn't do this work," to give the general tenor of several similar statements, "if we didn't like them." And that must be true. Only officers kindly disposed to the invaders could keep their tempers when arresting them by platoons. Rancor on their part would soon be reflected in difficult arrests and sulking prisoners in place of the relaxed and cooperative ones which most are observed to be.

The good nature of the PIs doesn't water the zest of the chase, though. That's the exciting part of a job which also has many routine aspects. Quest is an abiding delight, and that of the Patrol has a filip identified by Senior Patrol Inspector Allen E. Trenkel of the Nogales Station. "I've hunted every kind of game to be found from up in Canada to down in Mexico, and there's nothing to touch the thrill of a manhunt."

To have healthy work which is at all times held worthwhile and can be richly pleasurable. It is for these reasons that the Border Patrol is a body of which some members balk when threatened with more than just so much promotion. Their jibbing isn't due to any distaste for raises in salary but to what they have to sacrifice in order to get more than a Senior Patrol's Inspector's pay. Above that level loom sector headquarters posts and some inevitable confinement while directing and coordinating the efforts of the PIs out in the field.

Somebody has to do this important work, and it's nice to have recognition, rank and higher wages. But, as indicated, some patrolmen refuse promotion, which a dispensation of the Immigration Service enables them to do without turning down a specific responsibility. To qualify for advances in rank, they must be detached from the Patrol for a couple of years while they serve as Immigrant Investigators in some seaport city. If they refrain from accepting this tour of duty, they are ineligible for any command but that of a Senior PI in charge of a station.

"I thought it all out and made my choice long ago," SPI Albert Taylor of the Chula Vista Sector declared. "I didn't want to work in a city, and I didn't want a different job when I got back to the border. I'm doing just what suits me, and I want to keep right on doing it until I run out my time."

It has been stated that the retirement age for members of the corps is sixty-two. In the main, those invited to belong stay with the force until separated by the dates on their birth certificates. Still, the organization loses men to other Federal law-enforcement services with higher wage scales. Less frequently they accept industrial employment or branch out in business for themselves.

Yet such divorces are not necessarily permanent. A man of independent means, Senior Drexel B. Atkinson, of the Douglas Station, left the Patrol in order to invest his time in making more money, but he returned to border duty. "I found out," he reported, "where I wanted to be and what I really wanted to do."

Chula Vista's Assistant Chief Dale Swancutt spent plush years with the Immigration Service in the Pacific, his job to inspect the credentials of luxury liner passengers at sea in order to keep them from losing holiday time when in exotic ports. "It was a story-book job; a wonderful paid vacation." He shrugged. "But I gave it up and came back to the Border Patrol."

As in some other professions, the men that follow this one have to be careful whom they pick to take along with them. The wives of PIs have to believe in what their husbands are doing, for the Patrol is rough going for women, too. They have to get used to not knowing how long a shift will last or when their tuckered-out men will need meals. When their husbands are on the lobster watch, reveille comes while roosters are still knocking it off. And when a wetback-hiring community sours upon the corps, its womenfolk feel the brunt of popular distaste, plus the anguish of knowing that their children are being made unhappy as well.

But America's frontiers have never lacked women with the ick to take hardscrabble. From such statistics as are available, it seems safe to opine that the majority of patrolmen's wives like living in border communities. And it is certainly true that their children, when not victimized by silly local flareups, are lucky in their uncrowded playgrounds.

"I'd have to fight my whole family," Airpilot William Covington confided, "if I tried to move out of Marfa."

Riley Barlow, Intelligence Officer of the same sector, concurred. "I was Chief at New Orleans on the Gulf border and found the work very interesting, but I couldn't convince my West Texas wife and kids that a large city was a good place to be in." He slowed to let a chaparral cock—known as *paisano* on the border—lunge across the road with outstretched neck. "As they were unhappy, I was, too, so I applied to come back here. But it was also better for me, as I found out when I caught sight of those mountains yonder. The Big Bend is my country."

A proprietary feeling about some part of it, or of the entire border is characteristic of men identified with a portion of the earth to a degree that is true of few others today. They wear its brand and are peculiarly its masters.

Although they are members of a close-knit organization, they are called upon to act on their own responsibility more than most. For they are men, working alone or in pairs, that often encounter surprises and as frequently have to improvise in order to get results. As was made clear in the always engaging reminiscences of former Border Patrol Chief Nick Collaer, not all their methods have been orthodox, or accurately recounted in papers forwarded to Washington. Imagining a reunion of corps oldtimers, Collaer wrote, "We could walk from group to group and listen to stories, many of which would be difficult to match-up with official reports."

Collaer then gave a few sample narratives. One was the story of "the outwitting of 'El Airoplano,'" a Mexican smuggler who earned his nickname because of his sprinting ability: "El Airoplano used to cross in plain sight of the international bridge [at El Paso] about noon each day. He never wore any clothes and was he fast! The spotters were so efficient that we could not nab him.

"At that point on our side of the river there was a pipe from which warm water from a laundry ran into the Rio Grande and the hoboes used to go there from the nearby railroad yards and wash up. El Airoplano never paid no mind to those hoboes, so we let a couple of the fellows work nights until they had pretty good beards, put them with bundles on a freight train west of town and had them go to the river ostensibly to wash up. It was funny to see El Airoplano pass right by them and watch them nab him. . . .

"Another officer, identified as an old Mounted Guard, is telling about getting a letter from the Central Office: 'I was complimented for not shooting a smuggler. Jake took one side of a dry wash while I took the other while trailing this fellow. I decided to cut sign across his trail to be sure we had not passed him. When I rode through the brush to the wash there he stood with his rifle ready. He had heard me as I came through the brush. I didn't have time to turn my horse Smokey and get under cover so I kicked Smokey in the ribs and jumped at the smuggler, kicking him in the jaw as I went by. Later another fellow heard him tell a fellow prisoner while in line entering the courtroom at Tucson, 'Gee, that fellow (pointing at me) has a terrific wallop' at the same time holding up his right fist. He never knew what hit him and the Central Office never learned that the only reason I didn't kill him was because I was too busy at the time.' "

Collaer's memoirs also included the tale of a confession wrung from a suspected murderer. "The boss told me to stop all streetcars returning to Juarez, for most of the 16 smugglers ran to this side after Melton [PI Doyne C. Melton, slain at El Paso December 7, 1933] was killed. I went through each car, and from one, a fellow who looked suspicious jumped off the front end as I got off the back. I yelled to the bridge toll-collector 'stop that man' and just about then the smuggler ran into a piece of pipe which the toll collector conveniently held in his hand. It was of course all the smuggler's fault that he got hurt. He should have watched where he was going.

"His head was cut so we took him to the police surgeon who shaved his head and sewed up the cut. He then gave the smuggler a glass full of Epsom salts, saying, 'I just gave him a dose of truth-telling medicine. When you get him to the Chief tell him that this fellow in about half an hour will think that he is going to die, but he won't and that is the time to get the truth out of him.' It worked!"

One of the traditions of the corps is retired Fred Neale who extracted truth by subtler means. On the night of May 3, 1969, these were described by Senior Patrol Inspector Walter Tree of the McAllen Sector. Closer to the Rio Grande two young PIs were keeping line watch under his supervision. After making sure they were properly placed, Tree withdrew and told of a patrolman he was happy to remember. It seemed that Neale had worked for an oil company in Mexico and there had learned things about the psychology of peons which he later put to the use of police work.

"Old Fred Neale had one of these big glass paperweights that magnify anything stuck under it, and he used it as a crystal ball which the prisoner he was interviewing could look in, too," Tree began. "He had little cut-outs that he was slick at sliding under the glass without being seen. Then he'd let the Mexican take a peek, and he broke a lot of hard cases that way." Tree got up to peer around a bush, and so did his faint, moon-cast shadow. Then he seated himself once more on the blanket he'd spread as insulation from cold sand. "One of the cut-outs was the Devil, which would pop in sight if Fred thought his prisoner was lying, and under that magnifying glass he'd look awfully big and mean to a man with a sick conscience, you know. Supposing he coughed up what old Fred thought was the truth, then the Devil would disappear and the Virgin Mary would show up to let the smuggler know he was on the right track. Well, after he'd sweated out Hell and been rescued a couple of times, he'd decide he'd rather not see that old red rascal any more, so he'd talk straight."

Tree swatted a mosquito and chuckled. "Old Fred had another dodge that made honest men out of rough characters. He'd take one of these old Bon Ami boxes that sprinkled powdered soap, which he said would burn to the bone anybody who was lying. Then he'd dance around spilling out a little bit of that scorching powder every now and then and getting nearer to the Mexican with every few hops." As the moon and the mosquitoes and the Rio Grande's bottomland shrubbery looked on, Tree gave a convincing imitation of Neale in the guise of a menacing witch doctor. "Well, old Fred would have the fellow he was interviewing sitting in a corner, so he wouldn't back away. And as that Bon Ami box got closer and closer, the smuggler or whatever he was would watch that spilling soap powder until he couldn't stand the thought of it burning him any longer, so he'd yell for old Fred to stop and let him talk."

As the redoubtable Fred Neale has left the Patrol, his magic paper-weight and soap sprinkler are no longer in service. But psychology remains a field of study and practice of which some current PIs maybe aware. A certainty though, is that what former Patrol Chief Nick D. Collaer affirmed remains true today. Not all the force's exploits are matters of rule book, and it still would be "difficult to match-up with the official reports" the facts in some cases.

One such was related by Senior PI Drexel Atkinson, who neither named names nor was asked to. While driving along the cyclone fence, stretching for miles on either side of the Douglas port of entry, he remarked that wetbacks were sometimes smuggled through this heavy and expensive wire by dint of cutting holes in it.

"There was one smuggler," Atkinson went on, "who was doing this repeatedly, and we couldn't get a crack at him, because he never appeared on our side of the line. And naturally we couldn't apprehend him on his. The situation annoyed one PI so much that he stayed on the case until he learned from one of our informers in Agua Prieta that the smuggler planned to open a hole for a party of wetbacks in a certain vicinity. Moving to the Mexican side of the fence themselves, the PI and his partner laid for the wire-cutting expert but didn't close in until he had finished his work. Then they pitched him through the hole he'd made, skinned through it after him and arrested him for being illegally on American soil."

Yet about some things, there are no taken leeways. A patrolman's tongue may be hanging halfway to his belt—and coated with dust after a hot-weather shift on the desert—but while he's in uniform he won't touch so much as beer.

The force's chariness in the use of firearms has often been noticed. But men who have to qualify as marksmen, via sixty rounds fired every three months, are as skilled in the use of revolvers as they are careful about firing for effect. After citing patrolmen who had been National Pistol Champions or who had represented the United States in Olympic or Pan American pistol contests, Robert J. Seitz, the Southwestern Region's Public Information Officer, continued as follows: "National Police Pistol Combat Shooting—we have won the national team match each year since establishment of the match in

1966. We hold the national record. Thomas S. Gaines is the present National Individual Champion; past winners John C. Forman and Jerry L. Jackson also hold the National Individual Record."

The standard weapon of the force is the .38 Smith and Wesson snub-nosed revolver, but some now carry a .38 Magnum, a lighter revolver with an extraordinarily long effective range. "We can hit a torso-shaped target at two hundred yards with this gun." The speaker was William C. Joyner, Assistant Chief of the Tucson Sector. As a member of several Border Patrol pistol teams which have defeated the best in the nation, his words can be taken as authoritative.

Before closing, this profile must include a passage about the special Patrol division of airpilots. Some of the hazards they daily run have been dealt with; others have not. When they are searching for sign, they fly into canyons and draws which are so snug a fit that a bad air current could rub a wing against a neighboring ledge in Jack Robinson order. Then, the winds that toss small planes about can shatter a pilot's control. On a sufficiently windy day in March of 1969 while flying over mountains east of Tucson, Airpilot Harry Aitken reached behind him and held up a crash helmet. "When it's really rough," he said, "I put this on, so I won't be knocked out when my head's slammed against the cockpit's roof."

For men flying low to scout for sign, not enough atmosphere can be as dangerous as ozone in a rough hurry. That was the trouble in the first of two crashes experienced by Michael T. Box. "All of a sudden," he was remembered to have said, "there simply wasn't any air to hold me up." A low-slung air pocket may have caused his second disaster, but there was no report on that one. Airpilot Box was killed when his plane answered gravity's call near El Paso on August 29, 1950; and on December 18 Patrol Inspector Richard D. Clarke, who had been acting as the pilot's observer, died of the injuries then received.

Most of the Patrol's fatalities during the '50s were those of downed pilots and officers riding with them. On July 21, 1954, Airpilot William F. Buckelew and PI Donald F. Kee were killed in a plane crash near Rio Grande City, Texas, and on June 6, 1956, Airpilot Douglas C. Shute and Patrol Inspector James M. Carter were found amidst the wreckage of a plane near Comstock, Texas, in the Del Rio Sector. There is a suspicion, though, that in this instance nature wasn't the slayer. "Patrolmen familiar with the circumstances have always thought Shute's plane was shot down," now-retired John Eager said.

Another dangerous activity is highway traffic checking, either because drivers don't wish to stop or are insufficiently in control of their cars when they attempt to do so. One PI was seriously injured when an eighty-three-year-old woman with a learner's permit was driving a car at about seventy miles an hour that spun when she tried to halt. A car ricocheting from a collision at the check point of Oceanside, California, caused the death of Patrol Inspector Archie L. Jennings on April 16, 1960.

Then driving a scout car on rough roads or none can produce results as lethal as landing a plane unintentionally. Airpilot Kenneth L. Carl had that bad chance when a downdraft plummeted him one wing first near El Centro on June 18, 1961. For Richard A. Luco, fatal damage was done on May 5, 1967, by a blowout as he was wheeling a jeep along a levee in the Yuma Sector.

For fifteen years, meanwhile, or not since the mentioned death of PI Edwin F. Wheeler near Mathis, Texas, in 1952, Mexican guns had killed no member of the force. But murder is back in good standing as a Patrol hazard, as the corps struggles to deal with an emergency whose nature and causes will be set forth in the ensuing section.

PART

IV

━━━

*SOME
MEXICAN
INS
AND
CRIMINAL
OUTS*

──

13

UNTOWARD
TRENDS
SOUTH
OF THE
LINE

The drastic changes which took place in Mexico during the 1950s and '60s at first caused no upheaval along the boundary, nor were they viewed as harbingers of trouble there. One reason was that Mexico at last achieved the political stability to have bona fide national elections. For the first time in the history of the republic one administration succeeded the next without resorting to revolution as a means of assuming power. Then the 1950s formed a prosperous Mexican decade. Oil and mining contributed, but a nation whose wealth was still largely agricultural enjoyed a cycle of comparatively rainy years. This was a boon to a country where natural moisture was normally scant in many districts, and where irrigation—at last being tried in the interior on a major scale—was in many regions still in arrears.

But dams promotive of electric power as well as of irrigation water were building up Mexico, where money was also being wisely spent on an improved highway system. As far as the border was concerned, points along it were in the process of being connected with important internal towns—Chihuahua and Monterey being among them—and through them Mexico City.

A benefit derived from this program, as well as the expansion of irrigation, was the general employment of such laborers as did not cling to agriculture. These meanwhile had been encouraged and made modestly solvent by an agrarian reform movement which had mostly carried out the designs cried for, if not capably pushed, by Villa, Zapata, et al, forty years previously. For by the middle of the twentieth century approximately forty percent of the people engaged in Mexican agriculture were classed as *ejideros* or men engaged in farming the communally owned lands of what had been the encomienda villages. Off stage, however, and equally important to the economy of Mexico, were other Mexican farm workers. Employed in the United States, the braceros were both non-competitors in the Mexican labor market and productive of revenue which helped balance the general economy.

As it connected the American Southwest with Mexico's industrial centers in the interior, that country's new highway network originally loomed as an increment of the border's northern side. By becoming international channels of commerce, the line's United States cities seemed assured of profiting from activities in an awakened neighboring nation. Small notice was being contemporaneously taken of a development which had begun to become apparent as early as 1940.

This took the form of a population spurt in Mexican cities of the boundary which could be traced to no corresponding economic development in or about such communities. For while the Mexican cities of the line began to outstrip all their national competitors, all the important economic and industrial developments in that country continued to take place elsewhere in Mexico. Such untoward lines of progress were adumbrated first in *Migratory Labor in American Agriculture*, though the indications at the time of its 1951 publication were not strong enough to warrant ominous conclusions.

In the opening third of this century, the populations of the line's American towns were almost universally larger than those of their Mexican rivals. By 1940 the border communities of Mexico had doubled and tripled their 1910 size and were outstripping their opposite numbers in the United States. Ten years later a multiplication that had been thirty years in the making was repeated in spades. Between 1940 and 1950, that is to say, the population of Tijuana jumped from 16,846 to 59,117; that of Mexicali from 18,775 to 63,830; that of Nogales from 13,966 to 24,692; that of Ciudad Juarez from 48,881 to 121,903; that of Nuevo Laredo from 28,872 to 57,488; and that of Matamoros from 15,699 to 43,830.

The recent high fertility rate of Mexico has been dealt with in part. Between 1940 and 1950 the population of that republic swelled from approximately 19,600,000 to 25,500,000, an increase of 30 percent. "Compared with the United States birthrate of 25.3," writes *Migratory Labor in American Agriculture*, "the Mexican is 45.4 per thousand of population." While the industrialization of Mexico was progressing, it was not doing so rapidly enough to take care of such a population increment. A cause was the lag in developing the nation's human resources.

The following statistics and quotations are taken from the 1969 edition of *The Encyclopedia Britannica*. "As of 1950 43% of the population five years or more of age was unable to read or write any language . . . 46% of the population never ate bread made of wheat . . . only 54% of the population wore shoes."

To put it another way, about 45 percent of Mexico's population were living much as the Indians had prior to the Spanish conquest four and a half centuries earlier. They were living outside any coherent civilization, let alone the Industrial Age. Unqualified to participate by even the rudiments of education, they had no share of their country's culture, and no more knowledge of its daily news than of its history.

The extent to which many so much as knew the language of their country was called in question by a Mexican anthropologist named Alfonso Caso, quoted in the said edition of the *Britannica*. Caso's observations led him to believe "that almost all of those [citizens of Mexico] classified as bilingual in census tabulations in reality are persons who identify themselves with an Indian community, who speak one of the Indian languages as their native tongue, and who know only a little Spanish."

Just how many Mexicans now "identify themselves with an Indian community" is obscured by the fact that since the 1921 census, the practice of dividing the populace according to races has been discontinued. According to the guesses quoted by the *Britannica* relative to the 1960 racial partition, however, "estimates of 10% white, 65% mestizo and 25% Indian are about as accurate as can be obtained." As Mexico's 1960 population figure was 34,923,129, the approximate breakdown would stand at 3,492,312 whites, 22,600,028 mestizos and 8,830,780 Indians.

Where these groups predominantly dwelt was also related by the encyclopaedia. "A majority of Mexicans live in small rural villages . . . 49.3% in rural communities having less than 2,500 inhabitants."

The term "villages" as opposed to "towns" was used advisedly. Historically in Mexico it stood for communities outside the pale of civilization—overtly recognized as such in Spanish Colonial times, unofficially held as such, where not ignored entirely, during the first century of Mexican independence. In the nation's modern phase they stand less for deliberately ignored population clusters than for ones which well-intentioned but beset national administrations have largely been helpless to bring even into the outskirts of twentieth-century life, as understood in Europe and the rest of North America.

How remote from modernity people living within a few miles of the United States can be was indicated by the Marfa Sector's Intelligence Officer, Riley Barlow. "PIs pick up young wetbacks from villages near the line that can't name other Mexican burgs within ten miles of where they've lived all their lives. Even if they could read, they've never imagined such a thing as a newspaper. And they've never heard of radios, to say nothing of television. When our officers start talking to headquarters via the radios in our vehicles, you can see them trying to figure out what's going on and then the excitement, as they figure out in a general way what they've discovered."

Many Latin American natives of America's side of the border look down on the darkness of peons below the line. A case in point was cited by Airpilot Harry Aitken, now of the Tucson Sector but recalling service in Texas. While having coffee in some dispensary of it there, Aitken had passed the Spanish time of day with a Latin American who was chill in his disapproval of the superstitions degrading life south of the boundary. Bunched as foolishness by this apostle of enlightenment were witchdoctoring practices, such as flogging to force the retreat of evil spirits from possessed people, and faith in an assortment of supernatural personalities. From there on, the conversation thus proceeded:

Aitken: And you don't believe in anything like that yourself?
L. Am.: Of course, not! Well, except for El Demonio, that
is. He's real.

148

Aitken: Did you ever see him?

L. Am.: Sure, he tried to get me once.

Aitken: What did El Demonio look like?

L. Am.: He can look like anything he wants to, but that time he was like a man-sized cloud of haze or smoke. He was standing right in front of my door one night when I opened it.

Aitken: Did he say anything?

L. Am.: He didn't have to; I knew he was after me. Look, I ran for my pistol, which I always keep in only one place, and it wasn't there. *El Demonio had hid it before he came for me.* I ran for my rifle, which had *never* been any place but where I keep it ready. It wasn't there, because El Demonio had moved it.

Aitken: Wow! What did you do?

L. Am.: I knew I was a goner, if I stayed in my house, so I jumped out of a window, climbed into the window of a neighbor's home and hid under his bed.

When people who can so outmaneuver El Demonio form the comparative intellectual elite, it boots little to explore the mentalities of the lower crust. But such were the mentalities to be found in the "small rural communities" inhabited by "a majority of Mexicans" in the 1960s, and such were the mentalities of the wetbacks, who hailed from those communities.

Where these were near one of Mexico's industrial centers, some tincture of modern culture might rub off on them. But most of the villages were in isolated valleys of the Great Plateau, or salted in forests or jungles. The only thing which could have lifted them at all out of the most arrant type of rustic provincialism was a patently missing commodity. As of 1960, according to the *Encyclopaedia Britannica,* illiteracy was officially reckoned at 40 percent. But the picture wasn't as bright as that according to quoted unofficial experts, who declared that the truth was that only one in two Mexicans could read and write. Schools were not found among the "49.3% in rural communities having less than 2,500 inhabitants" to any pervasive extent. They were the luxuries of the cities and bona fide towns in contrast to peasant villages.

It was the people of these deprived rural communities who were caught between two social grinding forces in the decade referred to.

The increased industrialization of Mexico raised the cost of living at an even more rapid rate than was true of the United States. And concurrently a dry cycle impaired the yield of all but irrigated farms. The primitive tillers of *ejidos* about rural villages were at once earning less, and asked to pay more. Neither was there a place for them in Mexico's industry, insufficient as yet to absorb all the better qualified urban workmen.

For that last reason there was discontent in the cities of Mexico, mirrored in population pattern changes of so radical a nature as to reverse prior trends. In 1940 only four Mexican cities had populations of 100,000 or over. By 1960 seventeen communities were in that class. More significant than their number, though, was the location of some of the newcomers.

The great international calamity which culminated in the middle 1960s was the enormous population shift in Mexico at a time when that nation was clocking one of the highest fertility rates in the entire world. Cited is a 1960 headcount of 34,923,129, upped from a 1940 census of 19,653,508. The census of 1970 is expected to report that the people of the Republic of Mexico number about 50,826,100.

The older metropolitan centers were deep in central Mexico. The cities reflective of new conditions are, in several cases, strung along the border from sea to sea. The figures available stem from two generally agreeing estimates made in the middle 1960s by Mexican agencies. Matamoros had 15,699 people in 1940, 43,830 in 1950 and 122,680 in 1965. The populations of four other like cities will be given in east-to-west order, the same census dates being understood. Nuevo Laredo grew from 28,872 to 57,488 to 117,000; Ciudad Juarez from 48,881 to 121,903 to 385,000; Mexicali from 18,775 to 63,830 to 286,830; and challenging Tijuana from 16,486 to 59,117 to 244,000.

Then during that same period, Reynosa, opposite McAllen, climbed from a small town to a city of 74,100; Eagle Pass abruptly found itself looking across the Rio Grande at 44,992 inhabitants of Piedras Negras; and Nogales, Sonora, housed 37,657 people. Across from Del Rio, besides, 11,355 moved into a crossroads that became Ciudad Acuna; the settlement of Agua Prieta became a town of 15,339; and as it isn't represented by population figures on maps of Mexico, perhaps only Riley Barlow realized that 8,822 residents were dwelling opposite Presidio in Ojinaga.

As the respective rates of growth can be reckoned as irregular, the 1970 census figures for the cities in question are guesswork matters. But the conservative estimates, based on current trends, would set populations of about 160,000 for Matamoros; 100,000 for Reynosa; 175,000 for Nuevo Laredo; 65,000 for Piedras Negras; 20,000 for Ciudad Acuna; 11,000 for Ojinaga; 500,000 for Ciudad Juarez; 18,000 for Agua Prieta; 45,000 for Nogales, Sonora; 425,000 for Mexicali; and 410,000 for Tijuana. According to those calculations the Mexican population of the border would total about 2,000,000, counting only those living in the corporate limits of the named communities.

Growing themselves, the line's American towns were by no means keeping pace. To go by the 1960 census figures, Brownsville had 48,-040 residents; McAllen 35,411; Laredo 60,678; Eagle Pass 12,094; Del Rio 18,612; Presidio 1,062; El Paso 276,687; Douglas about 12,000; Nogales, Arizona, 7,000; El Centro and Calexico 35,000 between them, while Chula Vista was not to be reckoned with. Of them all only Del Rio was larger than its Mexican neighbor. Yuma's 24,000 were rivaled by nothing close to it, little San Luis being eighteen miles down river.

The Mexican side of the boundary, though, is the fastest growing section of Mexico. It was stated that as of 1940 Mexico had but four cities in the 100,000 inhabitants class. As of 1970 there are five with that rating on the border alone, and a sixth is probable. Juarez, Mexicali and Tijuana are among the largest cities in the land, far outgunning such former population centers as Vera Cruz, Tampico and Chihuahua.

Well, it could be asked, what's wrong with populous towns; haven't quite a few American cities in border states been booming during the same period? The difference is the cause of growth in the respective parts. Cities in California and Texas, for example, have grown swiftly as to population without outstripping an also rapid industrial expansion.

The Mexican towns along the border have an industry, too, but not one in the same universe with a healthy economic basis. It might be called wetbackism. Whatever its proper name, it speaks for no confidence in Mexico or any hope or intention of developing a self-sustaining society south of the boundary. As for the teeming cities, only Juarez ever had a real core of residents in any normal sense of the term, and they have been pushed out of sight by those with new views on how to promote civic development.

An authority on this subject is John L. Fouquette, for years an anti-smuggling officer of the Chula Vista Sector. "Outside of dope, whorehouses, dirty shows and souvenir shops, there's only one business here, and that's figuring out ways to sneak into the United States." While touring Tijuana in a sedan, he pointed to groups in huddles of various sizes. "That's all they're talking about, and it's the same story if you find heads together at a bar, a hotel lobby or a bus station.

"The men that aren't hoping to be wetbacks themselves live on the illegal alien traffic. They're smugglers, or guides, or make fake immigration documents, or peddle tips on how to cross the border and get past us when over the line. The owner of any service or shop that wants to do business has to keep posted on all the recent developments on both sides of the boundary, and some pin up bulletins telling where in America jobs are supposed to be open. The newspapers build circulation by publishing that kind of information, and by running ads of American firms which state that jobs are waiting for the wetbacks that can manage to get to this or that city."

So the economy of towns the size of Newark or Louisville is based on furtive schemes to get into another country on the part of men who do not aspire to live there but only to find money to take away.

If all the energy, ingenuity and even cash that is invested in bigtown wetbackism were put behind worthwhile enterprises, the population surge into northern Mexico could rank as a great advance for a previously empty region. As it is, the growth is as poisonous as demeaning.

The tragedy for Mexico is that what is probably now its largest industry is peopled by dropouts from the nation's economy. From this situation has emerged a population belt, threatening to be that country's dominant one, which owes nothing to national ambitions and is culturally a corpse.

The tragedy for the United States is that giant communities of a foreign nation function as parasitic growths attached to this country and infecting it with poisons. For they are channels for narcotics in addition to wetbacks, damaging America's social fabric as well as its economic fibre.

The health problem springing from the border's traffic in dope will be elsewhere discussed in this work. The other peril is two-headed, for not only Mexicans are involved. Their collaborators are industrial concerns in major cities of the United States which have come to take the same view of illegal Mexican immigrants as did the cotton growers of the Lower Rio Grande Valley prior to the day of cotton harvesting via machinery.

Urban businessmen welcome the docile fellow from Mexico who will cheerfully work any number of hours for any wage stipulated. And as ranchers of the border, managers of industries have come to feel that they have a right to the services of men whose legal position makes it impossible for them to argue about orders or demand pay raises. Employers of wetbacks don't have to bother with income tax deductions, social security payments or those covering workman's insurance. And it goes without saying that they can ignore minimum wage laws. Cherishing such aides to thrift, the supervisors of said companies resent Federal officers who try to deprive them of their wetback candy and resort to already described obstructionist tactics when Immigration Inspectors attempt to ferret out workmen illegally in this country.

For where wetbacks were once almost entirely farm laborers, they are now at home in a wide variety of trades. In border states alone they have been found working in automotive repair and paint shops, the building trades, lumber yards, television repair shops, service stations, laundries, cafes, bakeries and hotels. They have been found employed by manufacturers of brick, tile and concrete products, auto parts, structural steel and machine shop products, oil field and ranching equipment, aluminum products, drugs, garments and shoes. They have been found working at die casting, cabinet making, leather working, poultry dressing, peanut processing, and fish hatching.

As in agriculture, where he is still also prevalent, the wetback has dug in on many skilled labor fronts, and wherever he goes, he depresses the wage scale. What he is willing to work for becomes the local standard of pay for a given trade or service. As he is willing to work extra hours without bonus pay for overtime, that fair practice gets lost. Wherever the wetback prevails he worsens the plight of the entire laboring community.

The health rate goes down when wetbacks move in. Coming from communities without public health programs, they are carriers on a large scale of communicable diseases. Tuberculosis, syphilis, gonorrhea and dysentery are the most common, but some of the infections they bring into America are more dread than these. Take the case of a man who, at the time of his apprehension in the kitchen of a

Chicago restaurant, was mixing salad with his hands. Examined, he was found to have leprosy.

Above all, the illegal Mexican immigrant is the cause of unemployment for thousands upon thousands of American citizens. Wherever the wetback gets a job in the United States, the door is closed on an applicant who is in the country by right of native birth or naturalization. Of course, it can be urged that this would be true of a hired illegal alien of any race; but representatives of no further nationality are lawlessly present in numbers enough to radically affect the labor market. And the representatives of no other nationality, since the days when the Chinese of California formed an analogous problem, have established a reputation for being willing at once to work very hard and to ask very little.

So the wetback is a prime cause of American unemployment, which he brings about in two ways. In the upper reaches of the labor market he freezes out the skilled American citizen by underpricing him. In the labor market's lower level, the illegal Mexican immigrant brings the pay scale down to a point close to the offerings of Government welfare programs. By removing the incentive to work, he keeps men on the dole who then have few outlets for their energies but criminal ones.

14

THE
BUILDUP
OF THE
MODERN
INVASION

For ten years after Operation Wetback the influx of Mexican line jumpers was not a grave problem. The rate of apprehensions by the end of 1955 was described by General Swing as running about 200 a day or some 70,000 a year. Later, because of the bracero and Mexican road construction programs, the annual number of arrests by patrolmen dropped well below that level. The rest of the decade and the early 1960s found PIs confidently in control of their assignment.

The forces that triggered the change have been noticed above with the exception of a bad deal from nature. A drought problem, similar to the Dust Bowl Cycle that had ruined much of America's farmland in the 1930s, concurrently killed the livelihood of many. The trend created by all three began to be felt in terms of illegal migration to the United States with the tapering off of the international contracts for farm laborers. But in 1964, Patrol Intelligence Officers were startled by big percentage jumps in the arrests made in every border sector. In the Marfa one, for instance, the increase over 1963 was a resounding 54.9 percent.

Not realized as a trend at the outset, the fact became more apparent with the mounting apprehension totals of each successive year. To stay with the statistics of Marfa, the growth rate rose 26.2% in 1965, 65.4% in 1966 and 69.3% in 1967.

To put the steady increase in terms of figures, the records of the Chula Vista Sector will be used. At the beginning of wetback mobilization in force, its border crossing points were not much more popular than those of a couple of fellow sectors, but by the second year it was doubling the totals of any of the others. In 1964 there were 4,384 apprehensions. The 1965 figure was 10,365, a gain of nearly one hundred and fifty percent. In 1966 the number climbed to 15,228; in 1967 to 21,502; in 1968 to 26,206. As for the fiscal year ending in June of 1969, arrests were being made at the rate of 4,000 a month. In other words the monthly rate almost equaled the sector's annual total for 1964, when the second great wetback surge began.

And meanwhile, Washington was indifferent to the Patrol's needs for a reason not hard to find. Replacing Eisenhower, President John Kennedy had appointed as Attorney General Robert Kennedy. That director of the Patrol's destinies during the early and middle '60s presumably spoke for his brother's administration in a speech wherein he undertook to deplore the outcome of the Mexican War of 1846–48. Although Texans took that to be aimed at them, in as much as the Rio Grande boundary was the primary conflict cause, it could just as reasonably have been resented by residents of the other border states, which owned their place in the Union to that passage at arms. In any case, it was not to be expected that an administration so ill attuned to the Southwest would take an interest in the border or its wardens.

The situation got no better when John Kennedy was replaced in the White House by Lyndon Johnson. For although a Texan, Johnson had been hostile to the Patrol while a United States Senator. He had then been, as was earlier pointed out, the political tool of farmers who plunked for an open border and wished the Patrol to be denied operating funds. On that account nothing was hoped for by PIs when he took office as the nation's chief executive, and they got it.

In fiscal 1969 the number of Border Patrol apprehensions in the

Southwest was 159,395. To take in and process the equivalent of ten full strength military divisions, the corps had less than 1,200 men on the Mexican line. As the work load of officers mounted to the point where they were working sixty and more hours a week, as opposed to the forty-four set down in the rule book, they were hampered by played out equipment, much of which was daily tinkered with so that it would run at all.

But in spite of operational handicaps, wetbacks were at length being hauled into the collective sector headquarters at the rate of about 436 a day. And the news for the first half of fiscal 1970 was that the diurnal rate of arrests continued to climb.

If the daily catch of wetbacks is 100 or more men at a given sector, that many have to be hauled into headquarters, intensively questioned and reported on by the apprehending PIs. In the case of a captured smuggler the processing of one man may take several hours, as his statements have to be checked against those of the clients caught with him.

In the language of the border, smugglers are hailed as "coyotes" or *pateros*. Often residents of either a sector headquarters town or of a Mexican city just across the border, they are apt to be known, by repute at least, to the local anti-smuggling officers. On the other hand, some keep shifting their operation base, either because they feel the heat is on them or on account of a change in the wetback traffic pattern.

Any time a locally unknown smuggler is caught, application is made to the Anti Smuggling Center, a sub-division of the Yuma Information Center. Composed of the Air Detail Program (once at El Centro) and the Fraudulent Document Index, as well as the Anti-Smuggling Center, it was organized by Intelligence Officer J. W. Nowosielski in 1965.

That service keeps on file photographs and case histories of all alien smugglers who have been caught. Names submitted by phone from any other headquarters can be promptly checked out. Photographs could, too, were the Patrol equipped with radio devices for sending and receiving pictures common to newspapers. As it is, the photographs of newly apprehended men have to be submitted by mail, making it necessary to hold for a day or more prisoners who could otherwise be processed in a matter of hours.

When a smuggler is nabbed with a clutch of wetbacks, all are quizzed not only by the seizing PIs but also by the anti-smuggling specialists. Through their staffs of informers, these have such an accurate knowledge of the local probabilities that they know when they are being told the truth. Answers compared, there is a second round of questioning, if discrepancies make that necessary.

The questioning is firm but friendly, and sometimes interrupted with laughter, if the investigator points out a rank absurdity that the prisoner has tried to palm off. If faced with nothing worse than repatriation, most smuggled wetbacks respond to shrewd probing with eventual frankness. The ones who stick to inventions are men with bad records in this country or their own.

When patrolmen have pieced together the information supplied by informers as well as wetbacks, they are then ready to brace the smuggler with what they have learned. Whether or not he talks, which he may not choose to do until he's arraigned in a Federal District Court, the Patrol has a smuggling charge case which it is prepared to press in the same tribunal. For a first offense alone the penalty can be five years, but some courts are so lenient that the smuggler is out on probation and back in business within a few months of arrest.

The questioners of non-smuggled wetbacks try to determine such points as where he crossed, how he was financed, his sources of information about the United States and so forth. Of especial interest are the repeaters. These can usually be told from those making their first lawless visit by their clothes, comparative sophistication and knowledge of English. Another indication is their lack of nervousness. The greenhorns are jittery because of falling into the hands of peace officers. The old hands know they will be treated with consideration and are relaxed—if there's no other legal count against them, that is.

Not infrequently the cause of a wetback's arrest is that he unwisely made his presence known by trying to feed or finance himself at some American's expense. If such come back after having served appropriate sentences, they have the natural tendency to bring new names with them. They do not bring new faces, though, and their photographs are on file, along with their fingerprints. Anybody suspected of being a repeater is held in a detention center until it is determined whether charges have been filed against him in the past.

The Immigration and Naturalization Service maintains three such camps on the border, located at El Centro, El Paso and Los Fresnos in the Port Isabel Sector. Prisoners are detained at any sector headquarters for as short a time as possible. Then they are shipped out by bus to the nearest stockade. There, those with none but illegal entrant charges against them are returned to Mexico with a minimum of delay, provided they elect the time-saving device of "voluntary deportation." Some do not, because they think they have grounds, actual or cooked-up, for being allowed to stay in the United States.

These get hearings in Federal district courts, where their defensive statements and the evidence adduced against them by arresting PIs are carefully weighed. Preparing cases that will stand up and testifying in courts that are not right around the corner from a sector headquarters are other time-consuming Patrol duties.

Then there is the matter of reports from other sections of the nation. Often smuggled aliens are caught after the smuggler has left them. This might not be near the border at all, for the real money is made by those in the traffic who rush wetbacks from the line to big cities elsewhere. Some of these are in California or Texas; but favorite destinations include Chicago and Detroit. There is, indeed, no industrial region where the modern wetback cannot be found.

But however far from the boundary an invader may be apprehended, his story is sent back to the Border Patrol sector which includes his point of crossing. The anti-smuggling officers of the headquarters then try to identify the smuggler in the case by means of the testimony submitted by the investigators of the Immigration Service who caught the invader. And doing so might be complicated by the fact that the client of a coyote never knew his real name, having been told no more than a pseudonym.

Because the wetbacks involved crossed the border in the Laredo Sector, the following items were turned over to anti-smuggling officers Leslie D. Bell and K. R. Dunnigan. Matchable at other points along the line, they combine to show both how smugglers operate and how their contraband is located.

A wetback runner known only as "El Huero" charged a flat rate of $180 per head to drive aliens to Chicago. Of this fee the downpayment was $120; the rest, as will be seen, was paid in two installments.

Several arrested wetbacks testified that they went to El Huero's house in Nuevo Laredo at 4:00 P.M. on March 6, 1968. From there two men, one of whom was referred to as the brother of El Huero, drove them up the Rio Grande about twelve miles. The guides at that point led them afoot to the river, which they all waded a little after dark. Having passed the wetbacks into the United States, the coyote's brother claimed $20 from each for this service. He then led them afoot to a gate marking the private road of a nearby cattle ranch, by which they waited a half hour.

What this delay was for was not explained, but doubtless the guides finally got some signal which wasn't recognized by the wetbacks. In about thirty minutes, in any case, they were led to a paved highway. There a car blinked its lights twice, and all but the guides climbed in. The vehicle had two drivers who took turns during a non-stop journey to Chicago, which they reached at 7:00 A.M. on March 8, 1968. Their Windy City destination was a house whose address was 2327 South St. Louis Street. There each paid the remaining $40 due El Huero.

As has been shown, that smuggler never ran the risk of crossing the border himself. Others could not well help it, being residents of America as well as United States citizens. Instances in point involved the Garcia clan of Cotulla, Texas. Its members ran human contraband over and away from the line on numerous occasions before Bell and Dunnigan unearthed evidence which packed them all off to a Federal penitentiary.

These were real professionals; they had their lines out deep in central Mexico rather than waiting for potluck patronage at the border. On one occasion thirty-one wetbacks, applying from Yuriria, Guanajuato, arranged to be smuggled into the United States and north to Chicago for $200 apiece. Arriving in Nuevo Laredo on September 29, 1968, they called the Garcias from a hotel. As agreed during that conference, they met Gilbert, Jesus and Arturo Garcia in one of the houses of the city's extensive redlight district on September 30. Led across the Rio Grande by J. G. Ochoa (an alias of Jesus Garcia), they were guided through the brush to a paved highway where two pickup campers were waiting. Before they were packed in, Benito and Arturo Garcia collected $3,100 from the thirty-one wetbacks. The other hundred apiece was due to be paid at the Chicago end of the trip.

At least two of the Garcias had been caught up with on two previous smuggling counts, at the time of this undertaking. On March 26, 1968, Benito had been convicted in the Federal District Court at Del Rio and sentenced to six months, suspended for five years. On August 27, 1968, Jesus had been apprehended near Laredo and was

160

out on bail awaiting trial at the time of taking part in the venture of September 30. Then Arturo Garcia had been arrested on September 16 for having on his person a loaded .38 calibre revolver.

Gilbert and previously unmentioned José Garcia had also been stopped by officers who suspected them of making a local contraband run. But it seems they had really been bent on piety; their story was that they were returning from the Shrine of the Virgin at San Juan, Texas. Unfortunately for them, the court didn't believe this or anything else offered in mitigation, so it will be years before they will be in a position to make a pilgrimage, or meet clients in Nuevo Laredo's prostitution ghetto again.

Not all smuggled aliens are Mexican, naturally. On October 5, 1968, a Cuban named Julio Ortiz paid $500 to a man known only as "José" to get him into the United States. Met in Mexico City, they took a taxi for that town's airport, where José bought tickets for both. They left Mexico City at 7:00 A.M. on October 6 for Monterey, whence they went by taxi to Nuevo Laredo. In a hotel there they were joined by two men. José said he would meet Ortiz on the American shore of the Rio Grande. The guides meanwhile took Ortiz along the river, where a youth with a truck tire inner tube told the Cuban to remove his clothes and be ferried across. José met his client near Laredo just at dark and took him by taxicab to Corpus Christi. There the smuggler bought tickets for Houston on a plane leaving at 7:00 P.M. In Houston he bought tickets for Miami. Leaving Texas at 8:30 P.M., the pair reached the Florida city at midnight.

Another story involved entry by the use of fraudulent documents. Five aliens screened at the Los Fresnos detention center testified that they came to the border from San Juan de Los Lagos, in the State of Jalisco, to seek work in Chicago. Two of them had been in that American city before, having been brought there by a smuggler named Luvin Pina, whom they now contacted again at a Nuevo Laredo bar. An interesting aspect of the case is that the two Chicago old-timers had not been deported. They had returned to Mexico in January of 1968, evidently to visit their families, and in March of the same year they were prepared to crack the international line again. Pina asked his clients if they had border crossing cards, which all five of them said they did, in spite of the fact that they hailed from a Mexican state far to the southwest.

The coyote then said that, for $60 each, he would take the five men to Corpus Christi, where they could catch a bus to Chicago. However obtained, the crossing cards passed inspection, and the bridge at Laredo brought the wetbacks into the United States with dry feet on March 25, 1968. Meeting his clients near the bridge, Pina took them to the Rex Hotel. At 7:00 A.M. on March 26, he picked them up at the Rex and drove them to Laredo's Continental Trailways bus station. The invaders rode the bus to San Diego, Texas, where Pina, waiting in a car, transported them to Corpus Christi. Having taken the wetbacks to a bus station in that city, Pina collected the agreed $60 from each for faithfully rendered services.

The year 1968 was the one in which quotas for immigrants legally admitted to the United States were at last set up for Western Hemisphere nations. All combined were allowed an annual total of 120,000.

To return to the Ortiz case, he was but one of many Cubans who have come over the border, or attempted to. They have been encouraged to try by the official policy of the United States, which reads more like the rules of "red rover" or "prisoner's base" than a serious immigration plan.

To begin with, the United States grants political asylum to Cubans who can't abide Castro's Communist regime. So much sounds like an invitation, but the United States now only admits as many fugitives annually as fit into the Western Hemisphere's immigration quota. If Cubans in excess of the allowed number try to land in an American port, they will be sent back to their island homeland. Yet if one manages to sneak into the United States and report to a center for Cubans in Florida, all is well with him. The same American Government that would throw him out if he applied for admission openly, will reward his furtive entry by seeing that he gets supported.

So the game for anti-Castroites—plus some Cuban Communist agents that masquerade as fugitives—is to somehow get to Florida. Since Mexican officials will let such transients land, many prefer to attempt the border route rather than a more direct one. Their sound reason is that if they are stopped at the boundary, the United States will do no worse than return them to Mexico. As Mexico permitted their entry, the official American attitude re the caught ones is that they are Mexico's problem. The practical result is that these invaders are not repatriated but allowed to stay where it is convenient to essay future border jumps.

How heavy the Cuban traffic across the Mexican line has become can be gathered from a heading in the Phoenix *Arizona Republic* reading BORDER PATROL HALTS 42 CUBANS. Carrying a Nogales, Arizona, dateline and written by Harold K. Milks, the story was run on May 6, 1969.

> Forty-two Cuban refugees were seized here in the last two days as they attempted to enter the United States illegally through a rat-infested storm sewer beneath the international border.
>
> Their detention is believed to have plugged a vast underground escape route for Cubans which began in Havana and extended through Mexico to this border city. Nearly 300 Cubans have been detained here since January for illegal entry. . . .
>
> It was the largest seizure numerically, since a wave of attempts began in January to evade limitation of a new United States immigration law, officials said. This reduced immigration from the Western hemisphere to 120,000 annually.

The article said the refugees were detected because the Border Patrol had thought of the storm sewer's possibilities and equipped it with an electric eye. It also told the probable fate of the captives, as guessed by an Immigration Service spokesman. "Presumably . . . those who were 'clean' and could establish that they were bona fide refugees would be given conditional admission to the United States pending qualifications for permanent visas. Those not cleared would be handed back to the Mexican authorities . . .

"Security required a careful check to assure that no Cuban agents for Fidel Castro were able to enter as 'refugees' . . . ."

That more Cuban fugitives would soon be storming the border was also made clear in the news story. "Officials said the 300 Cubans seized since January were part of about 4,000 Cubans now waiting in Mexico for admission to the United States as refugees." These had "obtained temporary entrance visas into Mexico, good for 30 days. . . . Apparently there is an organized program in Mexico handled by Cuban refugee groups to use the underground route for those who face a long wait for legal admission to the United States. . . ."

A paragraph in the article scored the point that the well-heeled among the refugees planned to bypass the center which had been set up for them in Florida and go their independent ways. The ones caught in the Nogales storm sewer had equipped themselves with American transportation tickets, presumably arranged for by the mentioned Cuban organization in Mexico. "In all, the 25 adults and three children discovered Sunday and the adults and children found yesterday, obtained airline tickets before leaving Havana. These called for passage to Mexico City, then to Tucson and onward to various destinations, including Chicago, New York and Miami."

Canadians, surprisingly, have been caught crossing the line in some numbers, these being mostly the French-speaking ones. There are annually some illegal immigrants from Central and South American countries, as well as a scattering from Asian and European nations. But the boundary-jumping aliens of all the rest of the world lumped together remain as nothing compared to the wetback hordes. For seven successive fiscal years that invasion has mounted new floods whose full proportions are no more than suggested by the annual totals of Border Patrol apprehensions. Until a dedicated and furiously working force is sufficiently enlarged and adequately equipped, the story will continue to be that for every trespasser caught, a number of others will infiltrate and damage America's economic and social structures.

15

FALSE
DOCUMENTS
AND
REAL
VIOLENCE

Among the criminal industries of the border, schemes for certifying the American citizenship or legal entry of wetbacks stand second only to the various types of smuggling. On the simplest level, false claims to rightful presence in the United States may take the form of oral insistence on the part of a Mexican that his parents happened to be in this country at the time of his birth. Nor can such statements be lightly brushed aside. Because of historical episodes, covered earlier in this chronicle, there are possibilities in the wetback's favor which are not easy for patrolmen to disprove.

A great many of the difficulties stem from American generosity in granting asylum to the thousands of Mexicans fleeing from one faction or another during the gory decade that followed the fall of Diaz. As no thought was then given to the immigration problems of the future, no careful tally was made of just who stayed north of the border and for how long. Neither was there any count kept as to just which refugees begot American citizens by bearing children while in the United States.

If a Mexican of about the appropriate age claims that he was born in Texas in 1915, say, the fact that no record of his birth is discoverable cannot be used as a ground for disputing his citizenship. In that time and place the nearest thing to certification of birth for many undoubtedly native Anglos was a notation in the family Bible. Some births might have been supervised by doctors who could be expected to keep some sort of professional records. Most infants were delivered by illiterate midwives. Then the nearest thing to a record was the memory of a woman as perishable as other mortals.

Perhaps the most undocumented migration of the era was that of the mentioned town of El Mulato, opposite the border crossing point of Polvo, in the Big Bend region. To get out of the path of the warring agrarian reformers, the community pulled up stakes with tribal completeness and nested as individual families in the caves that conveniently pitted cliffs on the Rio Grande's American side.

How these transplants supported themselves is a secret of El Mulato's unkept annals. Probably they worked their fields on the Mexican side of days, retiring to troglodyte safety in Texas of nights, or whenever the grapevine said warriors were active near their abandoned home town. But their means of survival are not important here. They not only survived, they mated and multiplied.

The present population of El Mulato is reckoned at 615 by Big Bend specialist Riley Barlow. Perhaps there were half that number in 1913. But certainly there were quite a few more than had moved away when the town fathers decided that it would be safe to return to Mexico on an unrecorded day several years later.

Every one of the children born to those twentieth-century cave dwellers were automatically citizens of the United States, complete with the authority to pass that benefit on to progeny of theirs born abroad. Such do not instantly become American citizens, but if they choose to adopt the country where their parents were born, rather than the land of their nativity, they have naturalization rights which cannot be denied them.

So if a man stopped at the line by a PI asserts that he is the son of such and such an infant born to cave-dwelling refugees, he is in a very strong position, even though it is known that the claimants to be offspring of El Mulatoans in exile exceed the entire original population. The only recourse of the Patrol, as Barlow pointed out, was to query women who acted as midwives at that time. "We can kill a case if one of these will say of a citizenship claimant, 'No, he was born—or his father was born—a year or so after we moved back to Mexico.' Or, of course, she may substantiate the claim by saying, 'Yes, he was born in an exactly located cave; and give the approximate date."

The story of El Mulato is a picturesque representative of what went on less dramatically at other points along the line. Thousands of people moved north of it and bore children, with midwives presiding. But the testimony of surviving ones, as the Immigration Service has learned, is not universally reliable. "Investigations of the false birth registrations," according to the 1968 Immigration and Naturalization Service report, "has thus far identified seven Texas midwives who falsely registered births in the United States of several hundred children who were actually born in Mexico."

The subject of modern false claims to citizenship through nativity will be returned to. First, though, a glimpse of the consequences of one falsely established claim on the part of older people will be given. On file at the Patrol's Fraudulent Document Index at Yuma is a case in which three generations of Mexican aliens were involved. Feliz Martinez and his wife had eleven children, of whom four had produced progeny when the Immigration Service caught up with the family in 1959. Of this once-promising American dynasty a chart was made beside which there appears the following explanatory matter:

> The genealogical tree illustrated here is a portrayal of an actual case involving a family of some thirty-eight persons who had predicated their United States Citizenship upon the issuance of one delayed certificate of birth. The wife's claim to citizenship was based on a marriage to a United States citizen prior to 1922. The children claimed by derivation through United States citizen parents, and the grandchildren through their citizen parent. . . . Some of the grandchildren are residents of Mexico; however, in order to show the possible ramifications of one fraudulent delayed certificate of birth, they are included here as possible claimants to United States citizenship by derivation through their mother.

The odds urge that they would have made such a claim, had not a suit, boldly pressed on behalf of Feliz Martinez, collapsed as described in the chart's written matter: "On appeal to the United States

Court of Appeals for the Fifth Circuit, New Orleans, La., he was held to be an alien in a decision rendered on March 10, 1959."

About six years later the fraudulent document industry was given a boost by an amendment to the immigration laws which tightened the nation's entrance requirements at a time when Mexican employment in America was curtailed by the closing down of the bracero program. That ended on December 31, 1964. In 1965 a law was passed demanding Department of Labor certification of all immigrants. Applying aliens had to show, in other words, that their employment plans in this country were specific, and were not of a nature to crowd American citizens out of any corner of the labor market by accepting employment at rates harmful to the living standards of native or naturalized workmen.

Meeting Department of Labor certification is precisely what most Mexicans who desire to work in this country cannot do. They are all seeking jobs which could and should be filled by citizens, whether now actively trying to earn a living, hoping to do so when old enough, or marking time on the plea there is no available employment. The living proof that this last is nonsense, the wetback must be excluded in order to clear up the muddied labor and welfare pictures, if for nothing else.

Determined to have the rights of a citizen, the illegal Mexican alien tries a wide range of ruses to prove himself either a native American or entitled to consideration as a close relative of one. The false birth certificate racket may take the form of forged church records as well as documents based on the testimony of midwives. If the fraud is successful in deceiving an Immigrant Inspector, the whole family is as good as north of the border for keeps. For the parents of a citizen who is a minor can then claim "immediate relative status" and apply for visas on that basis.

A more direct method of achieving such status has been practiced, on a considerable scale, wherever it is possible for women in the final stages of pregnancy to secretly cross the boundary with midwives in attendance. If a woman can manage to bear her child before being detected and hurried back across the line, the United States has a new citizen. As such he cannot be ousted, nor can his parents be denied the right to bring in seven or eight other children when they enter legally to look after their American boy or girl. And the father, of course, cannot be deterred from securing the work he needs by way of shouldering his responsibilities.

168

As testified in the 1967 Immigration and Naturalization report, sham marriages are also resorted to as a means of sidestepping Department of Labor certification. A female American citizen cannot be ordered to leave the country in order to join a foreign fiance. And as the United States Government cannot be in the position of forcibly coming between a woman and her betrothed, it follows that he must be allowed to marry her wherever she lives and there support her by gaining such employment as he can find.

Because of these legal and social facts, wetbacks now try to remain in the United States by one of two matrimonial cheats. They either flourish false marriage certificates involving actual American citizens or they produce real certificates bearing upon trumped up marital contracts. There are professional arrangers of such fake marriages of convenience, and the I & N report cited shows that they do not proffer their services for nothing. "In one case, Lino R. Salazar of Los Angeles pleaded guilty in 1966 to arranging sham marriages between Mexican aliens and American citizens to evade labor certification requirements. Salazar, for fees up to $800, provided the United States citizen spouses and prepared all of the fraudulent documentation necessary to secure immigrant visas."

Draft cards, somehow obtained and passed over the border, form another branch of false documentation. In fiscal 1968 twenty-one wetbacks secured selective service cards based on the draft registrations of seven United States citizens. These American armed service vouchers were flashed when proof of citizenship was demanded by PIs or Immigrant Inspectors. The art of counterfeiting has been practiced in this connection, too, for an imitation draft card was found on an invader stopped for questioning in El Paso.

Not all document frauds are aimed at dodging labor certification, though. Artful shysters abetting them, some wetbacks try to show that they are manfully complying with the Labor Department's immigration rules. One way is to produce letters, purportedly from companies in America's interior, which attest that their bearers will be employed at standard wages and in select fields where they will not be competing with American laborers. Another method is to vouch for the responsibility of a man posing as a visitor who only wishes to tour the country. There are brokers in this department of crime, too, and "Luis Bonilla of Juarez," was found, as of 1967, to have "sold more than 80 sets of fraudulent employment offers and bank references to visa applicants for $225 to $300."

169

There is a common traffic in bogus visas, unsupported by other documents, and a rarer and more expensive trade in American passports. These, like some of the other ruses, may be either genuine in themselves but perverted to the uses of others than their original owners, or they may be completely counterfeit.

Cheaper and more simple than either of the others is the purveyance of forged or doctored border crossing cards. Or again a Mexican may legally obtain a short-term visitor's permit, which gives him access to transportation into America's hinterland. Once a ticket in any of these classes gets in circulation, there are efforts to make them serve any number of people. This is accomplished through a practice of sending cards south across the line on the part of Mexican invaders who can thus modestly profit. One of these will peddle his card to an international taxi driver or some other agent who will recognize its value and sell it to a coiner of false documents. That worthy will substitute for the original ones the name and photograph of the next wetback that applies to him and charge the price of a new piece of merchandise.

The drawback to the use of true or false border crossing cards is that they betray the lawless intentions of their bearers if found upon these while they are in transit away from the boundary. Men with the money to do so therefore prefer to invest in documents calculated to give them standing if challenged anywhere in the country. The ensuing statement in consequence appeared in the Immigration and Naturalization report for fiscal 1968:

> For the seventh consecutive year there was an increase in the number of false claims to citizenship encountered by the Border Patrol. The 2,052 cases developed were 22% above the 1,688 cases accounted for last year. The false claims were made by 2,025 Mexicans and 27 aliens of other nationalities.
>
> Various aspects of fraud were prevalent in a case developed in Brownsville, Tex., where officers apprehended an individual who was purchasing a copy of a baptismal certificate pertaining to Ascencion Sanchez. The apprehension was made as a direct result of liaison between the officers and employees of various churches in the area. A church employee . . . stated that she was reasonably sure the individual had, on several occasions, stolen blank copies of baptismal certificates from her desk.
>
> The subject admitted that he had purchased several copies of

the baptismal certificate of Ascencion Sanchez. He contended he had sold them to a man in Matamoros . . . known to him only as "El Negro." A check of the records at the Fraudulent Document Center revealed that the documents presented by Ascencion Sanchez had been presented by false claimants nine times before. . . .

County records are also rifled by Americans with enough political pull to assist wetbacks they wish to use. "In a case reported by Lubbock officers," the 1968 I & N report continued, "an alien presented a fraudulent Texas birth certificate, which was given to him by his employer. The certificate contained correct information concerning the alien's name, birth date, and his parents' names. The employer allegedly obtained a genuine blank certificate and had it executed by a county employee who had access to the county seal."

However felonious, the users of fraudulent documents are trying to carry their point by peaceful means. The great majority of wetbacks are not in this class. At their mildest they are pertinacious sneaks. Then come the petty plunderers, ready to help themselves to anything they can find as they make their way into a foreign country. In a minority, but still apt to be encountered on any day or stretch of the border, are the dangerous, marijuana-hot pachucos.

Though most of them are apt to be smugglers, their representation among clients of these, as well as individual crossers of the line, is attested by the 1967 I & N *Annual Report*. "Not since the early days of the wetback era in the early 1950s have service officers met with so much harassment and physical resistance in administering the immigration and nationality laws and in bringing law violators to justice. The defiance has ranged from verbal threats and assaults to physical violence culminating in death as in the cases of the two officers who were recently murdered. During the year, 46,734 aliens with prior violations of the immigration laws were apprehended and of these more than 3,500 with prior criminal records were taken into custody. Among those arrested were 58 persons in possession of weapons including 32 pistols, five rifles, two shotguns and 13 knives."

Some instances of fatal and near fatal violence perpetrated by lawless intruders from Mexico were cited by the same official document. "On May 22, 1967, the Zapata County, Texas sheriff requested assistance of the Border Patrol in the apprehension of an illegal Mexican alien who was wanted for murder. Patrol inspectors located the suspect in one of three small buildings located on a ranch about seven miles from where the murder was committed. The suspect was not armed at the time, but admitted the murder and showed the officers the weapon, a 12-gauge shotgun, located in another building along with . . . high powered rifles . . . .

"At El Paso, Tex., on July 6, 1966, a patrol inspector in a tower observed three Mexican male aliens carrying bundles from the levee on the American side to the edge of the river and then saw them passing additional bundles over the backyard fence of a residence. Mobile units were notified by radio. Two of the men fled to Mexico, one was intercepted. The alien struggled with the officer in an attempt to get the officer's gun. The alien had burglarized the residence and records indicate that he had been arrested by the Service for illegal entry on August 21 and November 15, 1960. The El Paso Police Department had previously arrested him as a burglary suspect on May 4, 1962, and again on April 29, 1965. . . ."

The incidence of violent immigrants moved upward in the next fiscal year, in which "there were 98 persons arrested who were in possession of dangerous weapons, including 78 pistols of various calibers, four rifles and 14 knives,

"The following cases are typical of situations where armed resistance was encountered by Service officers.

"Having been informed that the Milstead Ranch near Laredo, Tex., had been burglarized, officers from the Laredo Station, on November 17, 1967, promptly tracked down and arrested three aliens who had burglarized the ranch. One of these, when apprehended, had in his possession a fully loaded revolver he had taken from the ranch.

"On December 18, 1967, the Webb County, Tex., sheriff requested Border Patrol assistance to apprehend two persons who had abducted a citizen and had shot a deputy sheriff. Observation aircraft from the Laredo Sector located the wanted persons, notified ground units, and directed operations although one of the aircraft encountered rifle fire. Approaching ground units made up of Border Patrol officers, deputy sheriffs and public safety officers were also fired upon, but quickly subdued the two fugitives and took them into custody.

"On March 13, 1968, the Webb County sheriff notified Laredo Sector Headquarters to be on the lookout for a dangerous suspect, wanted for assault, threat to murder, and possession of a prohibited weapon. All units were notified and shortly thereafter patrol inspectors encountered the suspect on the highway 25 miles north of Laredo. A loaded .38 caliber revolver was located in his car. . . .

"A patrol inspector from Chula Vista, Calif., apprehended an alien illegally in the United States near San Ysidro, Calif., on September 23, 1967. Upon initial search, a loaded pistol was discovered on the alien's person, and a struggle for possession of the pistol ensued . . . Subsequent investigation developed that the alien had committed a burglary in the San Ysidro area, and the pistol was part of the loot. . . .

"Joint efforts of local police and the Indio Border Patrol Unit resulted in the arrest of an armed criminal alien on May 1, 1968. The alien, using an alias, had purchased a pistol at a local hardware store. Examination of immigration records showed he had an extensive criminal and immigration record and was using a false identity. He was soon located, and when taken into custody, the pistol was found loaded in the glove compartment of his car."

Not all instances of armed invasion are so successfully handled; nor do all PIs emerge from such encounters unscathed. In May of 1969 a Chula Vista patrolman was questioning one of two suspects when the other whipped out a pistol and got the drop on the officer. Bound to a tree by the handcuffs he carried, the PI only escaped being murdered because the owner of what was evidently a stolen handgun could not find and release the safety. His wiser partner led the foiled pistoleer away, but without releasing a man who remained shackled until fellow patrolmen instituted a search for their missing comrade.

A more disastrous case was recounted by David Brand in his *Wall Street Journal* feature of August 18, 1969. "Apprehended laborers sometimes can be dangerous. . . . Herman Moore, chief of the Patrol's El Paso sector . . . tells how one of his men was stabbed in the chest with a bread knife by a captured Mexican. As the officer slumped to the ground, he drew his gun and killed the man with a shot through the head. The patrolman, whose lung was punctured, recovered."

Two who encountered armed pushers—and users—of marijuana were not so fortunate. BORDER PATROL OFFICERS MURDERED was the headline of an official bulletin dated July 7, 1967:

Two young Border Patrol Inspectors, Theodore Lawrence Newton, Jr., 26, and George Frederick Azrak, 21, both of

Temecular, Calif., were found murdered in a remote, deserted mountain cabin on June 17, 1967, after an intensive 48-hour search after they disappeared while on official duty. The men were kidnapped from their post during a traffic check operation along Highway 79 near Oak Grove, Calif., in the early morning hours of June 17. The check point was located about 75 miles north of the Mexican border along a route where a large number of aliens have been apprehended.

The young officers failed to report in following an all night assignment at the road check, and a search for them revealed that the men and their two vehicles, a jeep and a Border Patrol sedan, were missing. Road "stop" signs which had been installed by the men were also missing.

The Service jeep was soon located about a mile from the road check point where it had been driven through two stock fences and left under a tree in an open field.

By evening of the 17th, some 400 men, including members of the Border Patrol, San Diego County sheriff's deputies, highway patrolmen and over 200 San Diego County sheriff's reserve members were engaged in a massive search operation. On foot and using planes, Marine helicopters, jeeps and horses, the men probed the rugged terrain near Palomar Mountain.

On June 19, the missing Service sedan was spotted about 9:00 A.M. by a member of a Jeep Club from Hamit, Calif. The sedan had been covered with brush. Fifty feet away was a deserted shack, and there the posse located the bodies of the missing Patrolmen. The cabin is located on the Bailey ranch, a mountainous brush area, off Highway 71 near Anza, Calif., and about 8 miles northeast of Oak Grove where the officers had been at work.

Left out of this account but attested in others are the details that Newton and Azrak had been handcuffed to the shanty's iron stove, seated on blankets which their kidnappers thoughtfully spread for them. From these circumstances it can be guessed that the original intent of their captors had not been murderous; but when something detonated the always unsteady tempers of marijuana fans, they had reacted by shooting helpless men in the back.

To continue with the wording of the official bulletin:

174

Immediately on discovery of the bodies, the FBI sealed off a vast area surrounding the cabin and an intensive search was begun for clues, and for the killer or killers who were believed at that time to be still in the area.

The Service sent its most expert trackers, who helped spearhead the intensive manhunt. The sign cutters . . . fanned out on foot and in jeeps over rocky and mountainous terrain which is part of an 18,000 acre Cahuilla Indian Reservation.

Trackers picked up shoeprints leading from the deserted cabin, and agents found fingerprints. Soil samples and other evidence was shipped to Washington to the FBI crime lab for study.

This proved rewarding scholarship. "So quickly and thoroughly did all law enforcement agencies work that by June 19 the FBI announced that complaints had been filed charging Florencio Lopez-Mationg, Victor Jerald Bono, Alfred Arthur Montoya and Harold Otto Montoya with the murder of the two patrolmen. . . ."

But it is often one thing to charge a man with a crime and another to bring him to trial for it. From informers, anti-smuggling officers had learned that the Montoya brothers had fled to a point deep in the interior of Sonora. There the FBI was not authorized to pursue, or negotiate even. Neither were Border Patrolmen when in uniform or official vehicles, so Assistant Chief Dale Swancutt and Senior PI Virgil Blivens donned mufti and flew below the line in the guise of tourists. They were not, to be sure, expecting to take active part in a manhunt south of the boundary; what they hoped to do was to put at the disposal of Mexican peace officers information which would make it easier for these to proceed with dispatch.

The patrolmen's enterprise paid off. " . . . on Saturday, July 7," the already quoted bulletin declared, "the Montoya brothers were apprehended by agents of the Sonora Judicial Police on a ranch about 100 miles south of Hermosillo, Mexico." It was the Montoyas, turning informers not as the killers, who supplied the information that the car fatally halted by Newton and Azrak had been carrying eight hundred pounds of marijuana.

The men who had slain the officers had, as the bulletin's next paragraph makes clear, chosen to stay north of the border. "On Sunday, July 16, 1967, a month after the double murder, the Federal Bureau of Investigation announced the arrest at Los Angeles, Calif., of Victor Bono and Florencio Mationg. Bono is also wanted for jumping a $100,000 bond on a narcotics charge."

Freed to smuggle and smoke "hay" and obey its crazy or malign impulses. Of the several kinds of "pot" producing plants cultivated in Mexico the favorite is *cannabis indica*, the same botanical culprit which produces hashish. The Old Man of the Mountain would have chuckled at the connection neatly established between assassination and marijuana by the untoward deaths of two young American peace officers.

16

CONTRABAND
AND
ITS
RUNNERS

The goods furtively passed over the border sometimes take shapes that wouldn't occur to the non-investigator. An item pushed across in the Del Rio and Marfa sectors is *candelilla* wax, produced from a plant of that name and prized by churches as the stuff of altar candles. Over toward the Pacific, lobsters are a frequent form of contraband. In parts of the border nearest to tropical Mexico, monkeys, boa constrictors and gaily colored birds are among the curiosities in which smugglers deal. The purchasers are black-market pet shops, to whose business the United States Government objects on two grounds. Such purveyors of livestock neither pay duty nor conform to the quarantine rules governing incoming wild life. Ever since the pernicious psittacosis epidemic which took so many American lives in the 1920s, the parrot has been a particularly unwelcome piece of contraband. But amateur as well as professional smugglers have continued to promote their entry into America.

"Smuggled Birds Given to Zoo," an item in the Laredo *Times* was headed on January 13, 1956. "The collector of customs at Laredo has received authorization from Washington to turn over to a San Antonio zoo 15 birds which were seized from tourists Tuesday night . . .

"Seizure was made in Laredo by U.S. Immigration Border Patrol, who detained the tourists and seized their 1953 Cadillac as well as the contraband . . .

"The birds consisted of 5 parrots, 4 toucans, 4 finches and 2 cardinals."

The popularity of duty-free and unexamined parrots can be gathered from an April, 1969 seizure described by Allen E. Fry of the Port Isabel Sector's Brownsville Station. "We got word from an informer that smugglers were going to push something across about ten miles downstream from Brownsville—by night, of course—so four of us got there early and hid out near the best crossing point. We had to wait a few hours, but sure enough men started wading the river, carrying bulky objects we couldn't identify in the dark. They put them beside a dirt road that paralleled the Rio Grande and went back across it for more. It was hard to wait without finding out just what sort of contraband was being moved; but we were less interested in smugglers from Mexico than in learning who was going to pick the stuff up on this side of the border. But after several hours more, a truck came along that road, and when it stopped by the contraband, we closed in." Fry shook his head at the recollection. "What we found were crates holding two hundred and thirty-nine parrots—worth $14,000 at going prices."

Run south across the boundary are such various items as gold, munitions and whiskey. But most contraband is northbound and is in the form of narcotics or humans. As the traffic in dope will be separately discussed, the ways and means of handling and moving wetbacks will be the subject of the rest of this chapter.

"There is no limit to the imagination of a smuggler," Paul K. Crosby, Assistant Border Patrol Chief, affirmed in an article published in a 1957 issue of the *I & N Reporter*. "Illegal aliens have been found hidden in automobile trunks, under the seats, between the radiator and grill and between the motor and hoods of vehicles. They have been found in gasoline tank trucks, in sprinkler wagons, in specially built compartments in cars and trucks, and in cramped spaces arranged within all kinds of cargo from lumber and baled hay to frozen fish."

At the headquarters of the Chula Vista Sector there are displays and portfolios of photographs showing wetbacks in all the situations described by Crosby, and more besides. Demonstrating in every case the position which a Mexican alien was actually in when apprehended, these form incredible testimonials to what the human frame can stand. Perhaps the most striking of them didn't involve a man. She was a girl who emerged from her ride beneath the hood of a car with an arm badly scorched from contact with a hot exhaust pipe.

Men shown in these exhibits were suspended from the chassis of automobiles by precarious slings, some so makeshift that they did not offer full support but required using one hand to grip some item in the machine's cellar. More dreadful to contemplate are numerous bodies crammed into—and locked in—such transportation as campers, making journeys of twenty-four hours and more in vehicles not notable for sanitary facilities.

One smuggler dreamed up something even more comfortless than that means of travel. It startled the Patrol's Southwestern Regional Headquarters, which issued a special, if undated, bulletin on the subject. ". . . a Mexican alien arrested in New Mexico was questioned as to his method of entry into the United States. He stated that he had been smuggled across the Rio Grande and placed by the smuggler with twelve other aliens inside a tank of a tank car. He said they spent the balance of the night in the truck, and that the following morning each alien was given a pint bottle of water to drink and then were driven over 200 miles across the desert of New Mexico to a farm area in the middle of the state.

"This story appeared to be preposterous because it was the middle of the summer and the officers knew that the temperature sometimes reached 120 to 130 degrees and the heat from the sun would be unbearable to anyone inside the metal tank."

But when another wetback told the same story, patrolmen investigated. "There were only two such trucks which could be found in the area and two aliens were permitted to see the drivers of these two trucks while they themselves remained hidden. Both positively identified one driver as the smuggler. The driver was arrested, admitted his guilt, and was prosecuted for the offense."

Meanwhile his vehicle had been examined. "The truck was brought to Border Patrol Headquarters and checked. It was found that the bottom quarter of the tank was filled with sand which was thoroughly soaked with water. The driver admitted that his purpose in soaking the sand was to permit water to drip from the sprinkler in the rear of the truck, and therefore cause any officer who stopped him to think that the truck contained only water."

But this coyote, as the bulletin made clear, was a scientist who knew by experiment what he could safely do. "He went on to say that he ran a test on the truck by placing a thermometer on the inside of the tank in order to ascertain whether it would be possible to carry the aliens across the desert in such a manner. He said he found that as long as the truck was moving, the temperature might only reach 140 degrees. He stated that on one trip with thirteen aliens in the truck he had a flat tire in the middle of the desert and before the tire could be changed, six of the aliens fainted from heat exhaustion. He blandly announced, however, that all six recovered as soon as he started up again."

Less careful smugglers sometimes overestimated the endurance powers of their clients. In April of 1969 an abandoned U-Haul trailer was found in San Antonio. From inside came anguished cries which had probably also been heard by the coyote who had towed the trailer from the border town of Del Rio. His decision to proceed no farther with his clients was apparently based on the belief that all was not well with them. There were grounds for such a conclusion. Of the forty-seven wetbacks found in the locked conveyance, three were dead and another ten or twelve had to be hospitalized.

Vinegar fumes on a massive scale couldn't be either soothing or healthful, but these were braved by one devoted band of invaders, according to the 1968 annual report of the Immigration and Naturalization Service. "In July, 1967, an immigrant inspector at San Ysidro became suspicious of the actions of the driver of an empty vinegar tank truck and decided to check the interior of the tank. As soon as the inspector climbed on the top of the truck, the driver fled to Mexico. The inspector opened the tank and found 40 aliens."

At least these were relieved from their misery early. Some that have been discovered—and doubtless many more who were not—must have spent days in wretched confinement. One such instance was related by the report above cited. "In January an Illinois State Trooper stopped a pickup truck near Morris, Illinois, because it was moving at a slow rate of speed and appeared to be overburdened. The vehicle had been topped with aluminum and wood. The trooper found 52 Spanish-speaking males jammed into the enclosed part of the van. Investigators from Chicago responded to the call of local officials, and it was ascertained that all the occupants, except the driver, were illegal aliens from the state of Durango, Mexico, who had entered the United States without inspection in the El Paso area. It was developed that the driver had contacted the aliens in Mexico and offered to assist them into the United States illegally for fees ranging up to $135 per person."

The same 1968 report demonstrates that not all smugglers are men. "A female resident alien was apprehended in the El Centro Sector and charged with the violation of the smuggling statutes. When she stopped her car just short of a traffic check point, two men who had alighted from the car were tracked and taken into custody."

According to the 1967 I & N report, couples are engaged in the traffic. "For $150 per alien, a man and wife team transported aliens in Mexico to an isolated border crossing point and instructed the aliens regarding the meeting place in the United States. The couple would then enter with documents through a port of entry and transport the aliens to a hotel in Yuma, Ariz. After purchasing railroad tickets and giving them to the individuals, the couple would leave for Indio, Calif., by auto to await the arrival of the smuggled aliens on a passenger train. The couple would then transport the group to the vicinity of Coalinga, Calif."

This pair of contraband runners gave honest service. A chance the wetbacks have to take, when entrusting themselves to coyotes, is that they will be cheated. A case in point was cited by a Border Patrol release:

An incident which occurred in the El Centro Sector is illustrative of how criminally inclined Americans attempt to victimize Mexican aliens illegally in the United States. In this case two young Americans had collected money from six illegal Mexican aliens, promising to take the six north by automobile for the sum of $50 each. The two young Americans collected the money from the six Mexicans and proceeded from Coachilla, California, north of Indio on the Dillon Road, which is the old Los Angeles Aqueduct Road now abandoned.

The two young Americans had arranged with another youth who had a spotlight on his car, to cover the spotlight with red cellophane and when they came to an isolated area the third party was to proceed from the rear and turn on the red light. When this happened, the driver and his companion of the car carrying the Mexicans were to tell them, "That is Immigration, we will stop and you get out in the desert and hide." The Mexicans waited for a period of time and proceeded afoot for the 10-mile stretch back to Coachilla. All six aliens were later apprehended. The three young Americans and four other persons involved in this smuggling operation were apprehended, pleaded guilty and were convicted.

An official report dated April 28, 1969, told of another bilking, this time by a man and woman who had posed as employment agents as well as smugglers. Specifically, they had bled three wetbacks of $300 each by agreeing to drive them to Los Angeles, where jobs, they swore, had been lined up for their clients. When they were near an actual or imaginary traffic checking point, they advised the wetbacks to walk around it. The pair who had set up that snipe hunt were not again beheld by the men they had set afoot.

Then there are smugglers who mean to deal honestly with their clients but blunder and wind up trapping themselves. A development of this sort was recited by the 1968 report also. It was a curious incident, as America's Navy wound up the captor of wetbacks. "At the close of the fiscal year, two individuals were awaiting prosecution after illegal entry and their involvement in smuggling five aliens into the United States in a boat. The group departed from Ensenada, Baja Calif., Mexico, in an outboard cruiser bound for the San Diego area. Although a large supply of gasoline was carried, adverse weather and the heavy load caused excessive fuel consumption and the five smuggled aliens were put ashore short of their destination. Unfortunately for the smugglers, the rubber raft used to ferry the five ashore landed at the United States Navy base at North Island, where they were promptly apprehended and placed in the custody of Chula Vista officers."

Thus much for overland smugglers, working alone or in pairs. When coyotes operate as members of gangs, one or more machines may be sent ahead of the car or truck carrying the wetbacks, the purpose of their drivers being to find which roads PIs are checking traffic on or otherwise watching. When a vicinity is scouted by guides in this manner, advice can be given the actual smuggler by inter-car communication systems as sophisticated as those used by officers. For as Assistant Patrol Chief Paul Crosby pointed out in the article above cited, "When a new method of transportation is devised, smugglers will use it. When a new type of communication is devised, smugglers will use that, too."

It is believably asserted that every smuggler who drives vehicles across the line—as opposed to using trucks or cars staked out north of it—has at least one lookout in the United States. Many coyotes are licensed residents or citizens of this country, and by no means all of these are Latin Americans. Anglos are now being found in this traffic, just as they are in that of narcotics smuggling. They have the advantage of protective coloration, being less likely to attract the notice of American officers than the swarthy drivers traditionally associated with the trade.

But if much has been learned about the operations of overland wetback runners, one thing is not known, or at least has not been made public by investigating personnel. And that is, what agencies in the interior's large cities act as the equivalent of fences for inanimate contraband? There must be depots, owned by metropolitan criminals, through which smugglers and the smuggled from the faraway border can make some necessary arrangements.

Specific destinations must be furnished to drivers arriving in big towns with fifty or so aliens. To keep from attracting undesirable notice, men with unspeakable travel stains must be hustled inside premises with several other functions. They must permit clients to make some sort of presentable appearance before applying for jobs; they must serve as bases of operation pending employment; and they must act as intelligence stations for wetbacks and hirers alike.

Such depots must also act as collection bureaus for coyotes, for one rather recent development is that many smugglers no longer demand the entire fee by the end of a long run. Instead they tell Mexicans who else could not afford to become clients that only down payments, supplemented by installments after employment has been found in American cities, are necessary.

There is, furthermore, the question of what intelligence system helps a smuggler decide whither in the United States to speed with contraband. To this a partial answer is that some American firms advertise for wetback help in the newspapers of Mexican towns on or near the boundary. And some of the advertisers were as far from the border as they well could be. An April, 1969 I & N bulletin noted that Ciudad Juarez journals had carried ads from the Green Giant Company and the Doughboy Company, located respectively in the states of Washington and Minnesota.

American employment agencies likewise advertise in suitable Mexican newspapers. Insertions in such journals have been found which refer wetback smugglers to helping hands in El Paso and Los Angeles.

An April, 1969 ad in *El Imparcial* of Hermosillo, proclaimed that companies in the United States were looking for both men and women eager for jobs. It promised advancement, stating that applicants could learn a trade while working.

Sometimes the American employer doubles as the smuggler, an instance being set forth in the 1968 I & N report. "Officers of the Del Rio and Marfa sectors shared in a case involving the use of an airplane to illegally transport Mexican aliens from Del Rio to Seminole, Tex. The arranger, a farmer and businessman, traveled to the border and back in a chartered aircraft to meet and transport the aliens so they could work on his farm."

There may be much more of such air smuggling—carrying men to distant industrial points rather than agricultural sites fairly close to the line. Though air smuggling is guessed as extensive, its dimensions will remain a mystery until the Patrol is furnished with pursuit planes.

For obvious reasons, however, the professional smuggler who drives wetbacks to points distant from the line is not interested in farmhands but only in men who wish industrial jobs. Men hoping for no more than stoop labor can afford to invest just so much of their wages in getting to the scene of employment. It is only the fellow who counts on higher pay in town who can afford to pay current smuggling rates of two to three hundred dollars. And it is certainly true that only an ambitious wetback would have a credit rating that would enable him to be transported far into the United States on an installment plan basis—complete with carrying charges, naturally.

The fact that such arrangements are now made says more about the volume of secret traffic than any other statistic. If a criminal feels that he can forego immediate full payment in favor of making a greater sum over a period of months, he must have strong grounds for believing that percentage is on his side in two ways. In the first place, he must feel that he has an excellent chance of not only completing the initial down payment run but of staying in business long enough to collect all the installments due him. Then he must be sure that the odds favor the wetback as to both promptly securing work and staying employed long enough to pay off a debt freighted with the underworld's interest rates.

So the 8,484 wetbacks found working in this country's industries in fiscal 1968 must have been greatly exceeded by the number added to the American industrial labor force in that year, or a percentage tempting criminals to risk losing most of their pay would not have existed. The same logic urges that the number of caught coyotes must be much smaller than the tally of the never arrested ones.

Of the former the Patrol alone apprehended 1,210 in fiscal 1968, while a few more were nabbed by other law enforcement agencies. Winners or not, they all took a chance on losing more than unfinished installment payments. "Smugglers of aliens," as Paul Crosby pointed out, "are generally prosecuted under Section 274 of the Immigration and Naturalization Act, which imposes a maximum penalty of five years' imprisonment or a fine of $2,000. . . . Section 277 imposes a penalty for five years or a $5,000 fine or both, for aiding or assisting a subversive alien to enter. . . . In addition, the general conspiracy statute, often used in connection with smuggling cases, provides a penalty of five years or $10,000 or both." Repeaters, of course, are liable to more severe penalties.

This puts wetback running in the category of hazardous occupations. But as winners can gross upwards of $1,500 for seven or eight clients crammed into a sedan, and upwards of five times that much, if driving a truck holding thirty-five or forty, the pay, if not the work, is respectable. Then the working conditions are not bad; after a wetback cargo has been assembled by soliciting frequenters of a Mexican border city's red light district, a stint calls for, say, twenty hours of hard driving to an interior city and an unhurried return when ready.

However chosen, the target cities are widely scattered. This is learned at the respective sector headquarters of the Patrol in two already noted ways. From smuggled wetbacks captured near the line, their expected destinations can be ascertained through interviews. Then it is the practice of the Immigration Service to extract from aliens arrested in the interior their points of crossing the boundary, and to notify officers of the affected sectors.

Analyzing the returns from a number of such reports, anti-smuggling officers at Laredo came up with the following figures. Of 137 wetbacks who had been carried into parts away from their sector, no less than forty had been caught in Chicago. The next most favored town was Miami, Florida, where thirty-five were apprehended. Twenty-nine were found in San Antonio, twenty-two at Dallas, seven at Hammond, Indiana, two at Milwaukee and two at Omaha. Other samplings proved that Detroit and Fort Worth were popular goals.

Most of the smugglers caught in the Laredo Sector, though, have been certified as Chicago-bound. And that finding matches reports turned in by anti-smuggling patrolmen of the Del Rio Sector, the next upriver. Emphatically this is true of its Eagle Pass Station, across the bridge from Piedras Negras. There the discovered traffic runs all to the Chicago area, and the official word is that "highly professional criminals" are conducting the smuggling along the Chicago-Piedras Negras axis.

That doesn't necessarily prove that the preponderance of the involved wetbacks are actually employed in Chicago. That city may be, rather, a clearing house for illegal Mexican labor in the whole great North Central industrial zone. This, in turn, could mean that Chicago gang leaders have moved into a crime field which is closely entwined with their old standby of importing and pushing narcotics. But of the links between the smuggling of human beings and dope running more will be set forth in a chapter to come.

Suffice it here to assert that wetback transporters can be classed as hard cases without putting other crimes to their account. Unlike most of their clients, the smugglers from south of the line are not rustics. They are big city toughs, with all the wiles and viciousness of the breed. They are habitually armed, and will use their weapons when the odds seem in favor of getting away with resisting arrest.

PART

V

OF
NARCOTICS
AND
MEXICAN
BORDER
JUMPERS

17

CUSTOMS
VERSUS
HARD
CUSTOMERS

For some reason never modernized to meet changing needs, the Mounted Customs Inspectors ran out their string in 1948. The history of these horsemen is so shadowy that little about them ever found a place in the files of the parent Treasury Department. The activities of one of its later members can be followed in detail, however. Alvin F. Scharf published some writings himself and became the subject of a biography by Garland Roark.

If not the first American to recognize the danger to this country of Mexico considered as a source of narcotics, he was the first to take any eradicating steps. The initial one had to do with a legacy by Chinese infiltrators below the line. It was here earlier told that in the early 1930s the Mexican administration of that day ousted them. But as they couldn't take along the fields they had sown with opium poppy seeds, these remained in a country where peons had learned to prize the drug they produced.

Discovering as much, Scharf undertook to alert Mexican officials to the danger. Gaining the cooperation of some, he was successful in seeing to it that poisonous crops were destroyed. By the close of the middle '30s a series of campaigns all but obliterated a menace which was not to be heard from again until recent years.

Not as successful in extirpating another malevolent crop, he wrote of its perils in a pamphlet titled *Mallihua, a story of marijuana*, which was published in the Sonoran port of Matzatlan in April of 1938. In that same year it was republished in a volume issued by the Texas Folk Lore Society. Edited by the late J. Frank Dobie, this was titled *Coyote Wisdom*.

The legend of the curse of marijuana itself was an Aztec allegory of unknown antiquity. In prefatory matter Scharf developed a number of points. Up in the stratosphere of scholarship, he adduced that the etymology of "marijuana"—itself a Spanish bungling of a lucid Indian term—was that the taker becomes its captive; is "hooked," as would now be said. Down to colloquial earth, he showed that marijuana was known as "the cockroach" for the same reason—once that aggressive insect is given the freedom of a house, it takes over.

For illustration he published several stanzas of a song which was a favorite of Pancho Villa's bandidos, one of whom may have been its author. By the 1930s it had moved as far north of the border as New York, to name but one of the cities where it was chanted by people who had no notion as to its meaning. Scharf translated the first stanza thus:

> *The cucaracha, the cucaracha*
> *He can't travel any more.*
> *Because he lacks, because he hasn't*
> *Marihuana for to smoke.*

"Cucaracha," as Scharf noted, was a "slang word for the *marihuanero*, the addict or smoker of marijuana—a drug that has come to be . . . a problem nearly as serious as that of opium."

When that was written cockroaches were to be found only on the fringes of American society. About the only users were thieves, whores and dropouts from the arts. At that time officers on the border thought of marijuana as a Mexican addiction. It will be remembered that when fifty pounds of the narcotic were seized by officers at El Paso in the '30s, a newspaper joked that it would have been enough to snogger all Juarez. Although the stuff had been found on the American side of the line, its relation to the United States wasn't recognized. Marijuana was something that Mexican criminals and opposite numbers among Latin American smoked. The better run of people from across the Rio Grande weren't cucarachas and Anglos of course, not at all.

The innocence of the period was shown, too, by the fact that a load of fifty pounds was described as one of the heaviest intercepted in years. That being so, drugs were not a serious problem to the Customs Agents who came more and more to supplant the outmoded Mounted Customs Inspectors. After the Prohibition Era most contraband was run through towns which had railroad connections with Mexico's interior, where most of the smugglerable goods came from. These were silver, handworked textiles, leather, jewelry and other products of handicraft.

But Customs officers have the job of foiling those who are trying to dodge payment of export duties as well as smugglers allergic to import tariffs. For a while, in the post-Volstead years, there was as much or more in the way of goods being pushed into Mexico than was traveling the other way. Notable among manufacturies from the north were the guns and ammunition of American make which were welcomed by Mexican revolutionaries.

But the comparatively harmless guns—which did few Americans, at least, any hurt—came to play second fiddle as border menaces. During the fifties the rise of the dope traffic made all other Customs problems minor ones along the line. The reasons could be easily read in the rewards supply could reap from demand.

According to Jackson Salter, Jr., the Customs Agent in charge at El Paso, 1,000 cigarettes can be rolled from one pound of "wheat" or marijuana. The reefers or individual cigarettes bring anywhere from fifty cents to a dollar each. On a pound of hay so retailed a sum of from five hundred to a thousand dollars can be realized. Thus at top retail prices one ounce of grass can fetch more than eighty bucks and a thousand pounds of it a million iron men.

Such are the possible financial returns from quantities of run-of-the-mill marijuana, a term that in Mexico covers several floral species with narcotic properties. The classical McCoy is *cannabis indica*, or the drug-producing variety of hemp; the hashish of the Near East and the bhang of farther Asian parts. Not native to Mexico, this has been naturalized where conditions are favorable and identified

191

with narcotics from plants that have no true kinship with it. Wherever in Mexico it flourishes, *cannabis indica* produces what is known as marijuana; but in Sonora, for instance, a drug identically labeled comes from *nicotiana glauca*, cousin of the tobacco plant.

The term "hashish" as now used by officers combatting the spread of cockroachism does not appear to distinguish between the sources of marijuana. What it means rather is a carefully processed marijuana of superior potency. Perhaps it is only possible to produce marijuana at its noxious worst from *cannabis indica*, but science has not yet pronounced to that effect.

Whatever its source, hashish is so precious that it is measured not in pounds but in grams. There are a thousand of this basic metric unit to roughly two and two-tenths pounds. The exact price of a gram is hard to fix, because hashish is a border pearl that is newly gaining admirers; but a sophisticated marijuanero would give for it many times the worth of ordinary wheat.

Not as much as a merchant could get for a like quantity of heroin, to be sure. This aristocrat of the drug field has a more or less established price. At its cheapest, according to Salter, it will bring thirty dollars a gram. That's the price of the Mexican variety, produced from the descendants of the poppies that Alvin Scharf didn't manage to destroy. Mexican heroin is brownish, while the better-prized European variety—which fetches forty dollars a gram—is white. Made largely in France, this increasingly enters the United States by way of Mexico. And so far it jumps the border in greater quantities than the home-grown pestilence

The smuggler of a quarter of a pound of this superior venom can exchange it for about forty-five hundred dollars, as opposed to a hundred and forty skins for four ounces of gold. And gold is cheap as compared with marijuana of ordinary good quality, capable as it is of retailing at two hundred and fifty dollars for a quarter of a pound. In between the high and low of the drug market stand not only hashish, as above defined, but cocaine and opium for smoking rather than intravenous injection.

The tremendous prices for poisonous plant essences are possible because of what Aztecs realized as to the original variant of marijuana. The takers become owned by it or any other mind-eating narcotic form. The cockroach has moved in and everything else is secondary to it.

"Addicts," as Don Whitehead observed in a book about the Customs Bureau titled *Border Guard,* "will beg, borrow, steal and kill to obtain money with which to satisfy the terrible craving for narcotics once they are hooked." The seller's market being thus a perfect one, smugglers moved into it in mounting numbers.

At first those along the border were all of the same Pachuco breed that had earlier run liquor. Later changing to human contraband, they doubled as dope smugglers or made narcotics their specialty when the growing popularity of drugs in America made that feasible.

Throughout the 1940s and '50s, the traffic consisted almost entirely of marijuana, and as far as the line's smugglers were concerned, it was local. As was true of liquor runners, they would bring "wheat" to some agreed point in one of the border states and let American handlers take it from there. But by 1960 the climbing prices changed that situation. Anxious to be in on the big killing instead of mere suppliers to such, Mexican smugglers began making deliveries to New York, Chicago, Detroit and other great hives of marijuaneros.

Conversely, dealers in big towns began visiting the border to inspect the quality of "hay" before purchasing instead of leaving the selection up to Mexicans. The outcome of one such business trip was related by Whitehead. The gist of his story was that a Laredo Customs Agent named Fred Rody, Jr., learned from one of his informers that an *Americano* was in the whorehouse quarter of Nuevo Laredo, shopping for twenty pounds of marijuana, about $10,000 worth. Following up the tip, Rody found that the shopper was a well-known narcotics dealer from New Orleans called John Vaccaro.

Stalking this fellow, Rody and a brother Agent named Simpson saw a man put a suitcase in the front seat of a car whose back seat occupants were Mrs. Vaccaro and a daughter. It developed that the gentleman from Louisiana didn't want to be caught. Feigning compliance when the Customs Agents drew abreast of him in their own machine, he gunned his own when they stopped to make the arrest. He had something to gun, too. The date being August 7, 1960, it was hot in Texas but not in a class with Vaccaro's rod. Rody worked his car up to the pretty good highway speed of 110 miles an hour and was still not in the race.

Summoned by radio and taking over was Agent Grady Grazner, tooling a special police-interceptor job. The runway being U.S. Highway 59, Grazner had revved his torrid heap up to a hundred and thirty miles per hour by the time he got near enough to the smuggler's to bump it. No man to take a hint, even in the form of four warning shots, Vaccaro waited until the front wheels of the Agent's crate were par with the rear ones of his own and abruptly veered. The move was so neatly made that it knocked Grazner's car aside without maladjusting the smuggler's job.

The road pulled out from under him, and it, Grazner rolled over and bounced for a total of 471 feet. Somehow surviving this, he was unable to resume pursuit, but the trailing Rody had used his radio to alert police farther out on Highway 59. Where it nears Ferret, Texas, they had rigged a roadblock which seemed to offer an exit, its form a dirt road. But Vaccaro was a city lad, and slick as he was on pavement, he didn't know how to handle the situation when his car started bumping along ruts. Caught up with, he got twenty-five years; but he can be allowed to have been in the class with the Argonaut celebrated in verse by Mark Twain. "He done his level best" in his last day of freedom.

While professionals from other parts formed a new border feature in the early 1960s, amateurs from all over the United States made up the novelty of the decade's latter years. But it is the nature of this new order of smugglers that startled Customs officers. "Narcotics smugglers in these parts used to be Mexicans or ignorant American trash," Jackson Salter mused on April 25, 1969, "but in the last couple of years American people from good homes are getting involved. And I said 'people,' not 'men,' for women from prosperous white families are engaged in the business, too."

The youth of many such law-breakers troubles Customs Bureau men, also. The following is taken from a Service news release dated October 17, 1968: "In an effort to establish the age group of the majority of persons arrested in connection with narcotics and marijuana smuggling, a review covering the last six months of the fiscal year was made.

"Of 442 persons arrested in marijuana cases, 92 were 19 or under, 266 were in the age group from 20 to 30, and 84 were over 30; 99 were arrested for heroin and cocaine violations, five of whom were 19 years of age or under, 53 were in the age group from 20 to 30, and 41 were over 30; 92 were arrested in connection with the smuggling of dangerous drugs [meaning here the not yet dealt with pills that float users on 'trips' of various lengths]. Of these 16 were 19 or under, 52 were in the 20 to 30 age group, and 24 were over 30."

Some of the young people, in particular, operate by mail. On April 25, 1969, Chief Agent Salter was notified by the international division of the El Paso Post Office that a parcel had arrived from Mexico which was thought to contain contraband. Not all line-crossing packages are inspected by the Postal Service, but spot checks are made to obtain a general idea of the extent to which the mail is used for lawless purposes, and when one is considered hot, the men of the Customs Bureau are automatically notified.

Salter put out an alert for Customs Agent Don Smith, who in due course showed up. Apprised of what was afoot, he picked up the camera the case called for and proceeded to investigate. The parcel in question had been sent by a Mr. Riley of Acapulco to a Miss Holden, of Boulder, Colorado, both doubtless students at the university of that state. What he had sent her, as a memorial of his trip to Mexico, was a papier-mâché statue of two embracing infants. This might have been held a cute souvenir but for one overlooked fact. In its natural state papier-mâché is light, and this sample of it weighed a lot more than its size warranted.

By inconspicuously puncturing one of the affectionate pair of children, Smith ascertained that their joint contents was marijuana. The hole adroitly sealed, the statue was weighed. By deducting the estimated weight of the papier-mâché container, it was found that a male cucaracha had expressed his admiration for a female of the species by purchasing her about four and a half pounds of pot.

The sender being out of reach, the receiver was the target of the El Paso Customs Agents. Of the twelve assigned to a district which includes New Mexico and Colorado, as well as Texas west of the Pecos, only eleven were stationed on the Rio Grande. The other, conveniently for Don Smith's next move, was staked out in Denver. As Boulder is suburban to Colorado's metropolis, all mail from out-of-state is channeled through the Denver Post Office.

Proceeding on that knowledge Smith marked the burdened infants in a fashion that would only be clear to an initiate of the Service. Next, he measured the statue with a tailor's care, photographed it from all conceivable angles, rewrapped the parcel and made a cameral record of it as well as the inscriptions thereon. With this information forwarded to the Customs Agent in Denver, the trap was about to close on the receiver at the Boulder end of the smuggle. Because duty must eventually be paid on them, packages from foreign parts go through special channels. Alerted to watch for this one by the Denver Customs Agent, inspectors at that city's P.O. would tell him when to proceed to Boulder, there to wait for Miss Holden to come and pay the tariff due on Mr. Riley's dandy gift.

Among the exhibits to be found in the offices of the El Paso Customs Agency is another papier-mâché toy. Its shape is that of an elephant, and on display beside it is the note that accompanied the small pachyderm when confiscated: "I hope my little niece will treasure this little Indian elephant from her loving uncle Ted and have a happy birthday." Uncle Ted's gift held one pound of marijuana, five ounces of hashish and three ounces of heroin. Since their combined value would add up to some few thousands of dollars, he must have loved his little niece very much.

This, too, must have been a matter of contraband-running by mail. Other lots of narcotics in all fields are known in some cases, and suspected in many more, to have been wafted across the boundary by airplanes. But until feathered with equipment to meet these birds on their own aerial level, Customs men of the border can only speculate as to the amount of flown contraband of this species and deplore their inability to meet its runners on their own lofty level. As was pointed out by the Del Rio's Assistant Border Patrol Chief, William Toney, the line's Customs Agents are allowed but one unspeedy machine to police the ether piled up above 2,000 miles of border.

But whether brought into the United States from Mexico by ground vehicles or winged ones, by professionals or amateurs, by Mexicans or Anglos, by young people or those advanced in years, the story is a consistent one. With the exception of smokable opium, which enjoyed a popularity in 1968 which was not at all reflected in the bracketing twelfmonths, the 1967 flow of narcotics over the boundary had jumped from a creek to a river three months before the end of fiscal 1969.

The seizures tallied for the region which includes the El Paso Customs District were as follows from June 30, 1966, to the end of March, 1969: For marijuana, the 2,103 pounds seized by officers in 1967 was more than doubled by the 4,552 pounds captured in 1968, and this total in turn was very nearly doubled by the 8,808 pounds impounded during only fiscal 1969's first nine months. Concerning heroin the report was more uneven, though the ending was similar. The 6,785 grams seized in 1967 overmatched the 5,900 taken from smugglers in '68 but were notably less than the 7,095 wrenched from smugglers in the first three quarters of '69. Far more dramatic were the gains achieved by hashish during the same period. In fiscal 1967, the confiscated total was but eighty-five grams. In 1968 that modest take was multiplied nearly nine times, the reading being seven hundred and sixty-five grams. The 2,899 grams impounded by the end of 1969's March more than tripled the take during the previous complete fiscal calendar run.

Not computed were LSD and a variety of lesser known but equally dizzying chemical preparations, lumped as "dangerous drugs" by Salter. During calendar 1968, he said, 14,657 preparations in this category had been found on smugglers caught in the El Paso area.

These are all newcomers to the field of dope, but downstream and around the Big Bend at Laredo a genuine North American old-timer is making a bid for recognition. This is the fruit of a turnip-shaped cactus common on the Great Plains of Texas and matching parts of Mexico. Scientists call it *lophophora Williamsii*. Spanish speakers know it as peyote and Anglos as mescal buttons or dry whiskey. The handle mostly used now is peyote, however.

The item and its properties are thus described in the old *Century* dictionary: "The tops of the plants are collected by the Indians and dried, forming button-like masses an inch or more in diameter and about a quarter of an inch thick. These buttons have narcotic properties and in Texas are sometimes called *dry whisky*. They are either chewed dry or added to tizwin, mescal or other alcoholic drinks. They produce a delirious exhilaration which enables the Indians to perform certain ceremonial dances for many successive hours without fatigue. The effect is that of opium, though in some cases a condition of exaltation is induced resembling that produced by Indian hemp [bhang-cannabis indica-marijuana]. Several alkaloids have been isolated from the plant, some of which resemble morphine, others strychnine, in their effects upon animals. . . ."

This dainty morsel was the subject of remarks by Walter J. Pardaen, Assistant Chief of the Customs Agency at Laredo. "University kids have discovered peyote, and we're in a bind about it because laws haven't caught up with it yet. The Navajos and other Indian tribes still use it ceremonially; as it's part of their religion they've always been allowed to gather peyote around here or anywhere else they can find it. It was never imagined that white people would want it, but kids have found a way to get free trips and pick the stuff like berries."

Important as narcotics and associated items are, they are not the sole concern of the border's Customs Agents. Chief among other sorts of contraband are munitions, watches, jewelry, hot money, gold and silver coins and bullion. On January 13, 1967, Laredo agents intercepted sixty bars of gold weighing a kilogram, or something better than two and two tenths pounds each. The value of the shipment was $68,700.

"That was the last of a string of intercepted shipments," Pardaen said. "There were twelve others, all of around the same size, and the total worth was about a million. We worked on the case in cooperation with Canada's Mounties and the Mexican Federal Judicial Police. The gold came from Canada and was shipped to a non-existent Mexican consignee in Monterey. We figured that the bullion was really supposed to be on its way to India or Pakistan where gold brings seventy dollars an ounce as opposed to thirty-five in this country."

Returning to the subject of narcotics, Pardean agreed with Salter that in recent years "people of good background have taken up dope smuggling. The age bracket of those involved has lowered, and lots of the kids caught with the stuff aren't hippies. They're of both sexes, and they come to the border to make their own deals with Mexican peddlers that don't always hang out in nice places. Worse yet, they're not interested in just grass; more and more of them are being found with harder stuff."

Mexico, he explained, is being increasingly used by smugglers from other parts as a channel for narcotics intended for the United States. Laredo agents made a 1969 haul of seventy-six pounds of white heroin which they are sure came from Europe, because of its purity and strength. European heroin is snow-white and 95 percent pure, but since Mexican laboratories have not yet mastered the process of extracting it from morphine, their brown produce is not of a strength to match the other.

As of May 2, 1969, cocaine was riding novelly high, there having been four recent Laredo hauls. Mexico produces no match for this breed of hop, which comes from a shrub native to Peru and Bolivia, albeit naturalized with success in Java and latterly in another mountainous island called Cuba.

The professional smugglers of all types of narcotics ford the Rio Grande with their wares, cross it in boats, walk and ride over it on bridges and fly above it in planes. The airborne smuggler need not trouble to land in order to make his point. He can drop his package in some vicinity agreed upon by phone, mail or personal conference with the operative who awaits its arrival on the American side. This fellow may be present to watch the contraband land or he may post a marker at a spot which he visits after the plane has passed and perhaps with darkness for cover.

"The air drop method is on the increase," Salter of the El Paso Customs Agency said, "and as the only Service plane on the entire border is in California, our best counter-measure is a radar screen. And sometimes that isn't good enough, for pilots who know about the device can fly under the screen by staying very close to the ground."

The only other means the Agents have for catching up with airborne smugglers is to get tips about their operations. Like the Patrol's anti-smuggling officers, each Agent has a staff of informers. As professional narcotics runners are a stop-at-nothing lot, those who spy upon them take long chances. The pay, as it has to be, is good. For each pound of marijuana seized because of an informer's tip, the reward is fifty dollars. For more valuable drugs, payment is scaled up accordingly.

Because of their fewness, the line's Customs Agents work largely in the towns where they are stationed and the Mexican supply base across the way. Out on the highways, accordingly, many of the seizures are made by patrolmen, acting in their capacity of ex-officio Customs officers. They, too, of course, have noticed the great pick-up in the dope traffic in recent years. In terms of dollar values, for instance, the amount of narcotics seized by PIs in fiscal 1967 was four and a half times the quantity captured in fiscal '66. Typical cases cited in minutes of various sectors will be briefed in the next paragraph.

On January 11, 1968, patrolmen from El Centro intercepted two Los Angeles-bound cars driven by wetbacks who had been hired in Mexico to drive the cars to said American city and leave them at an arranged spot. Search revealed that between them the machines carried 250 kilograms of marijuana valued at $55,000. . . . On Jan. 28, 1968, PIs from Laredo nabbed a driver who was transporting $80,000 worth of heroin to San Antonio. . . . During a traffic check on May 24, 1968, patrolmen from the Temecula, California, Station noticed that the bed of a truck had been raised above its normal position. Ordering the flooring removed, they found 224 kilograms of marijuana with a price tag of $49,280. Another find was a .38 calibre pistol carried by one of the truck's two occupants. . . . In the course of another traffic check operation—this one conducted at

Las Cruces, New Mexico, by officers of the El Paso Sector—PIs arrested automobilists who were on their way to Albuquerque with $50,000 worth of heroin. . . . On an undated but recent occasion PIs at Campo, California, apprehended eight Anglos in possession of 300 pounds of marijuana, 640 assorted drug capsules and six capsules of heroin.

Because of heavy involvement with the ballooning narcotics traffic, Patrol officials are as grimly concerned as those of the Customs Bureau. One commenter was M.E. "Buck" Hensley, Chief of the Del Rio Sector. "It was easier to understand the trade when the only people in it were professional crooks and bums trying to make some fast money, but when well-heeled people of education get their hands in that dirt for the fun of it, it's hard to figure out an answer."

Chief James Patrick Kelly of the Tucson Sector puts much of the blame on pundits pronouncing on the subject without benefit of knowing what they are holding forth about. "I keep reading articles by supposedly learned men who assure the public that they've probed the subject and there's not a lick of harm in marijuana." His face and tone were proofs that he wasn't a follower of the quoted swamis. "I've been in border police work for a long while and during that time I've seen any number of men so crazed with marijuana that they were beyond the reach of feeling, let alone reason. It's necessary to get rough when arresting a fellow out of his head, but men hopped up on marijuana don't know they are being hurt and only quit trying to attack officers when they're so tied up that they can't."

Fortunately for the country the heads of the Federal Government side with the viewpoint of Customs and Patrol officials rather than with doctors of the philosophy of cockroachism. In consequence, September 1969 saw the commencement of a drive against the border's narcotic traffic labeled Operation Intercept. News of it was broadcast in a United Press International dispatch datelined San Diego, September 22:

> The United States clamped a massive land, sea and air surveillance on 2,500 miles of the U.S.–Mexican border yesterday in a dramatic move to cut off the flow of marijuana and dangerous drugs. . . . The operation, utilizing radar, search planes, Coast Guard and Navy ships and a sharply augmented force of inspectors at crossing points, covered the border of Mexico where it adjoins the states of California, Arizona, New Mexico and

200

Texas. . . . In a split-second move in which "Operation Intercept" was not sprung until all agents were at their posts, the government launched intensified inspection of vehicles and persons crossing the border at 31 land points and at 27 airports at which international flights are authorized to land. . . .

Federal agents revealed that the pilot of a light plane carrying about 1,000 pounds of marijuana had been caught earlier and arrested after he flew over the border and was followed by a government plane when he landed at Bakersfield, Calif. . . . Officials identified the pilot as Michael Thomas Mitchell, 23, of Seattle, a student at the University of Washington. They said his rented Cherokee plane was loaded with suitcases and burlap sacks containing 532 bricks of marijuana of a kilo size, weighing about two pounds apiece. . . .

Federal agents said Mitchell told them he bought the marijuana in Mazatlan, Mexico, for $27,000 and planned to fly it to Berkeley, Calif., where it could bring an amount many times the purchase price when sold in marijuana cigarettes.

There are all sorts of means for making one's laborious way through today's universities, including the double duty of being at once amateur athletes and salaried hirelings. Some less dedicated students even work to pay their way, so perhaps an eyebrow should not be raised at a scholar, game to see what could be realized on $27,000 invested in grass.

In any case the government of Mexico was wise enough to wish to join the United States in a mobilization against what was recognized as a bilateral emergency. With the resultant proffer of assistance from Mexico City, the drive against the border's malignant promoters of narcotics was rechristened Operation-Intercept-Cooperation.

The Mexican share of the campaign was mainly a commitment to eradicating the source of marijuana by destroying *cannabis indica* and the several unrelated plants whence the narcotic known as marijuana is derived. If faithfully carried through, that basic part of the boundary's narcotic traffic would be ended. Unluckily, history remembers that earlier Mexican determinations to get rid of the grass on which marijuaneros love to graze have been in vain.

As for Operation Intercept, it was an experiment which was successful in two departments and may be expected to be followed by a general strengthening of the Border's Customs Agencies both as to personnel and equipment. The seizures cited by the Customs Bureau's Office of Information were "Marihuana—5,907.2 pounds; Hashish —78 pounds; Peyote—60 pounds; Heroin—3.85 pounds; Dangerous Drugs—578,506 five-grain units."

In commenting on the results, Bureau spokesman Gary E. Heath noted: "It was marijuana and such dangerous drugs as amphetamines and barbiturates that were mainly interdicted. . . . There certainly was a tendency of smugglers to lay low during Operation Intercept. . . . Amateurs might still take a chance, but professionals would not. . . . The Operation Intercept effort did affect the marijuana supply in particular. It was quite apparent that the supply was very limited and in many localities virtually unobtainable."

18

THE
WETBACK
AND HIS
MODERN
MEANING

In his book titled *Border Guard*, Don Whitehead wrote that nobody knows either the amount of narcotics smuggled into the United States or the share of it shortstopped by officers. "Some Customs agents," he continued, "estimate that law enforcement officials seize less than ten percent of the total."

What is true of the country as a whole can be assumed to be more or less true of the border. And what holds true with respect to narcotics applies with equal force to wetbacks. All that is known about the number who daily or annually try to sneak into the United States is that for every one foiled, many more succeed.

That will remain the situation as long as the Border Patrol is no better equipped than at present to meet overwhelming geographical odds. For however skilled and hard working PIs may be, they cannot change the fact that for every crossing point they watch there are numberless ones that stay unguarded. While they do a wonderful job of tracking men down within reasonable reach of a sector headquarters, they have not the means of plugging holes farther out in boundary frontages of immense extent. They can spot-check areas the size of half a dozen Eastern states, but until able to spare the men for roving task forces, they cannot patrol them in the sense of making regular investigations.

So, as of 1970, wetbacks swarm over the border in quantities that may be named by taking the guess of the above quoted Customs Agents as a talking point. If 100,000 wetbacks are apprehended in a given year, 1,000,000 may infiltrate the boundary and become entrenched in America. It was remarked that most of those caught after they had found employment were working on farms or ranches in some part of the country. But the ones that have abandoned farming are not as easy to spot.

Some things have earlier been said about the modern wetback; more will follow. He differs from his predecessors of the 1940s and early '50s in several respects. For one thing he never enters the United States as a family man. Women of the tribe are rarely present, and are as apt to be found with another job-seeking woman as with a man. What Mexicans learned from Operation Wetback was that a man immigrating illegally with a wife and children was too burdened to escape the Patrol. The new sort of invader came as a stag, and the mobility thus gained made other changes possible. The man with a family installed it in some sort of a den close to the line and was locked there. The singleton was not only able to move into the interior but indulge his curiosity about cities.

Then many wetbacks of the 1960s had earlier been braceros. Thus migratorily employed, they had learned that there was much more to the United States than the international boundary zone. They had doubtless visited some sizable towns and found the pay was better. Certainly many had found that away from the border, patrolmen weren't forever showing up to check the status of field hands.

Moving north to get out of reach of PIs, wetbacks first commenced to abandon the border and next began to cease being largely rural. The drift away from farms may have started simply because it was possible to get steady work in cities. The word may have been passed that an illegal alien was less apt to be caught doing indoor work. In cosmopolitan and polyglot towns he was less apt to be noticed and he was safe from mass inspection by airplane. But whatever the factors, the wetback of the middle and late sixties was an urban fact.

Not all wetbacks enter the United States merely because the employment grass is greener north of the boundary. There are subversives about whom the Immigration Service is chary of talking and such runagates from justice as a pair described in the 1968 I & N Report:

> José Cruz-Gonzales was apprehended in Chicago for illegal entry and transferred to the detention facility at El Paso. Remarks made by him indicated that he might be wanted in Mexico, and the Chief of Police at Juarez was notified. . . . He advised that they had been looking for him since 1961 for killing a man with a .32 caliber pistol. . . .
>
> Mario Quesada-Lujan brutally murdered a schoolteacher in Mexico on December 4, 1966. Early in November, 1967, Mexican authorities informed the Service that Quesada was believed to be living in Los Angeles. Investigators from our Los Angeles office located him within a short time and took him into custody for illegal entry. . . .

It will be noted that one of these dangerous felons was at large in this country for some six years before he was caught up with. That fact introduces the question as to why wetbacks, once they succeed in getting beyond the Patrol's sphere of authority, are hard to root out. Some of the answers can be found in national statistics.

The forty-eight connected United States contain 200,000,000 of the least surveyed people in the world. It is possible to traverse most of the multimillion lineal miles of highways which criss-cross their 3,000,000 square miles without meeting policemen. Encountered, these are no problem to any but flagrant cut-ups and criminals for whom lookouts have been posted.

In transit to his chosen point, the well-behaved invader will arouse no curiosity in the citizens he passes. Vague when it comes to differentiation—most couldn't tell a wetback from a Levantine or a Hindu—Americans are sophisticated as to the idea of foreigners and are startled by encounters with none, whatever his hue or costume. So if his conduct doesn't cause police to wonder about him, an illegal alien can count on plain highway sailing until he finds cover in a city. Of communities in this class America has about seventy with a population of a quarter of a million or more, counting only those huddled in their corporate limits. In such teeming communities, the problem for most people is to be noticeable rather than be robbed of identity by submersion in the swarm. Conversely, the metropolitan man whose sole ambition is not to be discerned can be very inconspicuous indeed.

That is above all true if he has no known identity to begin with. It is one thing to look for Juan Gomez or John Smith, wanted by the law for specific offenses, and another to be on the hunt for faceless and nameless committers of a crime that never attracted public attention to begin with.

Then, there is the fact that the wetback is often able to blend with people resembling him in appearance and language, who have every right to be in the United States. In addition to white Latin American citizens, there are hundreds of thousands of dominantly Indian ones. And there were, as of the close of fiscal 1968, 684,533 Mexican nationals, most of them dusky, who are legally in residence north of the border.

In general, the only Americans who are aware of wetbacks in their midst are the employers who choose to keep mum on the subject. With the odds heavily in his favor both at the line and north of it, the Mexican peon becomes the confident man of two countries, described by Virgil Bliven of the Chula Vista Sector. "When one of 'em's picked up on his first try, he's straight paisano, right off the farm and not really knowing where he's going, let alone how he's going to get along. By the time he's stopped at the border again, he's been in the United States and gone back to show the people at home his American clothes; and he's only a little nervous when nabbed. By the time he's caught the third or fourth time, he's a man of the world. He's been around. He's been arrested before and knows that nothing's going to happen to him except to be sent back to try it again, so he'll laugh and kid with you when you're questioning him."

But whether he's a scared neophyte or an amused veteran, the wetback has ways of financing trips to the United States which range from primitive to up-to-date contracts. The matter was discussed by Intelligence Officer James F. Gray of the El Paso Sector. "Some of them put their women in pawn in cat houses. By such deals men both raise the travel money they need and arrange for their wives' support while they're away. But financing trips for men who intend to work in the United States has become a regular business down there, and loan sharks and even banks with clients that have venture capital to invest will back experienced wets."

In common with the smuggler who makes an installment plan deal with his passengers, Mexican money lenders—who probably know the inside arithmetic of the traffic across the line better than any American officers—trust the odds they find piled high on their side. So the sponsoring of Mexican prospectors of American industrial fields has become a standby, as harmful to the nation with one half of the border as its other owner. For the Republic of Mexico, no less than any other country in the world's history, cannot but be debased when investments of energy and capital are aimed at nothing higher than bloodsucking another land.

Details of the damages inflicted by these trespassers have been offered in earlier caustic terms. But one thing must be said in admiration of the wetbacks. And it should drown out all the political claptrap and professional sobbing about America's "disadvantaged" people who can't find employment in their native country. Courtesy of Federal and state governments, the out-of-work United States citizen has money to house and feed himself while looking for employment, assuming that is really his mission. The language of the country is his native one. He is not handicapped by being subject to arrest and deportation if found at salaried work by investigating authorities. And he lives, unchallenged and rightfully, where jobs are available on a major scale, *in as much as untold thousands of wetbacks annually find them, forfeit them, when minded to visit their homeland and seek renewed American employment in the confidence, based on experience, that it will be found when sought for.*

Now for the situation of the Mexican invader who beats an American city dweller to a job only a mile or so from the latter's home. Some live farther away from the Chicago area, say, but the earlier dealt with Guanajuato Joe has two thousand beeline miles to negotiate before he can begin to compete with a man living figuratively or exactly right around the corner from possible employment. On his first trip, especially, the wetback is "disadvantaged" in other ways. He speaks English brokenly, if at all; and sometimes the Spanish of exploring wetbacks isn't much better, for their real fluency lies in some Indian jargon.

He may have a much rougher row to hoe, but first he will be considered as a fellow who has managed transportation as far as the border, plus the capital to hire the services of a smuggler by full or partial payment. Unless he can also afford fraudulent credentials, getting across the line itself is no luxury. If not called upon to downright swim or ford the Rio Grande, he negotiates it in any weather via an inflated inner tube, a log, a canvas boat or one fashioned of automobile hoods. Such cruises differ from rides on some form of municipal transportation inasmuch as they are undertaken in the full knowledge that Patrol spoil-sports may be lurking near all the most convenient crossing points. Assuming that all is well, though, the wetback has made up 500 of the miles he was behind the "disadvantaged" American at the beginning of the race for employment.

The anguish and even mortal dangers which he may have to endure while being conveyed from the line to an interior city by a coyote are subjects of marvel. Sardines have plenty of fresh air and elbow room compared to many of the wetbacks who pay to be transported through the United States already occupied by "disadvantaged" Americans. The gruesome details were presented in the chapter covering smugglers.

Now for the invader who couldn't afford the luxury of being smuggled to some big American town. Coming from more primitive parts of Mexico than the lads who had it easy, he hoofed it across the Great Plateau to the border, living on tortillas, cactus fruit and small game knocked over with a slingshot. Arrived at the border, he may find himself confronted by fifty to seventy-five miles of desert wilderness. His equipment for such rough jaunts consists of the tatters he's standing in, a bag of tortillas, a plastic water bottle—a disused Clorox jug is the favorite cantina—and what the Marfa Sector's Riley Barlow defines as "a built-in compass." At the conclusion of this march he must ride the rods or thumb rides for a thousand or so miles in order to get where the going is still bound to be tough for him.

Whether smuggled or making it on his own, the wetback making his first trip to America doesn't speak or understand English. He's either dead broke or, at the most, has a few dollars to carry him. Half the time he has no clothes but the one's he's roughed it in for weeks. He has had no experience at any type of work but that of a farmer or chore boy. He's a fugitive, besides, who has to be very careful where he shows himself in a foreign city until he can afford to buy American clothes and blend with the scenery. But unless caught up with right after his arrival, he is found in possession of a job—and one that's often no more than a few blocks from the home of the "disadvantaged" American who reports year after year to some Government welfare agency that there's simply no work to be had.

The foregoing typical case histories are bound to inspire respect for the pluck and enterprise of the wetback. But that doesn't alter the fact that he remains a menace to the welfare of the United States that cannot be overestimated. Every year he invades the nation's interior in ever multiplying numbers. No census has been taken between 1964 and 1969, of course; and it is probable that the 1970 one will tell little about evasive criminals sheltered by law-breaking employers.

Yet one statement can be used as a yardstick. It has been estimated by immigration officials that if the wetback could be eliminated, so could America's entire crippling welfare program, barring only aid to the physically incapacitated.

With wetbacks out of the way, the gaps in labor's ranks would be so wide that neither Americans who do not wish to work, nor the Government officials who thrive on covering up for them, could hide behind the cry of "We can't find jobs." Denied the use of wetbacks at bargain prices, industrialists, businessmen and farmers would clamor for American workmen. And no longer able to break laws by paying substandard wages, employers would be forced to offer United States citizens salaries which they could not turn down without confessing that they had no lust for any way of life except to be supported at public expense.

It goes without saying that the wetback himself would be better off, were he denied a furtive and unnatural order of living and be required to turn his in many ways admirable energies towards constructive goals within his own country. And the Mexican nation would profit from directing purposefully the initiative, determination and adaptability which the wetback now squanders on a futile way of life. Mexico's stake in the matter is only incidentally a subject of this chronicle, however.

Here the paramount point is that the illegal Mexican immigrant should be kept from remaining any considerable part of the American social pattern. To do so demands strengthening the watch on the border and cracking down on habitual employers of criminals.

These have been treated as the smashers of immigration laws only, and they seem to be able to evade any penalty, if they compound their felony with the flick of a forked tongue. But they are guilty of far more than breaking the law against hiring illegal aliens. They are smashing tax laws by hiring men who pay no taxes, and which employers cover up—while saving money themselves—by dodging social security payments. They are breaking health laws and are guilty of maintaining a nuisance by hiring men who pass the border without being ascertained as physically fit, and often bring communicable diseases with them. They are breaking a host of labor laws, including ones that regulate wages, hours, insurance and workman's compensation in the event of accident.

The Federal departments of the Treasury, Labor, and Health, Education and Welfare are therefore as concerned in the matter as the Department of Justice. It would seem that these four great divisions of the national administration could promote a jointly sponsored legislative act that would take all the profit and fun out of hiring wetbacks.

Related legal action could usefully take the form of authorizing a large task force of Immigrant Inspectors, moving from city to city, empowered to sift commercial premises for criminal aliens. By transferring Operation Wetback from rural regions near the line to industrial ones apart from it, the invaders could be weeded out of town diggings. A simpler but also necessary maneuver could separate them from America's migratory farm labor force.

Should the Border Patrol's men and machinery besides be multiplied, the source of wetback supply could be reduced from a flash flood to a rill. The combination would whittle a now major problem down to one of unalarming size, if by no means guaranteed to eliminate it entirely.

Thus much for the policing of the Mexican boundary during the first seven decades of the twentieth century. As to the future, only one thing can be safely affirmed. Whether or not the proper steps are taken about narcotics as well as wetbacks, the border is an intrinsically wild area with annals of ill behavior that will not end here.

BIBLIOGRAPHY

Bailey, Philip A. *Golden Mirages*. New York, 1949.

Barnes, Will C. and Raines, William McLeod. *Cattle*. Garden City, N. Y., 1930.

Collaer, Nick D. Letter Published in *Guardian at the Gate*. Vol. XXI, No. 2, New York, May, 1949.

Corle, Edwin. *The Gila*. New York, 1951.

Dobie, J. Frank (Ed.) *Coyote Wisdom*. Dallas, 1938.

Fergusson, Harvey. *The Rio Grande*. New York, 1937.

Garber, Paul N. *The Gadsden Treaty*. Philadelphia, 1923.

Gilliland, Maude T. *Horsebackers of the Brush Country*. n.p., 1968.

———— *Rincon*. Brownsville, Tex., 1964.

Gresinger, A. W. *Charles D. Poston, Sunland Seer*. Globe, Ariz., 1963.

Haley, J. Evetts. *Jeff Milton: A Good Man with a Gun*. Norman, Okla., 1948.

Harper's Encyclopaedia of United States History. New York, 1907–1910; 10 vols.

Hollon, Eugene W.   *The Southwest Old and New.* New York, 1961.

Horgan, James.   *Great River . . . The Rio Grande.* New York, 1954; 2 vols.

Idar, Ed., Jr.   *What Price Wetbacks?* Austin, Tex., 1953.

McClintock, James H.   *Arizona, Prehistoric, Aboriginal, Pioneer, Modern.* Chicago, 1916; 2 vols.

McWilliams, Carey.   *Southern California Country, an Island on the Land.* New York, 1946.

Myers, John Myers.   *The Alamo.* New York, 1948.

—— *The Deaths of the Bravos.* Boston, 1962.

—— (Compiled and Annotated by) *The Westerners.* Englewood Cliffs, N. J., 1969.

Poston, Charles D.   *Building a State in Apache Land*, with a Preface and Explanatory Notes by John Myers Myers. Tempe, Ariz., 1963.

Raines, William McLeod and Barnes, Will C. *Cattle.* Garden City, N. Y., 1930.

Rak, Mary Kidder.   *Border Patrol.* New York, 1938.

Roark, Garland.   *Coin of Contraband.* New York, 1964.

Sonnichsen, Charles L.   *Paso Del Norte.* El Paso, Tex., 1968.

Timm., Charles A.   *The International Boundary Commission, United States and Mexico.* Austin, Tex., 1941.

U.S. Department of Justice.   *Annual Report of the Immigration and Naturalization Service,* 1954, 1955, 1967, 1968.

—— *I & N Reporter,* October, 1957; October, 1959; October, 1961; January, 1963; April, 1964; January, 1968; April, 1969.

U.S. Department of Labor.   *Migratory Labor in American Agriculture.* Washington, 1951.

U.S. Department of the Treasury.   Undated Bulletin Titled *The Old Border Patrol* (The Mounted Customs Inspectors).

Webb, Walter Prescott.   *The Great Plains.* New York, 1931.

—— *The Texas Rangers.* Boston, 1935.

White, Owen P.   *Lead and Likker.* New York, 1932.

Whitehead, Don.   *Border Guard.* New York, 1964.